The Politics of Force

The Politics of Force

Media and the Construction of Police Brutality

Regina G. Lawrence

UNIVERSITY OF CALIFORNIA PRESS
Berkeley · Los Angeles · London

University of California Press
Berkeley and Los Angeles, California

University of California Press, Ltd.
London, England

© 2000 by the Regents of the University of California

Library of Congress Cataloging-in-Publication Data

Lawrence, Regina G., 1961–.

The politics of force : media and the construction of
police brutality / Regina G. Lawrence.
    p.   cm.
Includes bibliographical references and index.
ISBN 0-520-22191-5 (alk. paper).—
ISBN 0-520-22192-3 (pbk. : alk. paper)
1. Police in mass media.   2. Police brutality.   I. Title.
P94.5.P64 L38   2000
363.2'32—dc21   99-053115
                                            CIP

Manufactured in the United States of America

09 08 07 06 05 04 03 02 01 00

10 9 8 7 6 5 4 3 2 1

The paper used in this publication is both acid-free
and totally chlorine-free (TCF). It meets the mini-
mum requirements of ANSI/NISO Z39.48-1992
(R 1997) (*Permanence of Paper*).

To Steve

Contents

Illustrations

FIGURES

TABLES

Preface

This book is an attempt to better understand how dramatic news events shape the problems we pay attention to as a society and the way we think about those problems. Through close analysis of news coverage of one event-ridden topic—police use of force—I develop a framework for understanding why some events become major news stories and how those events shape public discourse about policing. I argue that event-driven problem definition is an important political phenomenon in today's media environment. By zooming in on certain news events they see as particularly newsworthy, journalists become key mediators in ongoing struggles of various social groups to designate problems and shape how we define those problems.

This study reflects my fascination, as a political scientist and as a news-consuming citizen, with the question of who is allowed to speak in the news and what perspectives on reality can be found there. These questions have intrigued me since I first read the work of Lance Bennett, Herbert Gans, Gaye Tuchman, and other pioneering critical scholars of the news. The rich intellectual legacy of these scholars' work has revealed how the news, by inviting some groups to center stage and relegating others to the wings, confers legitimacy and authority on certain perspectives on reality—usually the perspectives of officials or other societal elites. My small contribution to this legacy, I hope, is to shed some light on dramatic news events as centerpieces of struggles among competing perspectives on reality. I suggest that we analyze unexpected, unplanned, and highly newsworthy events as moments when elite dominance of the news is most vulnerable. Doing so illuminates the full range of news dynamics, and identifies an increasingly important institutional role that the mass media play in politics and policymaking. While these moments may be few and the opportunities they provide for wider-ranging public debate limited, event-driven openings in the news represent one of the few real battlegrounds available for the marginalized to take on the powerful.

I am drawn (perhaps at my peril) to analyze media coverage of police use of force because it is fraught with ambiguity, clashing perspectives, high emotions, and deeply divided perceptions of the world. As my opening comments may suggest, my personal political sympathies tend to lie with those groups in society who have a difficult time being heard. More important, as an academic I am interested in political dynamics in which marginalized ideas gain symbolic and rhetorical advantage over their more powerful opponents. Therefore, this study is implicitly structured around the difficulty that police critics have in advancing what I call "systemic" claims about police brutality. Put simply, it is tough to get the general public thinking about police brutality as a serious public problem. It is tougher still to persuade the public that the roots of that alleged problem lie not in the occasional bad behavior or poor judgment of individual police officers but in entire institutionalized systems of police training, management, and culture; in a criminal-justice system that discourages prosecutors from pursuing police misconduct vigorously; in a political system that responds more readily to police than to the residents of inner-city and minority communities; or in a racist political culture that fears crime and values tough policing more than it values due process for all its citizens. To generate serious, sustained attention to these problem definitions is an uphill battle indeed, which makes this an irresistibly interesting subject to me.

At the same time, I have been impressed throughout my research by the profoundly difficult situations that police officers face in using force appropriately and effectively. As this preface is being written, a friend reports that his son, a police officer, shot and killed a man who in an apparent fit of suicidal rage brandished a gun at a phalanx of armed police officers. What is most painful and disturbing about such events is that quite often, no one can know if a split-second decision to use force could have been avoided and lives saved or if hesitating to use force would have brought greater tragedy. Thus, throughout the book, I make no claims about the objective "truth" of incidents in which police use force, lethal or nonlethal. In fact, it is the very uncertainty and ambiguity of these events that makes them so politically volatile and that generates the event-driven debates in which I am interested. Even more than I am drawn to the difficulties faced by grassroots groups in defining policing problems, I am drawn to the difficulties our society has in talking fully and openly about the deep dilemmas inherent in policing a democratic, violent, and fear-ridden society.

Many colleagues deserve acknowledgment for their careful reading and trenchant criticisms of my work; I relieve them of responsibility for anything but its strengths. First and foremost I wish to thank Lance Bennett, who has been the intellectual inspiration for this book in many ways and who has continually offered me invaluable ideas, guidance, and humor. He and my other advisors at the University of Washington—Bryan Jones, Peter May, Michael McCann, and Stuart Scheingold—created a crucial mix of challenge and support that made the conceptualization and completion of this project possible. The manuscript benefited enormously from the critical eyes of Tom Birkland, Timothy Cook, Robert Entman, Doris Graber, Susan Herbst, Steve Livingston, David Paletz, and Gadi Wolfsfeld. The argument was sharpened and my thinking challenged by my colleagues at Syracuse University, including Kristi Andersen, Gavan Duffy, Steve Macedo, Grant Reeher, and Richard Sherman. This project was also nurtured by a particularly insightful and collegial group of fellow graduate students at the University of Washington—Megan Dahl, Mark Donovan, Shane Fricks, Valerie Hunt, Tom Lewis, Lisa Miller, Sheila Rucki, and Steve Sandweiss. In addition, Valerie Hunt and Lisa Miller provided crucial help with the tedious tasks of coding.

I also acknowledge with gratitude the reporters, policing experts, and activists who took the time to speak with me candidly about their work: Christie-Lynne Bonner, Ralph Blumenthal, Paul Chevigny, Andrea Ford, William Geller, Diop Kamau (formerly Don Jackson), David Kocieniewski, Clifford Krauss, Morton Levine, Jim Newton, Martha Plotkin, Rick Rosenthal, and Peyton Whitely. The book was significantly enriched by the insights I gained from them.

This project was made financially possible in part by the Goldsmith Research Award from the Joan Shorenstein Center on the Press, Politics, and Public Policy at Harvard University. I also thank Reed Malcolm and the editors and staff of the University of California Press.

Finally, I thank my mother, my father, my aunt Cindy, and my aunt Yvonne for inspiring me to work hard, aim high, and always listen to the other side. My deepest thanks are due as well to Paul Landraitis and to Ken Masters, whose wise advice made the difference more than once, and most especially to my husband Steve. He has been more generous, supportive, and forgiving than any partner has a right to expect, and I hope that he will be proud of what his support has accomplished.

ONE

Mediating Realities

The Social Construction of
Problems in the Media Arena

On July 4, 1996, New York City police officer Paolo Colecchia shot and killed Nathaniel Levi Gaines on a dark subway platform in the Bronx. Gaines, a 25-year-old African American who was unarmed, had served in the Persian Gulf War and had no criminal record. He was shot in the back. Officer Colecchia claimed that Gaines had struggled with him, attempted to take his gun, and tried to push him onto the tracks.

Gaines's death raised considerable controversy in the pages of the *New York Times*. Gaines's parents attributed the shooting of their son to racism. "We didn't want to say that his life was taken because he was born with his skin dark. But there is no other explanation," said his father (Herbert 1996). Columnist Bob Herbert asserted that the Gaines shooting showed that the New York Police Department "has never adequately addressed the brutality in its ranks" (ibid.). New York Police Department officials countered this critical news by telling reporters that "there's far less force used by the police now than in the past—the Rodney King stuff that you used to hear about a lot. . . . Some recent cases make the public think the problem is more wide-ranging than it really is." But another *Times* columnist answered that "a batch of cases from this year alone suggests [police misconduct] is wide-ranging enough" and observed that "it is hard to accept on faith the Police Department's assurances that bad-apple officers are being dealt with more firmly than ever" (Haberman 1996).

The news about the death of William Retana, a 26-year-old unarmed

Mexican American, recipient of the Purple Heart in Vietnam and a staff sergeant with the U.S. Air Force Reserves, was less controversial. Retana died after two-and-a-half weeks in a coma caused by skull injuries sustained during a confrontation with Los Angeles police in November 1985. In a brief *Los Angeles Times* story buried deep in the back pages, a Los Angeles Police Department spokesman told reporters that a drunken Retana "approached [the officers] in a hostile manner shouting, 'Shoot me, shoot me,' " and attempted to grab an officer. In response, police said, an officer struck Retana with a "two-handed power stroke" of his baton, accidentally hitting Retana in the head (Severely injured suspect resisted arrest, police say, 1985). Retana's death never became major news, and alternative narratives that might explain his death were never explored—until 1991.

Then, in the wake of the widely televised beating of black motorist Rodney King, William Retana's death again briefly entered the news, this time on the *Times'* editorial page. In an op-ed piece, Retana's brother James, a former veteran LAPD police officer, observed that "The [police] press release describing the investigation of William's death was standard fare.... The press release ... used the standard buzz words to describe William's behavior—'resisting arrest' and 'hostile manner.' Fact was that William never touched or hit any officer" (Retana 1991). He then offered an alternative scenario of his brother's altercation with police in which the officers became the aggressors and the police account of his death a rhetorical cover-up. Retana wrote that he left the LAPD after his brother died, concluding that "The LAPD has one unofficial-official rule I did not know about when I joined: The department puts symbols ahead of human lives. The squeaky-clean badge, which separated us from them, was now covered with blood" (ibid.).

No critical news followed the death of a third man, Louis Segura. On May 13, 1990, the *Los Angeles Times* reported that Los Angeles police officers had "killed a reputed gang member" the evening before in South-Central Los Angeles. Two of the four paragraphs on the incident read as follows:

> Louis Segura, 27, was shot and killed in South-Central Los Angeles when officers said he pulled a handgun from beneath his jacket after being stopped on Broadway near 69th Street.
>
> Officer Richard Ludwig, who told investigators he feared he was about to be shot, fired two rounds at Segura, hitting him in the throat and shoulder, police said. Segura died at the scene.

No other sources offered additional perspective on the incident, and after this brief news item the *Times* made no further mention of Segura's death.

These three cases illustrate the subject of this study: struggles among competing groups to define the meaning of news events and the news narratives about public problems that result from these struggles. The news events this study focuses on are incidents of police use of force; as we will see, these incidents are subject to a range of interpretations in the news. As in many use-of-force incidents, the actual details of the deaths of Gaines, Retana, and Segura were murky and potentially subject to widely divergent perceptions. The news offered socially constructed public definitions of these events, which drew upon official and, sometimes, nonofficial voices. With different degrees of success, police attempted to control those definitions by providing reporters with narratives that defended their use of physical force. Police were successful in controlling the news narrative about Louis Segura. The police version of events and the label "reputed gang member" were not challenged in the news pages. Similarly, the police version of William Retana's death initially remained unchallenged in the news—until the Rodney King incident opened the *Los Angeles Times'* editorial page to James Retana's alternative scenario. In the Nathaniel Gaines case, competing public definitions were more prominent in the news from the beginning and sparked questions in the news about the performance of the NYPD. Gaines's death thus became a defining event in the continuing struggle among different social groups making competing claims about policing and police brutality.

THE NEWS AS AN ARENA
OF PROBLEM CONSTRUCTION

Understanding the shifting representations of groups, events, and issues in the news requires thinking of the news as a socially constructed representation of reality and as an arena of problem construction in which struggles to designate and define public problems are waged. The social construction of news has long been of interest to scholars of political communication, while the social construction of public problems has become an area of increasing interest to political scientists and public-policy scholars. This study melds those two lines of research by viewing the social construction of the news as part and parcel of larger political competitions to designate and define public problems.

This approach begins with questions that have long fascinated scholars of the media: How can we explain why different issues rise and then fall in the news and on the public agenda? And how can we explain the variations in the news coverage those issues receive? We know, for example, that for many years nuclear power received relatively little attention in the news, and when it was covered it was treated in a mostly positive way as a benign harbinger of technological progress. But in the 1970s a shift occurred, and the media began to focus on a more sinister face of nuclear power. Nuclear power became a "problem" in the news, rather than a solution for other problems (Gamson and Modigliani 1989). This study employs a constructionist approach to explain how one public problem—police brutality—rises and falls in the news and how it is talked about in the news across time.[1]

This social-constructionist approach assumes that "problems" may not exist objectively as much as they exist in perception. That is to say, what qualifies as a "problem" for any given society on any given day may have less to do with the objective breadth and depth of problematic conditions in society than with the things people are paying attention to and how they are perceiving them. What becomes understood as a problem—a societal condition that people believe is unacceptable and should be addressed with new or invigorated public policy—can depend upon what perspectives on societal conditions are highlighted in the news.[2] The news is a main symbolic arena in which "various social groups, institutions, and ideologies struggle over the definition and construction of social reality" (Gurevitch and Levy 1985). Journalists are "managers" of that arena (Gans 1979).[3] As they construct the news, journalists give some voices, claims, and symbols wide exposure by admitting them to center stage (Wolfsfeld 1997). News organizations thus play a vital role in the social construction of public problems. Like other political institutions, news organizations constrain which problems are attended to and who participates in constructing them (Hilgartner and Bosk 1988). In the process, problems are defined (or ignored), claims-makers are empowered (or marginalized), and some realities win authority and legitimacy over others.

Most studies of this kind have argued that the social construction of public problems allocates resources in ways that benefit the "owners" of those problems (Edelman 1988; Gusfield 1981). When officials are able to designate a "terrorism" problem, for example, the president and the institutions responsible for national security gain greater leeway to utilize military force abroad and to arouse public support for terrorist-fighting activities (Livingston 1994). Likewise, when drug abuse is defined as a problem of criminality rather than of addiction, power is conferred upon crime-fighting institutions such as the Drug Enforcement Agency to pursue a criminal-justice solution to the problem, while medical institutions are relatively disempowered to pursue therapeutic solutions such as drug treatment programs (Edelman 1993; Zimring and Hawkins 1992). While many studies of the social construction of public problems have focused on how problems confer power, this study is premised on the notion that *warding off* problems confers power as well by deflecting critical public examination of social conditions that might demand greater governmental action and accountability.

Which problems are either designated or warded off depends upon how the news simultaneously confers and denies power to different groups' perspectives on reality. Different groups of people often "take quite different 'realities' for granted" (Berger and Luckmann 1967, 2). Some people's realities become authoritative and widely shared while others' realities remain isolated and marginalized. When this perspective is applied to the study of public-policy issues in the news, the question becomes: What kinds of "realities" are represented in news coverage of policy issues? And whose realities are they?

A well-established answer has been provided by what I will call the "official dominance" model of the news—a perspective that is engaged critically by this study. One of the clearest findings of decades of communication research has been the role officials generally play as "primary definers" of events and issues in the news (Hall et al. 1978). Journalists rely heavily on institutionally positioned officials for the raw materials of news, and these elites act as "authorized knowers" that are considered by journalists to be the most legitimate sources of news (Bennett 1996; Cook 1998; Tuchman 1978). Officials' interest in routinizing the daily business of governing and communicating with the public, combined with journalists' interest in routinizing news production, creates a well-recognized symbiotic relationship between reporters and official sources (Cohen 1963; Gans 1979; Sigal 1973). Consequently, the news usually quite faithfully reflects the views, concerns, and activities of political elites. Journalists "select the sources through whose eyes the public views the world," and those eyes are predominantly official (Graber 1993, 111).

By the same token, according to this model, when nonofficials appear in the news they are often marginalized and rarely act as "primary definers." Marginal groups—those journalists view as lacking political power or a sizable constituency—are generally accorded minimal news coverage (Paletz and Entman 1981). "Unknowns" rarely enter the news unless they stage some unusual activity or somehow attack or challenge "knowns" (Gans 1979). Nonofficials and grassroots groups are usually marginalized *from* the news, in that they are rarely drawn upon as primary news sources, and marginalized *in* the news, in that such groups, even when they do become primary news sources, are usually treated differently than official sources. Indeed, even when a social movement becomes a major news story, news organizations often cover it in ways that undermine the movement's message (Entman and Rojecki 1993; Gitlin 1980).

This study seeks both to develop and to challenge that model of the news. While the news usually does present officially sanctioned realities, it does not do so exclusively or inevitably. Rather, the news is best viewed as a product of (unequal) struggle among competing news sources who often press competing politically charged claims about issues and events.[4] A key factor in the outcome of struggles among competing sources to shape the news, I argue, is the appearance and use of dramatic, unplanned news events. Such "accidental" events present challenges to officials who must work to contain these events' publicly shared meanings. Such events present opportunities to journalists to construct critical news coverage of public-policy issues. Groups who compete to shape the news can be rendered somewhat more equal when dramatic events become major news stories. Consequently, "accidental" events can reshape news discourse about public-policy issues.

MAKING MEANING OF NEWS EVENTS

Events are the raw materials for daily news content, and the primary way journalists represent reality is through reporting on events. But journalists do not simply report events, they imbue events with meaning(s) in the process of converting them into news. As Hall et al. (1978, 54) write,

> If the world is not to be presented as a jumble of random and chaotic events, then they must be identified (i.e. named, defined, related to other events known to the audience), and assigned to a social context (i.e. placed within a frame of meanings familiar to the audience). This process—identification and contextualization—is one of the most important through which events are "made to mean" by the media.

Different sorts of events, however, provide different raw materials for journalists to work with. Especially important is the distinction between "routine" and "accidental" news events (Molotch and Lester 1974). Routine news events generally dominate the news. These are news events that are planned by politicians and other officials to manage the news and communicate with the public. The nominating convention, the Rose Garden bill-signing, the summit meeting, and the campaign trail baby-kissing are all routine news events provided by officials largely to build and perpetuate particular public images. These are predefined news events, so to speak. As Molotch and Lester (1974, 108) argue, these routine events that form the basis of so much daily news are the "purposive accomplishments" of elites, "the generating of a public experience by those in positions to have continual access to asserting the importance and factual status of 'their' occurrences." The predominance of elite voices in the news occurs in large part because officially sponsored events constitute much of what becomes news.

Some news events occur unexpectedly, however, and are not humanly planned (tornadoes and earthquakes, for example), not intentionally planned (oil carriers grounding or space shuttles exploding), or not planned as news events (presidential gaffes or sexual scandals). These "accidental events"[5] often violate standard assumptions about the way things are and ought to be, and they do not come to journalists predefined in the way that routine events do.

Accidental events appear in the news fairly often: buildings collapse, terrorists strike, planes crash, crazed killers open fire. Even these nonroutine events are subjected to routines of newsgathering and routine news scripts, thereby allowing journalists to tame the unexpected and bend it to the requirements of news production (Tuchman 1978). Given their privileged access to the media arena, officials can often take advantage of these news routines to authoritatively define accidental events and so to "contain" their meaning. Such events may be crises for the persons involved, but if managed successfully by officials, they will not be treated by the media as *public* crises. When successfully managed, the news script about an accidental event will read, "some official action wins out, the day is saved, and the story ends with a return to 'normal' " (Bennett 1996, 25).

But some accidental events become the centerpieces of struggles to designate and define public problems, as other groups vie to provide journalists with frames and claims to define these events. As journalists try to make sense of troubling news events, news routines may extend to underutilized news sources and marginalized perspectives. Occasionally, therefore, focused through the prism of a dramatic news event, a new problem gains currency or a recurring problem resurfaces with new urgency in the news. Events that crystallize deep political and cultural tensions can become "news icons" that dominate the news and become etched in public memory while they "mainstream" marginalized ideas. For example, as journalists covered the infamous garbage barge *Mobro* that wandered the high seas in 1987 looking for a port that would accept its cargo, they cast it as an indicator of a looming garbage crisis. Environmentalists seized on the barge as a symbol of a nation quickly burying itself in trash, while officials played "catch up" with the barge story by promoting recycling as a solution to this newly perceived problem. Consequently, trash and the culture of wastefulness became recognized as "problems" and recycling as a viable solution (Bennett and Lawrence 1995).

As this example suggests, the news is an arena of struggle over the meaning of events, the existence of problems, and the search for solutions. Events can play a dynamic role in these struggles because the news assigns definitions and significance to events whether or not officials successfully control that process. Officials must work to frame and contain the definitions journalists construct around evocative news events such as wandering garbage barges or shocking events such as police shootings. Thus, key battles in the competition to construct public problems are fought with and around accidental events. Indeed, what is designated problematic by the public is often driven by its association with some key news event, and how we understand public problems is often influenced by the way these events are defined in the news. The key questions considered in this study, then, are how journalists construct public definitions for "accidental" news events and how those definitions both stem from and influence the ongoing social construction of policy issues.

EVENT-DRIVEN PROBLEM CONSTRUCTION

What this study proposes, then, is a model of problem construction that differs from that offered by the official-dominance model of the news: event-driven rather than institutionally driven problem construction. Institutionally driven news is cued by official activities in official arenas. It is pegged to institutional news beats, official actors, and institutionally defined decision points. For example, issues that Congress is currently debating are more likely to be in the news than are issues not on the Congressional agenda; such issues are especially likely to win news coverage if Congress is about to vote on some relevant legislation. If the issue is being debated vigorously by legislators, the perspectives in the news are likely to be more varied than when Congress is in wide agreement (Bennett 1990).

Event-driven news is cued by the appearance of dramatic news events and the "story cues" for reporters that arise out of those events. Event-driven discourse about public issues is often more variable and dynamic than institutionally driven news, ranging beyond established news beats and drawing on a wider variety of voices and perspectives. In institutionally driven news, political institutions set the agendas of news organizations; in contrast, as event-driven news gathers momentum, officials and institutions often respond to the news agenda rather than set it.

Institutionally driven news is news in which society's problems are those that officials wish to "own" (or that they must own, given their political responsibilities and current political realities). The public problems presented in institutionally driven news are often defined in ways that help officials to set the public agenda, shore up their political legitimacy, mobilize key constituencies, protect or acquire political turf, and win elections. The problems and problem definitions arising out of event-driven news, by contrast, are more volatile and difficult for officials to control or to benefit from and are more open to challengers. Thus, event-driven news discourse takes on special significance in the policy-making process: the media become a kind of informal screening mechanism for the policy process, a key arena in which the competition over problem definition is played out.

THE "EFFECTS" OF DEFINING EVENTS

This study seeks to explain how news organizations represent reality to the public but does not directly analyze how the public makes sense of those representations. The ability of the news to impose particular meanings on individual news consumers has been hotly debated. Many scholars have argued that while the news may attempt to designate preferred meanings of issues and events, audiences are the ultimate arbiters of the private meanings they make of the news (Fiske 1994; Morley 1992; Neuman, Crigler, and Just 1993). As Cappella and Jamieson (1997, 50) correctly argue, "content differences are not effects." Variations in news content over time, in other words, do not necessarily produce variations in individual perceptions. Yet at the same time, an impressive body of "agenda-setting" research has shown that the news often does designate for people what is happening in the world, what is important, and how events and issues should be understood (Iyengar 1991; Iyengar and Kinder 1987; McCombs and Shaw 1972). Thus, while the media may not succeed in imposing preferred meanings on individual consciousness, the news does provide cues that guide the construction of private understandings of the world.

More important, perhaps, the news establishes a key basis for public meaning and, ultimately, popular beliefs. The media establish the public symbolic terms upon which political players struggle while organizing the spectacle for their audiences with cues about the importance and legitimacy of competing players, claims, and problems. Journalists can decide that some issues and events are not worthy of public attention and thus routinely marginalize the concerns of various groups. At the same time, the media can bring issues and events to the forefront of public attention, compelling politicians to respond (or appear to be responding) to them. These two facets of the power of the news media—marginalization and agenda setting—are central concerns not only of media scholars but of most competitors in the political process as well. On a daily basis, the news helps and hinders different groups that wish to construct or to ward off particular public problems. Thus, the content of the news matters even when it cannot be traced to individual-level effects. The news both reflects the power of the groups who struggle to shape it and constitutes one aspect of their power.

This study shows how the news generally provides a rather narrow range of voices and perspectives on the issues of police use of force and police brutality but occasionally expands to include a wider range of voices and perspectives. Significantly, this broadening of the news about policing generally occurs in the aftermath of particular use-of-force incidents. The news often allows police and elected officials to ward off the construction of policing problems but occasionally becomes a "site of struggle" (Hall 1980) among competing perspectives—a struggle that officials must work to win.

RESEARCH STRATEGY

The research presented here is based on content analysis of *New York Times* and *Los Angeles Times* coverage of police use of force from 1985 through 1994. The findings are bolstered by an analysis of coverage of the Rodney King beating in a larger group of newspapers and newsmagazines from across the country and by interviews with reporters and police experts in New York, Los Angeles, and other cities.[6]

While examining print-media coverage in great detail may seem less than relevant in this increasingly televisual era, studying how use of force is presented in newspapers offers many advantages.[7] First, newspaper reporters, much more so than their television counterparts, are in constant contact with police sources; indeed, the "police beat" is an integral part of the daily newspaper business in a way that is not always true of television. Newspapers therefore offer a better site for studying something of prime interest here: the processes by which police (along with other officials) attempt to manage the daily news and the processes by which journalists adopt or depart from police-supplied narratives. Second, local (and, with increasing frequency, national) television news often sacrifices discussion of public-policy issues for sensationalized and "human interest" news. Analyzing newspaper coverage captures a greater range of news coverage, from daily crime-beat reporting to serious, thematic coverage of policing problems. Third, premier newspapers such as those analyzed here continue to provide cues to other types of news organizations about what is newsworthy. Their importance therefore extends beyond their own readership to the content of other news media. Finally, despite the advent of television as most news consumers' primary news source, there is evidence that newspapers remain a crucial information source for well-informed citizens. Indeed, "despite dwindling readership . . . newspapers remain America's premier source of public affairs information" (Robinson and Levy 1996, 135), and newspaper readership is strongly correlated with political knowledge.

The *New York Times* and the *Los Angeles Times* are chosen for intensive study here for several reasons. Both are the premier news organizations in their respective locales as well as respected national newspapers; both are well endowed with resources for gathering and reporting news; both aspire to high journalistic standards. Moreover, these news organizations cover two of America's largest, most emulated, and most controversial police departments. Thus both have played key roles, at various times during the period under study, in designating and warding off policing problems in their respective locales and across the nation.

Because this study opts primarily for intensive analysis of two news organizations rather than more superficial analysis of many, it cannot speak to one of the key dynamics of local news coverage: the competitive interaction among news organizations in a single locale (see Kaniss

1991). Nor can the findings reported here be unproblematically generalized to all other news organizations across all locales. To some degree, the dynamics of news coverage reported here are the product of the specific historical relationships between the news organizations studied and the police departments they cover.

What the study sacrifices in breadth, however, it gains in depth, allowing for careful analysis of the specific dynamics of specific news contexts. Closely analyzing two news organizations' coverage of one issue over a long period of time allows us to see the full range of coverage produced on the ambiguous and controversial topic of police use of force and thus to produce more subtle and nuanced theory of mediated political communication. Moreover, the similarities in the coverage produced in these two different settings are as striking as any differences this analysis uncovers, pointing toward underlying dynamics that are likely to be found in a great number of news organizations.

Two specific challenges are encountered by the researcher wishing to study news coverage of police use of force. One is the difficulty of gathering independent data about police use-of-force incidents, as discussed further in chapter 2. Although the NYPD and the LAPD make public some statistical overviews of some categories of use-of-force incidents (e.g., police shootings), it is not possible to obtain specific records pertaining to a large number of specific incidents.[8] Yet the lack of independent data does not pose a fatal difficulty, for the purpose of this study is primarily to understand how "problems" arise out of these incidents rather than to ascertain whether reporters represent those incidents "accurately." As should be clear from the discussion in the next chapter, quite often there is no "accurate" representation possible.

The second challenge is that the task of explaining patterns of news coverage ultimately becomes a task of explaining the normative structure of mainstream news reporting. Demonstrating how norms structure news coverage is not a simple task. Norms are socially enforced and habitual approaches to news construction that produce patterns of representation in the news. Norms are unobservable, and their existence can be inferred only from these patterns and from how journalists explain their news-construction decisions. Yet uncovering journalistic norms is not entirely problematic, because within the news are numerous clues indicating norms at work: what journalists find most newsworthy, what sources they consult, what questions they find important to ask, and how past news events shape the coverage of current news events. Comparing a large number of cases over a long time period and across two news organizations also allows for greater rigor. Thus, careful analysis can shed light on the "rules" that govern the construction of the news.

Finally, a few words about the time period covered by this study, a period marked by key events in the history of aggressive policing as a political phenomenon and, occasionally, as a public problem. In 1985, the Supreme Court, in *Tennessee v. Garner*, struck down a state statute that allowed police to shoot fleeing, nondangerous suspects, ruling that shootings to apprehend "fleeing felons" in some circumstances violated Fourth Amendment protections against unreasonable search and seizure. That same year saw the appointment of New York City's first black police commissioner, Benjamin Ward. Ward moved to strengthen administrative and civilian oversight of the NYPD in the aftermath of a major police brutality scandal in which officers in several precincts were discovered to have tortured suspected drug dealers with electric stun guns to obtain confessions of drug dealing. Reform efforts continued during the administration of Mayor David Dinkins, who successfully battled for the establishment of an all-civilian review board to review allegations of NYPD misconduct.

Meanwhile, public concerns about drug-related crime increased, as cocaine and crack appeared in the streets and flooded the headlines, fueling the latest national "war" on drugs. New York City and Los Angeles became major battlefields in this war, a role pursued with particular fervor by LAPD chief Daryl Gates, who presided over 1,453 drug- and gang-related arrests in April 1988 alone (Davis 1990, 268). In both New York and Los Angeles, the tensions between police and urban, minority communities, and the dangers of the drug war to those communities and to police themselves, were revealed in two dramatic events. In 1991, videotaped images of the beating of Rodney King filled televisions screens around the world, leading eventually to a shake-up of the LAPD, the departure of Chief Gates, and the conflagration of 1992. And in 1992, the arrest of NYPD Officer Michael Dowd for drug dealing led to a two-year-long investigation of police corruption that uncovered dozens of New York City police officers involved in drug use, drug dealing, and brutality as well.

These events became big news just as traditional American policing was undergoing much critical scrutiny and attempts at reform. The "crime attack" strategy epitomized by the LAPD under Daryl Gates was being reexamined, and "community policing," championed by another new NYPD chief, Lee Brown, was gaining adherents, even as calls mounted for intensified wars on drugs, gangs, and violent crime. In New York, Dinkins lost his seat to Rudolph Giuliani in a race in which police misconduct was a pivotal issue, and with strong support from police, Giuliani ushered in a new get-tough era. Media representations of police use of force during this period thus became a site of struggle among these various groups over the future of American policing—a struggle that has continued to play out around dramatic news events in both California and New York.

ORGANIZATION OF THE BOOK

The news about police use of force is filled with "accidental" news events. Most use-of-force incidents reported in the news are intentional events but are not staged to generate media coverage. This is not always the case, of course. During his tenure as chief of the LAPD, for example, Daryl Gates turned some shows of force into media events, as when Gates rode his department's innovative battering ram, designed to break through the walls of alleged crack houses, into the evening news (Davis 1990). But most instances of police use of force are spontaneous, and the vast majority do not occur in the glare of television lights, although many occur in public places. Such events are potentially problematic for police and political officials, who must authoritatively frame and contain their public definitions by providing reporters with narratives that explain and rationalize them.

These use-of-force incidents are often controversial because they are perceived differently by different groups. Moreover, the issue of police brutality itself is subject to widely divergent perspectives. The ambiguity of the subject is heightened by the lack of concrete data on excessive force as well as by the difficulty of defining what constitutes excessive force. Consequently, struggles to define use-of-force incidents are often highly volatile and efforts to determine if we have a brutality problem in the United States are often frustratingly difficult. These underlying ambiguities that shape the struggles over meaning in the news about policing are discussed further in chapter 2.

Most of the time, as chapter 3 demonstrates, when a use-of-force incident enters the news, officials retain control of its public definition. Officials generally try to control the news by "individualizing" these incidents, claiming that those subjected to police use of force brought that force on themselves with their deviant, violent behavior; occasionally, when an incident looks particularly bad for the officer(s) involved, officials describe excessive force as a problem of a few rogue cops. These individualizing claims contrast with "systemic" claims about police brutality, which are typically made by nonofficials. These claims cast brutality as an endemic and patterned problem arising from poor police management, inadequate police accountability, a hostile police subculture, or a racist culture more generally. Systemic claims are much less common in the news. The typical news story about a use-of-force incident is structured around individualizing claims provided by officials—news that normalizes what some might see as evidence of a policing problem.

This normalization, as I argue in chapter 3, results from three "constants" that shape news coverage of policing: privileged official access to the news, access maintained and virtually guaranteed by the "beat" system of news gathering; a norm of journalistic professionalism, which encourages journalists to privilege the police perspective in stories about policing; and a larger cultural discourse of crime control, in which crime is believed to be a rampant problem of deviant individuals against whom we should "crack down." These three factors create practical and ideological limitations on what is commonly said about police use of force in the news.

But occasionally, a case of alleged brutality initiates the construction of policing problems, and the news about police use of force spins out of official control. Chapter 4 examines this opposite end of the news spectrum by analyzing *Los Angeles Times* coverage of the beating of Rodney King by officers of the LAPD in March 1991. That event thoroughly escaped the effort of LAPD officials to portray it as an "aberration" and thereby control its public definition. While the fact that the beating was videotaped was obviously a primary factor explaining how it escaped containment, the analysis reveals additional key factors, including how the incident was captured by George Holliday's video camera as well as the political dynamics it set in motion. Thus, the case of Rodney King offers clues to the construction of the news about police brutality in other settings.

Chapter 5 draws on the propositions generated by the King case to develop an explanation for variations of news coverage of police use of force. The key explanatory variable identified by comparing hundreds of news stories is the presence of "story cues" that emerge out of some use-of-force incidents. Certain cues encourage journalists to recognize a "good story" in the making and provide the raw materials for dramatic storytelling about potential official wrongdoing. This chapter presents a typology of story cues that help to explain why some cases of police use of force become the centerpieces of problem construction while many others do not.

Events marked by these story cues often become the subject of intense struggles over meaning. News coverage of these few incidents widens, and critical societal voices—activists, community leaders, residents of inner-city and minority communities, and academics—can momentarily take center stage to become "primary definers" of those events and the problems they allegedly represent. Chapter 6 analyzes coverage of three high-profile use-of-force incidents in the *New York Times* in order to explore how the struggles set off by such events play out. One part of the story told in these pages is that of news which expands in response to dramatic events, as sources compete to push and pull the news narrative in opposing directions; the other part is the story of how officials regain control of the news and troubling events are, perhaps imperfectly, normalized.

Chapter 7 concludes the empirical analysis by returning to the King beating, this time to analyze the kinds of definitions and problems that were constructed around it in print media from around the country. The analysis shows that as news organizations drew upon the voices and claims of antibrutality activists and black leaders, and upon the strong symbolic associations of that event with past moments in the history of American struggles over civil rights, the news linked the King beating not only with a contemporary pattern of police misconduct, but also with an historical pattern of police abuse of minorities. By evoking larger cultural themes associated with race, civil rights, and progress, the King beating stimulated a national public debate about brutality which momentarily overcame the many constraints on problematizing police brutality. The analysis also reveals how the King beating helped to popularize the concept of "community policing," redefining it as a solution not only for the crime problem, but for a newly perceived police misconduct problem.

Finally, chapter 8 offers a theoretical approach integrating the empirical analysis presented in this study into a broader framework of theorizing on social problems in the news, and points to the increasing significance of event-driven news in our public life. As I hope this study will show, an event-driven model of the news about public problems can illuminate an important dynamic in politics today. In an era in which news organizations converge ever more quickly and intensively upon dramatic news events—from terrorist bombings to environmental catastrophes to presidential sexual scandals—it is crucial that we better understand the dynamics of event-driven news.

TWO

Making a Problem
of Brutality

Crime is a problem that preoccupies the news and the public. As the nation has engaged in "wars" on crime and drugs over the past several decades, crime has become an ever-more prevalent staple of news reporting. A variety of studies of media content have estimated that as much as 25 percent of the daily news is devoted to crime (Surette 1992) and that crime is the largest major category of stories in the print and electronic media (Chermak 1994, 103). As with other kinds of news, the most privileged perspectives in most crime stories are those offered by officials, particularly the police (Chermak 1995; Ericson, Baranek, and Chan 1989). In fact, media interest in "crime waves" can be the product, at least in part, of official efforts to create, sustain, or exploit public concern about crime (Fishman 1980; Hall et al. 1978). Privileged access to the media offers police and other officials abundant opportunities to shape public images of themselves, their work, and the nature of the crime problem.

Police use of physical force is a particularly controversial issue in American crime fighting. Given the considerable ambiguity that surrounds the issue, whether police use of force is presented as police brutality[1] and whether brutality is understood as a problem depend greatly upon which voices and views the media emphasize. Moreover, the kinds of problem definitions that arise in the news after a highly publicized incident of alleged brutality both draw upon and shape the various groups, demands, and social values engaged in the policy process.

THE AMBIGUITY OF POLICE USE OF FORCE

Police use of force is often highly controversial because it raises questions about a government's use of coercion against its citizens. In a democratic society that prides itself on ideals of civility and equality before the law, police use of force is often an inherently troubling phenomenon. As one scholar has observed, "Justifying police and what they do has always been problematic in democracies, and this has been particularly true in the United States, where ambivalence about government authority is a persistent force" (Mastrofski 1988, 61). Yet whether police brutality constitutes a public problem is a question whose answer depends largely upon who is asked.

Of course, the nature of policing requires police at times to use physical coercion against civilians; indeed, "police are sometimes morally obliged to employ force" to accomplish legitimate ends of controlling crime and maintaining order (Skolnick and Fyfe 1993, 238). Yet police use of force is often highly controversial precisely because it is nearly always ambiguous. As legal scholar Paul Chevigny (1995, 139) observes, while "the power to use force is a defining characteristic of the [police officer's] job, . . . the line between excessive and justifiable force is difficult to draw." Indeed, he suggests, "Much of the problem in understanding the work of the police lies in the fact that what they do, and what they should do, when they are 'doing their job,' is always contested" (ibid., 9).

Police and criminologists draw conceptual distinctions among the terms "use of force," "unnecessary force," and "brutality." The use of force, according to experts, is a necessary and legitimate tool of the police officer's job. In contrast, "brutality" is "a conscious and venal act by officers who usually take great pains to conceal their misconduct," while unnecessary use of force "is usually a training problem, the result of ineptitude or insensitivity, as, for instance, when well-meaning officers unwisely charge into situations from which they can then extricate themselves only by using force" (Skolnick and Fyfe 1993, 19–20). "Excessive force" can thus be brutal, involving malicious intent, or merely unnecessary, involving poor judgment.

While these lines may be relatively easy to draw in the pages of academic articles and police manuals, whether the behavior of individual police officers in any particular altercation constitutes excessive force or brutality is often a difficult question to settle definitively. In fact, "spokesmen for some police departments [are] not able to give a clear

definition of what is considered 'unnecessary force' in their cities"
(DeStefano 1991, 5). This is not because police have no clear policies
on excessive force, but because defining excessive force is highly
context-dependent. By the same token, allegations of brutality often involve the alleged victim and the officer(s) in a "swearing match," especially since many use-of-force incidents have no outside witnesses.

Even the presence of witnesses often does not resolve the ambiguity
of these events. Civilians who witness police using physical force to
subdue a suspect are often surprised and discomfited at what they see.
Police often must use serious coercion to subdue people who do not
wish to be subdued, they experience physical sensations of fear and
surging adrenaline, and they generally believe they are paid not to
"coddle" but to capture criminals. For these reasons, even the appropriate use of force can seem to observers to be out of proportion to the
danger presented by suspects.[2] As criminologists and police often observe, police use of force "rarely, if ever, photographs well" (Skolnick
and Fyfe 1993, 37). In cities across the country, use-of-force incidents
have led to prolonged investigations and trials that never fully resolve
questions in the public mind. Indeed, two different trials of the Los Angeles officers charged with beating black motorist Rodney King did not
fully resolve the ambiguity of that event.

This is not to suggest that all use-of-force incidents are ambiguous.
When police shoot a gunman holding hostages or a sniper terrorizing
pedestrians, few observers are likely to call it a case of excessive force.
But many use-of-force incidents are not quite so clear-cut. In fact, police
often face situations in which they decide to apprehend or subdue
people who appear to them to be dangerous, threatening, or "out of order" yet whom observers may not perceive as particularly threatening.
Quite often, when police use force, as one police officer observed
bluntly, "it looks terrible" (Bonner 1996). This is precisely what makes
many police officers so ambivalent about the use of force: a crucial tool
of their jobs and a sometimes necessary means of saving themselves,
their fellow officers, or civilians from harm, it is also likely to be perceived differently and perhaps more critically by the public.

Mirroring the ambiguity of individual use-of-force incidents, the issue of police brutality is often the subject of sharply divergent perspectives. For police officers, especially the street cops who daily face the
deterioration of urban life, the issue is met with strong feelings. Police
generally believe that "right conduct in a policing situation requires an
intuitive sense of the situation and that there is no way to do the job

that cannot be criticized from a different point of view" (Chevigny 1995, 90). And they are generally aware that their own attitudes toward the use of force and the public's can diverge fairly dramatically. For physical coercion "is part of the daily life of the police officer in a way that is very difficult for an outsider to grasp" (Scheingold 1984, 102). As one police officer put it, while police use of force may easily be criticized by the public, "police are not paid to fight fair" (Bonner 1996). Therefore, police officers tend to give each other the benefit of the doubt when it comes to the use of force,[3] and they tend to believe that the public should do the same.[4]

Yet the subject of police brutality has been a steady source of public relations woes for many police departments and a serious source of friction between police and particular communities. And while it would be simplistic and misleading to attribute single perspectives to entire social groups, divisions between whites and minority groups, particularly African Americans, on the subject of brutality have often been sharp. Indeed, African American communities across the country have for decades voiced complaints about police brutality and have often perceived it as a tool of racial oppression. In 1935, a Harlem Riot Commission report stated that "The insecurity of the individual in Harlem against police aggression is one of the most potent causes for the existing hostility to authority" (quoted in Skolnick and Fyfe 1993, 78). The National Advisory Commission on Civil Disorders wrote in March 1968 that "Negroes firmly believe that police brutality and harassment occur repeatedly in Negro neighborhoods" (ibid., 19) and reported that "all the major outbursts [of civil unrest] of recent years were precipitated by arrests of Negroes by white police for minor offenses" (78). Scholarly studies by Scheingold (1991) and Lyons (1999) have confirmed the persistent tendency of minority communities to be more suspicious of police and more critical of how they use force.

This gulf in perceptions manifested itself in public reactions to the beating of Rodney King in March 1991. A U.S. Civil Rights Commission report undertaken after the King incident found that blacks experienced "a real or perceived pattern of widespread, endemic racism and physical and verbal abuse" by police in Washington, D.C. (Thomas 1995, 6), mirroring beliefs around the country. Indeed, a common response among blacks was that, contrary to LAPD chief Daryl Gates's assertion that it was an "aberration," the event was unique only in that it had been videotaped, televised, and responded to by the public and officials (NAACP 1995; Lawrence 1996b). A *New*

York Times/CBS poll conducted after the King video had saturated the airwaves found considerable differences between white and black beliefs about police. For example, "while 28 percent of blacks said the police would give them a 'harder time' than they would give other people stopped for a minor traffic offense, that figure was nearly five times higher than the 6 percent of whites who held that view" (Holmes 1991, A16).[5] More recently, a Gallup poll found 60 percent of blacks agreeing that they generally are "treated less fairly by police" (Gallup Organization 1997) than are whites; only 30 percent of whites agreed with that statement. Of six situations, including access to and treatment at jobs, while shopping, while taking public transportation, and while eating at restaurants, blacks rated encounters with the police as the worst for unfair treatment. In a 1998 poll, 62 percent of African Americans reported having only "some" or "very little" confidence in police, in contrast to 37 percent of whites (Public Agenda 1998).

As the gap in perceptions between minorities and whites continues to loom deep and wide, incidents of alleged police brutality continue to spark conflict across the country. In New York City, for example, the deaths of Anthony Baez in 1995, Nathaniel Gaines in 1996, Kevin Cedeno in 1997, and Amadou Diallo in 1999, and the brutalization of Haitian immigrant Abner Louima in 1997, raised continued outcry from minority communities. In August 1996, a videotape that saturated television news showed Riverside, California, county sheriff's deputies beating Mexican immigrants who had led them on a high-speed chase; in December 1998, another Riverside case angered the black community: the police shooting of Tyisha Miller, who had been sleeping in her car with a gun in her lap while she waited for help with a flat tire. In other cities around the country, police use of force continues to be the subject of intense controversy: in St. Petersburg, Florida, where a 1996 police shooting of a black motorist led to days of civil unrest; in Prince George's County, Maryland, where an off-duty officer was accused in 1995 of beating a black man wrongly suspected of murdering a county officer; in Seattle, where the 1996 shooting of Edward Anderson was labeled an "execution-style killing" by local NAACP leaders; and in Pittsburgh, where in March 1997 two police officers were found not guilty in the 1995 death of African American businessman Johnny Gammage, who died from suffocation as one officer allegedly stood on his neck. In June 1996, the Pittsburgh chapter of the ACLU filed a class-action suit on behalf of 51 plaintiffs who alleged all manner of police misconduct, including harassment and brutality. By the late 1990s, the federal government was investigating at least ten police departments around the country, including New York and Los Angeles, for alleged patterns of brutality and other civil rights violations (Weiser 1999) and had filed lawsuits against departments in Pittsburgh, Columbus, and Steubenville, Ohio, alleging such patterns.

The gap in perceptions also continues to fuel larger political conflicts. In September 1995, for example, the Congressional Black Caucus asked Attorney General Janet Reno to investigate police abuse in a dozen communities, including New Orleans, Philadelphia, and Prince George's County. This call was echoed by the National Urban League in November 1995, which urged President Clinton to create a federal commission to address police misconduct. Meanwhile, in October of that year, Nation of Islam Minister Louis Farrakhan told hundreds of thousands of participants in the Million Man March that racism was "pervasive in police departments around the country" (Thomas 1995, 6). As a regional director of the U.S. Commission on Human Rights recently commented, there is in many urban areas "a tremendous amount of mistrust between the police department and members of the black community. Any spark can lead to a major eruption" (Navarro 1996, B6).

Race does not neatly capture all the dividing lines in public perceptions of the issue of brutality, nor is brutality exclusively a white-on-black phenomenon. Other ethnic groups often complain of police misconduct, as do homosexuals and the poor, while minority officers are just as capable of brutal behavior and just as vulnerable to perceptions of brutality as white officers. Nor is the black community monolithic in its concerns about police misconduct. Yet minority communities, particularly African Americans, often have a particularly ambivalent relationship with police. Precisely because their communities are often more crime-ridden, minority and inner-city residents often desire a strong police presence. But many African Americans and other minority groups fear both the violent crime that threatens their communities and the police who are supposed to protect them (see Lyons 1999; Sadd and Grinc 1994). For these communities, life is sometimes lived between the lines: between violent drug- and gang-related crime and violent police forces deployed to fight crime; between the rightful and appropriate physical force officers guard the right to use and the oppressive, racially charged policing many citizens perceive. As Randall Kennedy has observed,

> The communities most in need of police protection are also those in which many residents view police with the most ambivalence, much of which stems from a recognition that color counts as a mark of suspicion relied upon as a

predicate for action—stopping, questioning, patting down, arresting, beating and so forth. This causes people who might otherwise be of assistance to police to avoid them, to decline to cooperate with police investigations, to assume bad faith on the part of police officers, and to teach others that such reactions are prudent lessons of survival on the streets (1997, 153).

CONSTRAINTS ON PROBLEMATIZING POLICE USE OF FORCE

Despite the consistency of complaints about police brutality and the durability of the gap in perspectives on the issue, groups who believe that police brutality is a serious public problem find it difficult to win authority for their reality. This difficulty is due to rhetorical, informational, and political constraints that limit the construction of police brutality as a public problem.

RHETORICAL CONSTRAINTS

The power to construct or to ward off public problems depends upon rhetorical struggles over images, claims, and symbols: what some scholars have labeled "the politics of problem definition." Scholars have discovered a typical vocabulary that political contenders employ as they try to construct or ward off problems. This vocabulary includes claims about the causes of problems, how severe their effects are, how frequent or prevalent they are, the social groups they most affect, and the solutions that would best address them (Rochefort and Cobb 1994). Competing claims about causality, severity, incidence, affected populations, and solutions lie at the core of most struggles to define public problems. Those who wish to construct public problems out of troubling social conditions generally portray those conditions as widespread, as affecting large and diverse populations, or as harming groups that are positively stereotyped, such as children, or "hard-working Americans" (Schneider and Ingram 1993). They also seek to present troubling conditions as the product of identifiable causes that should be addressed through public policy.

These basic rhetorical components of problem construction present challenges for those who would designate police brutality as a serious public problem. While minority communities have continually asserted that they are subjected to police brutality on a regular basis, the bulk of the white, middle-class population does not usually feel threatened by police brutality. In fact, the white middle class is often geographically and culturally isolated from those populations who typically experience more aggressive police tactics and police misconduct. At the same time, those groups most likely to perceive brutality as a serious problem, such as ethnic minorities and the urban poor, rarely benefit from positive social stereotyping. In other words, it is difficult to make a problem out of brutality not only because much of the white middle class does not feel threatened by it but because it most affects the very groups the white middle class often does feel threatened by.

INFORMATIONAL CONSTRAINTS

Moreover, it is difficult to make compelling claims about the severity of brutality because conclusive data on its incidence is lacking. Put bluntly, there is no reliable or uncontested data to tell us how widespread and serious police brutality is. Reliable data about the incidence of brutality throughout the nation and the performance of particular police departments in comparison with others is simply not available. This is partly because what constitutes brutality is, again, inherently contestable and partly because of the way information about police use of force is recorded by police agencies.

For example, many police departments keep records of the number of people shot by police each year, and some track even the number of times police guns are discharged. But departments across the country categorize and track police-involved shootings in different ways, while other uses of physical coercion, even some that are deadly (such as deliberate ramming of vehicles during police chases), may not be tracked at all. Meanwhile, the data on the use of deadly force that police departments provide to the Justice Department under the Uniform Crime Reporting system is provided voluntarily, and differences in reporting procedures across departments seriously limit the comparability of the data. These limitations are multiplied regarding nondeadly force, about which police records are generally much less systematic.[6] Furthermore, until very recently, police departments were notoriously unwilling to make public what information they did have about police use of force (Geller and Scott 1992, 29–30). All of these difficulties with establishing the incidence and severity of police brutality are summed up—and compounded—by the fact that the Justice Department has not maintained a national database of incidents of police misconduct. After Congress mandated in 1994 that the department begin compiling such data, the department sponsored a workshop of over 40 experts to discuss how to begin. The workshop participants "noted that acquiring data on the use of excessive force would be difficult because there is no single, consensual definition of 'excessive force' among police, researchers, and legal analysts and there is little agreement about the best sources for obtaining data relevant to the incidence and prevalence of excessive force" (Greenfield, Langan, and Smith 1997, 2).[7]

Therefore, police statistics on the use of force offer little help to those who see police brutality as a prevalent problem in the United States, but they do not conclusively disprove a brutality problem, either. Other sources of data are equally problematic. For example, most police departments have procedures for processing civilian complaints against officers, and most major cities have at least one civil rights or police-monitoring organization that collects police misconduct complaints. But these data do not necessarily provide a more accurate picture of the prevalence of police brutality. Both individuals filing complaints and the groups monitoring those complaints may have motives for exaggerating the scope of the problem (just as police-provided data almost certainly underreports it).[8] But more important, there is often a counterintuitive relationship between a department's conduct and the prevalence of misconduct claims: more complaints can actually signal a department that is more open to investigating complaints.[9] Therefore, the official complaint rate may not be a reliable measure of police performance but rather an indicator of the particular administrative culture of different police departments (ACLU 1992).

Thus, it is not that there is no data on police use of force upon which various claims-makers can draw but that there is no fully objective and verifiable data that can unambiguously demonstrate either the presence or absence of brutality problems.[10] For example, the Christopher Commission, charged with investigating allegations of widespread brutality in the LAPD in the aftermath of the King beating, found that of 2,152 citizen allegations of excessive force from 1986 to 1990, police investigators listed only 42 as "sustained" (Christopher Commission report excerpts 1991, A12). Does this mean that there were 2,152 incidents of excessive force by the LAPD during those years, or only 42? The answer depends on many factors that either cannot be known or cannot be definitively settled: Did everyone who believed they experienced brutality file a formal complaint with the department? Did everyone who filed a complaint tell the truth? Did the department fully investigate all the allegations? And were the department's grounds justifiable for concluding that over 2,000 of these complaints could not be sustained?

Whether brutality is a "problem" is therefore difficult to establish in the statistical terms that our society usually finds authoritative, and any claims about the prevalence of police brutality are likely to be highly contested. This lack of conclusive data presents a serious informational constraint on the construction of brutality problems.

POLITICAL CONSTRAINTS

Finally, police critics find it difficult to persuade the public that police brutality is a serious problem because police and political officials generally have an interest in keeping the issue out of the news and off the political agenda. For police departments and local elected officials, allegations of brutality are politically vexing. Especially in the increasingly diverse, conflicted, and economically hard-pressed environment of America's major urban centers, allegations of excessive force are a potential match in a tinderbox. A cursory glance at the history of civil disturbances in the past three decades reveals that many have been sparked by incidents of alleged excessive force; the list includes disturbances from the mid-1960s through the mid-1990s in San Francisco, St. Louis, Dallas, Chicago, Detroit, Memphis, Cleveland, Atlanta, Houston, Newark, Miami, New York City, St. Petersburg, Washington, D.C., and, of course, Los Angeles in both 1965 and 1992 (Geller and Scott 1992, 3–10). Potential political crisis in the wake of police use of force is therefore a serious concern for police and political officials alike, and when racial dimensions are involved, the stakes are even higher.[11]

Moreover, there is rarely any political benefit to officials in "owning" a police brutality problem. Instead, police often fear that losing control of the brutality issue will lead directly or indirectly to decreased police autonomy if the public's "second guessing" becomes institutionalized in more restrictive use-of-force policies or in more formal processes for civilian review of allegations of police misconduct. Consequently, police often see allegations of brutality as dangerous invitations to the public and political officials to circumscribe police authority and discretion. Meanwhile, challenging the power of police departments and their supporters is often politically unappealing to politicians. In an era in which it is fashionable to "get tough" on a crime problem seen as growing ever worse, it is much more appealing to politicians to focus public attention on crime fighting than on the crime fighters. Police unions, moreover, can be powerful political allies—or enemies, as former New York mayor David Dinkins discovered. Dinkins's response to a police shooting in 1992 lit a firestorm of police protest that helped Republican candidate Rudolph Giuliani to unseat Dinkins in the 1992 election.[12]

For all of these reasons, rhetorical, informational, and political, police brutality appears on the public-issue agenda only rarely. Indeed, when police brutality does land on the agenda, it is generally propelled by highly publicized and controversial incidents rather than by clear statistical trends or clear political consensus about the existence of policing problems. Hence, its status as a problem is socially constructed, and the news is the construction medium.

POLICE USE OF FORCE IN THE NEWS

The media largely determine what the general public learns about street cops' daily experience with criminals and the underclass, as well as what the middle-class public learns about other groups' experiences with police. While the news media are generally preoccupied with crime, they are not generally preoccupied with police behavior in fighting crime.[13] Police brutality therefore usually becomes an "issue"—in the news as well as in other public arenas—only occasionally, in the aftermath of certain dramatic and controversial use-of-force incidents.

Police use a wide variety of coercive practices in their daily work, only some of which involve physical force—everything from using an authoritative tone of voice to applying handcuffs to striking or occasionally shooting people. This study is concerned only with news coverage of what I call "use-of-force incidents": altercations in which police use significant physical coercion, such as striking, kicking, beating, or shooting people. By this definition, "use-of-force incidents" involve a level of coercion greater than simply handcuffing people and taking them into custody.[14]

While some use-of-force incidents become highly publicized centerpieces of public debate, the vast majority never become news at all. For example, New York City police shot (either fatally or nonfatally) 101 people in 1990, 111 people in 1991, 90 people in 1992, and 86 people in 1993, according to the best available records (Chevigny 1995, 67). Only a fraction of those shootings became news: the *New York Times* published news stories about six police shootings in 1990, one in 1991, eight in 1992, and five in 1993. Similarly, Los Angeles police agencies (the LAPD and the county sheriffs' department) together shot 124 people in 1991 and 126 people in 1992 (ibid., 46). The *Los Angeles Times* published news stories about 32 local police shootings in 1991 and 12 in 1992.

In other words, roughly 17 percent of police shootings in the Los Angeles area and only 5 percent of those in New York City were the subject of news stories in these cities' major newspapers.[15] Moreover, New York City's Civilian Complaint Investigation Bureau reports that over 27,000 complaints of excessive force were lodged against New York City police between 1986 and 1995 (NYCLU 1996, 26). Of the unknown number of these altercations that actually occurred, only a tiny fraction became news: the *New York Times* reported on a total of 198 instances of police use of force between 1985 and 1994. Similarly, 3,107 excessive-force complaints were filed with the New York City Civilian Complaint Review Board in 1994 (Civilian Complaint Review Board 1996, 4); in that year, the *Times* reported on 29 use-of-force incidents overall.

The key phenomenon of interest in this study is how news organizations construct the public definitions of those use-of-force incidents they do report.[16] As subsequent chapters will show, most use-of-force incidents that do gain news coverage do so only fleetingly, and their public definitions are successfully contained by officials. Yet a handful of these incidents become major news stories, centerpieces in struggles among nonofficial sources seeking to designate brutality problems and official sources seeking to ward them off. It is in these few cases that news organizations at least tentatively construct new (or reconstruct old) brutality problems.

THE NORMATIVE DILEMMA

The deep divides in public perceptions of police promise to fuel further mistrust, hostility, and violence, especially if the general public's fear of crime continues to grow, economic and social conditions continue to deteriorate in urban centers, and police continue to search for effective ways to convince the public they can control crime. In this context, the media offer one of the few public arenas in which divergent perspectives on policing can hope to confront and learn from one another. Yet the news about brutality hangs on a dilemma created by the ambiguity of police use of force: The media's response to incidents of alleged brutality can look either too aggressive or too passive, depending upon one's presuppositions about the police and the troubled communities that often criticize them.

Those who believe that police brutality is a pervasive and endemic problem feel persistently marginalized by the mainstream news, which, in their view, rarely if ever grapples seriously with fundamental questions about excessive force. People whose lives have been scarred by violent encounters with the police often charge that the media help to shield police from public scrutiny. They often feel unable to effectively challenge the official claims that define use-of-force incidents for the general public. As the mother of Johnny Gammage, who died in police custody in Pittsburgh in 1995, lamented, "They are trying to make it sound like he caused his own death" (Meredith 1996, A10). Moreover, they believe that the news media simply help existing policing practices to remain unchallenged. Ronald Hampton, an antibrutality activist and past president of the National Black Police Association, argues that the mainstream media play a greater role in the continuation of police brutality than in alerting the general public to the problem. Because of their tendency to ignore voices within the communities most subject to brutality, and their tendency to "side with the police" by relying almost exclusively on official sources, Hampton claims, the media actually contribute to an ongoing brutality problem (Hampton 1996).

In contrast, some people who see police as the vulnerable thin blue line between order and chaos resent what they see as the media's willingness to make an issue out of police brutality on the basis of isolated incidents and possibly fraudulent claims of excessive force. Police, who are paid to put their lives on the line in frightening and sometimes life-threatening situations, and whose split-second decisions can trigger ugly controversies that linger for years, often view the media with suspicion and even hostility. As the lawyer for a Miami policeman acquitted in the shooting death of a black motorcyclist—an acquittal that touched off days of rioting—indignantly told reporters, "If the headlines had read, 'Twice-convicted drug dealer shot while trying to run over officer,' there wouldn't have been any riots" (Bearak and Harrison 1989, 1). As another critic put it, "Hundreds, thousands of arrests are done competently. When you have an incident like L.A., and it gets in the media, it's like a magnet sucking up little filings. The incident becomes a lightning rod for other issues," such as allegations of police racism (Charles Friel, quoted in Harrison 1991, A1). And in the aftermath of the highly publicized shooting of Amadou Diallo in New York in 1999, the city's deputy police commissioner publicly blamed negative news coverage of police for a rise in the city's homicide rate (Blair 1999). Critics on this side of the divide believe that, rather than unduly upholding police legitimacy, the media unduly erode it.

The findings of this study offer a response to both sides of the divide.

As subsequent chapters will show, the news media help to create and sustain the legitimacy of the police, but they also sometimes subject police to critical scrutiny that erodes police legitimacy. At the same time, critical citizen voices are not completely absent from the news about policing, but they are generally not granted the same place in the news as those of police and other officials, and often are subtly undermined by the ways that reporters frame news stories. Thus, critical perspectives on policing rarely earn a lasting place in the news—except in the circumstances that surround extraordinarily high-profile use-of-force incidents such as the Rodney King beating.

These findings will not satisfy either camp of critics, no doubt. Nor will they resolve a deeper normative question about the news: whether news coverage that problematizes police behavior is "good" or "bad." Whole segments of the American public believe—and have believed for decades—that police are racist, that they systematically target, harass, frame, brutalize, and even kill certain classes of people, and that their behavior stems from deep roots in the criminal justice system and American culture. The key question considered in this study is not whether this perspective is right. Rather, the key question is: Who gets to participate in the mass-mediated conversation about public issues such as police brutality?

Neither can other daunting normative questions be settled here once and for all: Should the media be more responsive to police voices than to their critics? Could society function and order be maintained if police were not usually given the benefit of the doubt? On the other hand, can order be maintained, over the long run, if the news (and thus the general public) ignores the beliefs and perspectives of those most often on the receiving end of the night stick? Is any objective definition of "police accountability" possible, given that some societal groups will probably always view police with suspicion and that police will probably always believe that they should be given greater latitude and benefit of the doubt? Indeed, the ultimate question may be, What would constitute an open and fair public deliberation on the issue of police brutality?

Addressing the question of the quality of today's mass-mediated public deliberation, Page (1996) writes that, for normative standards of public deliberation to be met, "it is probably *not* necessary . . . that the mass media meet hard-to-define, and difficult-or-impossible-to-enforce, standards of perfect balance or absence of bias" (123, emphasis in original). After all, Page asks, "From what ideal kind of representativeness should bias or deviation be measured?" This question is particularly pertinent—and particularly vexing—in regard to issues as highly charged and polarizing as police brutality. It is not clear that there is any standard for news coverage of policing upon which all societal groups could agree, nor does this study seek to impose such a standard. But this study does contribute to that normative debate by performing a crucial empirical task: measuring the prevalence, prominence, and treatment of competing perspectives on policing in the news.

THREE

Normalizing Coercion

*Competing Claims
about Police Use of Force*

In its July 1994 issue, *New York* magazine featured a piece by media critic Jon Katz entitled "Is Police Brutality a Myth?" The article examined what Katz called "an increasingly familiar urban ritual":

> A young black or Hispanic is killed by police or dies in police custody. People who say they are eyewitnesses appear live on local TV newscasts, giving accounts that diverge wildly from the police's and one another.
>
> Extra cops gather in riot gear. People identified—by themselves and the media—as community activists appear at the family's side along with lawyers, calling for investigations, all too predictably claiming that the police committed brutal and unprovoked murder. They demand justice, lead marches, file lawsuits. The accusation hangs in the air: *racist killer cop*. (Katz 1994, 39)

The media, Katz claimed, are all too eager to publicize these activities and claims and to overreact to such events. Have the media, he asked, "become easy prey for lawyers and spokespeople now fully adept at the art of racial media manipulation?"

Katz's questions are valid, and to residents of New York and similar urban centers his portrayal of the news about police brutality may seem accurate. Certainly, that portrayal is consistent with the perspective of police departments across the country. A recent survey of police officials found that most believe that news coverage of police brutality is sensationalized, unfair, and inaccurate and that the news media have "a habit of jumping on isolated instances of police misconduct and blow-ing them up into national stories" (Corrigan 1994, 19). Similarly, an internal survey of Los Angeles police officers conducted in the aftermath of the Rodney King incident found that 92 percent of officers identified "the media and outspoken community leaders" as causing "negative interaction between the police and the community" (Murphy 1991, B3).

Critical media scholars, however, would bring another set of questions to this "familiar urban ritual": How does the news usually represent police use of force? How many instances of police use of force become major news stories of the sort Katz describes? And if the media are "becoming easy prey" for a new set of voices, then whose voices have more typically influenced the news about policing?

Several decades of scholarly research suggest that the news typically represents most faithfully the perspectives of officials and other elites. Institutionally positioned officials provide reporters with the bulk of the "routine" events that become news. Political and social elites are generally the most audible voices in the news and, therefore, heavily influence the public definitions of news events. Moreover, the news is generally episodic (Iyengar 1991) and fragmented (Bennett 1996), skipping from event to event, providing little thematic context. This episodic focus and heavy reliance on officials, scholars have argued, create news that is biased in favor of official control over the definitions of public problems.

This chapter demonstrates that the same is true of much news coverage of policing. The data presented here illustrate that the typical news story about use of force is brief, episodic, and structured around claims provided by police spokesmen and politicians. Crucially, these same sources usually "individualize" police use of force, focusing public attention on deviant, violent criminal suspects who threaten officers and the public and, occasionally, on "rogue cops" who lose control and cross the line between acceptable and unacceptable force. This kind of coverage normalizes what some might call brutality and marginalizes competing perspectives on the existence of brutality problems and the causal roots of police violence. Later chapters will explore how some use-of-force incidents become the kind of highly charged "rituals" Katz criticizes. This chapter demonstrates that the vast majority of incidents that receive any coverage at all disappear quickly from the news pages and are successfully contained by official communication strategies.

CLAIMS, FRAMES, AND CAUSAL STORIES:
THE TOOLS OF PROBLEM DEFINING

As outlined in chapter 2, the distinctive vocabulary of problem definition includes claims about what causes certain problems, how severe or
widespread their effects are, the groups that are most affected by them,
and the solutions that are needed to address them. In other words,
groups seek to construct (or ward off) public problems by making
claims about reality. When societal groups disagree about the nature of
conditions and problems, whose renderings of reality "win" is a question that is largely decided in the media arena. What problems the news
presents to the public, therefore, is largely a function of which voices
and views journalists amplify and which they marginalize.

Much attention has been paid to the way the news "frames" issues
and events in the news. In fact, the term "frame" has been used by so
many scholars in so many contexts that its precise meaning has become
unclear (see Entman 1993). Despite the many uses of the concept, the
same fundamental elements that are central to the rhetoric of problem
definition are also central to news frames. As Entman (1993, 52) writes,
frames are communication devices that

> *define problems*—determine what a causal agent is doing with what costs
> and benefits, usually measured in terms of common cultural values; *diagnose
> causes*—identify the forces creating the problem; *make moral judgments*—
> evaluate causal agents and their effects; and *suggest remedies*—offer and jus-
> tify treatments for the problems and predict their likely effects.

The way the news frames events and problems, therefore, depends largely
on the claims provided by the sources journalists rely most heavily upon.

A common way in which claims-makers advance their claims about
public problems is in the form of causal stories (Stone 1989). A critical
task of the claims-maker is to argue that certain events and issues are or
are not within the realm of human causation and intention. Moreover,
different claims-makers may assign different causes to a problem, since
the nature of its causes can determine its status as a public problem.
Therefore, "political actors use narrative story lines and symbolic devices to manipulate . . . issue characteristics, all the while making it
seem as though they are simply describing facts." Problem definition is
thus "a process of image-making, where the images have to do fundamentally with attributing cause, blame, and responsibility" (ibid. 282).

Police use of force is typically framed in the news in terms of two distinct sets of causal claims. "Individualizing" claims are generally

(though not always) made by police and political officials, while "systemic" claims are typically made by nonofficials, particularly those I will call "critical nonofficials": activists, community leaders, residents of minority and urban communities, and many academic experts.

In brief, the essential difference between these claims lies in whether they frame police brutality as a public problem—an unacceptable social condition that needs to be addressed with new or invigorated public policies. Whether police use of force is seen as a problem depends on how its causes are understood: as a necessary police response to violent deviants and criminals or as police violence stemming from deep roots within the criminal justice system, the political system, or widespread societal attitudes. Problematizing police use of force also depends on whether police brutality is understood as a common and widespread phenomenon or as something that occurs only occasionally and randomly.[1]

If police use force to defend themselves and protect the public against violent criminals and other deviants, then the use of force cannot be labeled "brutality" or understood as a public problem. Even if people agree that particular use-of-force incidents appear to have involved excessive force, the status of police brutality as a public problem is still far from certain. For to be problematized, excessive force must be understood as something caused by systems, not merely by individuals. If excessive force is caused by individual renegade cops, it can be addressed adequately by existing legal and administrative remedies: bad cops can be tried in criminal court, sued in civil proceedings, or subjected to departmental discipline. As long as those remedies are thought to be operating reasonably well, the scope of any perceived brutality problem is confined, and individual officers' wrongdoing can be addressed without resorting to fundamental reforms. In contrast, an excessive-force "problem" that is systemic in nature can be addressed only by moving beyond these typical remedies; indeed, the ineffectiveness of these remedies may be seen as part of the problem. Before providing data showing the comparative prominence of individualizing and systemic claims in the news, the following sections describe these claims in more detail.

OFFICIAL VOICES AND INDIVIDUALIZING CLAIMS

The most common voice in the news about police use of force is an official voice. When talking to reporters, those officials—police officers, police brass, and local elected officials, along with attorneys who de-

fend officers against excessive-force suits—typically assert that the suspects apprehended or killed were uncooperative, combative, violent,
and threatening. In other words, they place responsibility for the use of
force with the suspect. Of course, individualizing claims are not exclusively official. Witnesses to a use-of-force incident may attest that a suspect threatened officers; members of the general public may believe that
alleged victims of brutality deserved their treatment at the hands of police. But, most typically, it is officials who focus attention on the behavior of suspects rather than on that of officers, asserting that officers
were obliged to use force to accomplish legitimate crime-control and
order-maintenance goals. Officials also typically portray the use of
force as consistent with departmental policies and with public expectations of how officers should behave in dangerous situations. By adopting these claims as the basic structure of news stories, the news commonly frames police use of force as necessary and defensive behavior,
and certainly not a public problem.

> Los Angeles County district attorney's investigators concluded Wednesday
> that three sheriff's deputies acted in self-defense when they shot and killed a
> 50-year-old woman armed with a knife in a Lancaster fast-food restaurant
> in April. . . . [The investigators concluded that] "The evidence indicates that
> the deputies showed considerable restraint" until [the woman], a robbery
> suspect cornered by six deputies, lunged at them with a butcher knife.
> (Rotella 1989, 8)[2]

> When police tried to arrest him for public intoxication, [the suspect] began
> kicking, biting, and punching the officers, [Inglewood Police Sgt. Harold]
> Moret said. . . . Eventually, the officers tied his ankles with a nylon rope and
> handcuffed him. He was carried to a police car, where officers discovered he
> had stopped breathing. (Lacey and Maharaj 1989, B3)[3]

> Given the circumstances, given the facts that we could have had an armed sus-
> pect and given the fact we had a violent crowd, I think the level of force we
> used was not only appropriate, but minimal. . . . I've been in lots of situations
> where officers have been hurt, including myself . . . and this situation was def-
> initely progressing to where an officer was going to be hurt. (Serrano 1989, 7)[4]

When police and other officials offer individualizing claims to reporters, they manage the public image of the police by establishing
simple news narratives that may reduce the ambiguity and complexity
of real incidents. Many police-citizen encounters are straightforward
incidents of police responding appropriately to suspicious or threatening behavior. Police are often obliged to use force to restrain violent
people. Police must operate in situations that are often unpredictable

and dangerous, and the nature of their work requires them to exercise considerable discretion in deciding what incidents and behaviors to respond to and how; moreover, the cues that alert police officers to potential trouble or to possible crimes in progress may not be immediately obvious to the untrained eye. Moreover, when cops do use force, they are sometimes responding to situations in which split-second decisions may mean the difference between life and death. The behaviors that indicate to an officer that it is time to pull the trigger, to take the most extreme example of use of force, may be difficult to reconstruct into a narrative that sounds well reasoned and convincing to people after the fact.

Indeed, use-of-force incidents may escalate to violence through a chain of events and perceptions. Scholarly research has shown that the reasons police might decide to approach or arrest someone, and the reasons people might choose to defy police, are more complex than is often assumed (Chevigny 1969; Muir 1977; Skolnick and Fyfe 1993). Perceived challenges to their authority often make cops bristle, and those challenges may not seem great, or even evident, to outside observers. At the same time, it is perceived abusiveness on the part of officers that can lead civilians to defy and resist police commands to comply and submit (Skolnick and Fyfe, 1993, 102–3). In the heat of the moment, both police and suspects can do things that seem irrational to outside observers, sometimes with tragic consequences. For example, inexperienced or inadequately trained officers may escalate the level of physical force they use beyond that which is strictly necessary to control the situation at hand.[5]

Regardless of what "really" happened between an officer and a suspect, in most cases police retain the power to define those events for the public. As one legal scholar has put it, "the police shape the facts [of use-of-force incidents] to justify what they have done" (Chevigny 1995, 74) in order to manage public perceptions.[6] It can be difficult to know if the individualizing narratives police tell are reasonable accounts of what occurred or if they are the public-relations equivalent of the "cover charge," in which those the police have roughed up are subsequently charged with disturbing the peace or resisting arrest (Chevigny 1969; Mollen 1994; Worsnop 1991).[7]

Officials tend to frame the use of force in individualizing terms even when evidence arises that police have indeed used excessive force. Officials then tend to blame the individual officers for inadequate attention to proper procedure or for losing control of themselves. According to this type of individualizing claim, excessive force happens randomly and is not a problem that warrants departmentmental reforms or structural changes in policing or the criminal justice system. Rather, they suggest, these "rogue cops" need to be dealt with through regular departmental or legal proceedings. And while police spokespersons sometimes acknowledge that officers are to blame for incidents of excessive force, they also often emphasize that police are human and make mistakes. As one lobbyist for police organizations told a *Los Angeles Times* reporter, the public "has the right to expect a high standard from police, but they don't have the right to expect [police] to be gods all the time" (Al Cooper, quoted in Rainey 1989b, 4).

Finally, officials ward off the construction of brutality problems by denying that brutality is either common or patterned. For example, when Kerman Maddox, a prominent African American and former aide to Los Angeles mayor Tom Bradley, complained of racially motivated police harassment by the LAPD in 1989, a department spokesman replied, "We are looking into it. But if Mr. Maddox is alleging that there is some institutional bias in this department or that any community is being treated differently by the Police Department, then it's absolutely wrong" (Garcia 1989, 3).[8] This type of strategy was repeated in LAPD Chief Daryl Gates's assertion that the beating of Rodney King was "an aberration."

Individualizing claims, therefore, are preemptive damage control strategies. Portraying the use of force as a necessary response to violent criminals and deviants, or as a result of bad officers who lose control, can ward off the construction of policing problems in the news. Ultimately, what is at stake for police and politicians in defining use-of-force incidents is the ability to legitimate themselves and government policies in public discourse. Indeed, political legitimacy "depends on the ability of authorities to make convincing claims, arguments that they are acting in accordance with social norms" (Ericson, Baranek, and Chan 1991, 7). For police, whose job allows and sometimes requires the use of violence, this is a crucial task indeed.

NONOFFICIALS AND SYSTEMIC CLAIMS

Of course, individualizing claims are not the only possible perspective on police use of force. Sometimes nonofficials—persons subjected to force, their families, or witnesses, for example—view those events as unjustified. These nonofficials appear in the news fairly regularly; indeed, much reporting on use-of-force incidents is driven by nonofficial "competing accounts" of these events (see chapter 5). Yet when these kinds of sources talk to reporters, they tend to make claims about particular events rather than about any systemic underpinnings of police abuse. Typical of such claims are the following, taken from two *Los Angeles Times* stories:

> An El Cajon man said Wednesday he was shot in the back of the neck for no reason after he raised both arms in the air and attempted to surrender to police.
> Randall Cary Geiger, 30, said he was hiding under a table in his apartment on South Magnolia Avenue in El Cajon on Tuesday morning when two police officers kicked in the door.
> Geiger said he was coming out from under the table with his arms up when one of the officers grabbed him, pinned him to the floor face down, put a gun to his neck and shot him. (Sanchez 1988, 1)[9]

> Witnesses said that when [tow truck driver John] Daniels tried to give officers papers regarding the truck, they refused to take them.
> Daniels swore at the officers, jumped into his truck and turned on the ignition, the witnesses said. When the officers tried to pull him from the vehicle, Daniels clamped his hands on the steering wheel and would not get out, according to testimony.
> [Officer] Barnett [claimed] that Daniels pushed one of the officers, knocking him almost under the truck's wheels, but witnesses disputed the description. (Ford 1993, 1)[10]

Thus, in the news the most common type of nonofficial claim about police use of force does not offer an alternative reason for police behavior. Rather, such claims emphasize the "unreasonableness" of police responses to civilians' behavior. In contrast, claims that cast brutality as patterned or systematic aggression, and which locate the roots of police violence in systemic aspects of American policing, criminal justice, and culture, appear more sporadically in the news. These claims are typically made by groups I will call "critical nonofficials": activists seeking police reform, residents and leaders of minority and inner-city communities, and some academic experts; occasionally, such claims are also made by victims of alleged brutality who seek legal redress.[11] These groups cite several kinds of systemic problems that, in their view, create police-brutality problems.

First, critical nonofficials often claim that police administration, local political officials, or both are at some level responsible for the conduct of rank-and-file officers. Police brutality becomes a systemic problem, according to this view, when those leaders fail to establish firm oversight and discipline, when they provide poor examples of public decorum and respect for the community, or when they are insulated from civilian control. According to this claim, police brutality can be solved only by changing the leadership of police departments, establishing civilian oversight of police, or otherwise instituting better political accountability of police. This kind of claim gained wide currency in the aftermath of the Rodney King beating. As one editorialist wrote in the *Los Angeles Times*, "The Los Angeles Police Department sanctions brutality by enforcing an implicit code of silence regarding misconduct by officers. The beating of Rodney Glenn King was an aberration only because a bystander made a video recording of the incident" (Watson 1991). This systemic problem definition was ratified by the Christopher Commission, who in its recommendations for reform of the LAPD asserted that "the problem of excessive force in the LAPD is fundamentally a problem of supervision, management and leadership" (Christopher Commission report excerpts, 1991, A12).[12]

Similarly, critical nonofficials often contend that existing institutional checks on police brutality do not function properly. According to this claim, departmental review procedures and legal remedies are seriously weakened by conflicts of interest and racial bias. They argue that prosecutors are notoriously unwilling to bring excessive-force charges against police, both because their success in other cases depends upon police testimony and evidence and because prosecutors generally initiate only those cases they believe they can win. Given the reluctance of police to cooperate in rooting out brutality, and the reluctance of many juries to convict police officers, critical nonofficials argue, prosecutors have little incentive to pursue excessive-force cases. Consequently, many antibrutality activists favor the establishment of independent special prosecutors to handle police abuse cases. For example, minority activists claimed in 1989 that Los Angeles District Attorney Ira Reiner had failed to file charges in over 15 cases since 1985 in which black or Latino men were killed by local sheriff's deputies or police officers. "We need prosecution outside the hands of his office," claimed Geri Silva of the Equal Rights Congress. "We're just whistling in the wind, if we think he'll prosecute" (Merina 1989, 3).

Critical nonofficials also often argue that a clannish police subculture encourages police hostility and violence toward the communities they serve and erects a "blue wall of silence" that keeps even good officers from helping to stop or uncover brutal officers. For example, as one academic expert told a *Los Angeles Times* reporter in 1991, "The cops (in Los Angeles) are trained that they are soldiers in the war on crime, rather than members of the community who are there to arrest people and bring them to court" (James Fyfe, quoted in Tobar 1991, A1).

Finally, critical nonofficials often claim that police brutality is an expression of racism, an inevitable output of a political and legal system corrupted by—or actively engaged in—the continued oppression of racial and ethnic minorities. Police brutality, in this view, is just one particularly blatant way that dominant groups keep oppressed groups "in their place." Generally, when critical nonofficials make this claim about police brutality, they contend that brutality is systematically aimed at particular groups, indicating a problem that extends beyond individual prejudices to institutionalized racism within the department and the society as a whole.

Claims about racially motivated police abuse are the most common criticisms of police conduct raised in public discourse. These claims are common because, first of all, they are strongly entrenched in the African American community, in particular. The belief that police routinely single out blacks for everything from traffic citations (for "DWB—driving while black") to search and seizure to gunfire is widely shared among African Americans. These perceptions may be exaggerated, and nationwide patterns of such institutionalized racism may be difficult to prove, but it is a fact that police use force, particularly deadly force, disproportionately against blacks as compared with force used against whites (Geller and Scott 1992, 147). In fact, black Americans tend to have different kinds of encounters with police than do whites. As black journalist Ellis Cose (1997, 81) has observed, "it's hard to find any black adult in America who has not had an unpleasant encounter with the law, who has not been stopped, for instance, by disrespectful police spoiling for a fight or perhaps a bit too eager to assert their authority over members of a race they view indiscriminately as a threat to the civil order." These embittered attitudes toward the criminal justice system, so revealing of America's continuing racial gulf, explain the strongly divided public reactions to events such as the not-guilty verdicts in the Rodney King and O. J. Simpson criminal trials.

Claims about police racism also are relatively common because they are confirmed by iconic moments in our collective memory. Many Americans can easily draw on images of Bull Connor-style tactics of racial oppression when thinking about the civil rights movement, for example. Indeed, claims about police racism resonate with a civil rights "master frame" (Snow and Benford 1992) that has profoundly shaped the political culture of America. While racism in many forms is certainly alive and well, its most blatant forms have become taboo, and so, paradoxically, it is easier to talk about racism as a cause of police brutality than about causes that have been less thoroughly aired in public discourse.

Finally, racism is the most common systemic explanation for police brutality because it is simple and translates into easily understood news scripts. In fact, though critics often intend it as a critique of the entire system of criminal justice, racism is easily personalized and individualized, traced to individual maladjusted cops rather than to the police culture or societal attitudes toward minorities. For this reason and others, racism can be an incomplete and even problematic basis for thinking about the causes of police violence, as will be discussed in subsequent chapters. But it is undoubtedly the most widely shared critical perspective on police misconduct—and the most politically volatile.

TYPICAL NEWS ABOUT THE USE OF FORCE

Analyzing the content of the news about police use of force demonstrates that official voices and individualizing claims predominate. Of approximately 8,000 total *New York Times* (*NYT*) and *Los Angeles Times* (*LAT*) articles regarding U.S. police published between 1985 and 1994, 1,192 *NYT* articles and 1,439 *LAT* articles addressed police use of force specifically. (Most of these were stories about particular use-of-force incidents, but some were stories about subjects such as police policies regarding the use of force or legislative debates about police weaponry.) As shown in table 1, close to 80 percent of all articles relied on official sources. By comparison, nonofficials were less prominent, and "critical nonofficials" such as activists and community leaders were rarely cited.[13]

Individualizing claims about police use of force were also much more common in the news than were systemic claims. Moreover, individualizing claims were much more likely to be given prominent placement. Such claims appeared in the lead paragraphs of 17 percent of the *NYT* items, while systemic claims appeared in only 2 percent of story leads; in the *LAT*, the figures were 21 percent and 5 percent, respectively.[14]

EPISODIC COVERAGE, EVANESCENT EVENTS

The analysis also reveals that the news about police use of force is highly episodic in nature, focusing primarily on the who, what, where, when, and how of particular incidents.[15] In 84 percent of *NYT*

TABLE 1. RELATIVE PROMINENCE OF VOICES AND CLAIMS IN COVERAGE OF POLICE
USE OF FORCE, *NEW YORK TIMES* AND *LOS ANGELES TIMES*, 1985–94

Newspaper	Percent of stories mentioning officials*	Percent of stories mentioning nonofficials*	Percent of stories mentioning critical nonofficials*	Percent of stories mentioning individualizing claims[†]	Percent of stories mentioning systemic claims[†]
New York Times	79	47	19	61	19
Los Angeles Times	77	42	17	57	26

*Based upon coding of all index entries regarding police use of force appearing between 1985 and 1994; *n* = 1,192 in the *New York Times* and 1,439 in the *Los Angeles Times.*

[†]Based upon coding of the full text of news coverage of a random sample of 56 police use-of-force incidents reported in the *New York Times* and 58 reported in the *Los Angeles Times*; *n* = 423 news and editorial items.

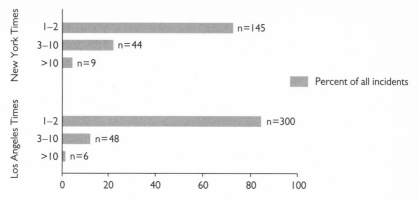

Figure 1. Amount of News Coverage of Use-of-Force Incidents, *New York Times* and *Los Angeles Times*, 1985–94. Source: Data are compiled from the *New York Times* and *Los Angeles Times* indexes. Incidents are grouped by the amount of coverage received; lengths of bars correspond to the percentage each group represents of all use-of-force incidents reported in that newspaper.

articles and 89 percent of *LAT* articles over the ten-year period examined here, an episodic focus was clear, and the bulk of these articles—75 and 79 percent, respectively—simply reported the details of individual use-of-force incidents. News items that had at least some thematic focus on police use of force as an issue were much less common. Twelve percent of *NYT* and 8 percent of *LAT* items were partially thematic in focus, using some discrete event as a starting point for a broader focus on the subject of police use of force. Only 4 percent and 3 percent, respectively, were purely thematic explorations of police use of force.

Thus, police use of force is represented in the news primarily through the prism of events. Reflecting the typically fragmented nature of daily news (Bennett 1996) and the underlying journalistic "epistemology of the particular" (Ettema et al. 1991, 96), the news doesn't often address questions such as the prevalence of police violence, patterns in how it occurs, or the acceptability of police tactics in fighting crime and maintaining order. Rather, the primary question addressed in the news is, "When and where did police use force against whom?"

Not only is most news about police use of force highly episodic in its focus. Most use-of-force incidents that are reported in the news disappear from the news pages quickly. Figure 1 illustrates this point by grouping all use-of-force incidents reported in each paper according to

the number of news stories and editorials in which they were mentioned. Fully 73 percent of incidents reported in the *NYT* and 85 percent of those reported in the *LAT* were mentioned in only one or two
articles.[16] Thus, the news about police use of force is highly fragmented,
briefly focusing on various incidents, only occasionally covering one incident beyond the initial police report, and only very rarely examining
the issue in broader thematic context.

SIMPLIFIED NARRATIVES OF POLICING

That the news about police use of force is both highly individualized
and highly episodic is no coincidence. Police and other official sources
typically provide reporters with simple narratives that encourage minimal contextualization and minimal follow-up. Accordingly, most use-
of-force incidents are covered in brief, episodic news items that depend
heavily upon official claims, usually including no nonofficial voices or
explicitly marginalizing their claims, as the following lead paragraphs
suggest:

> An unidentified man was shot to death last night in a gunfight with two po-
> lice officers in East New York, Brooklyn, the police said. The officers spotted
> the man firing into the air about 10 P.M. near the intersection of Fulton and
> Cleveland Streets, said Sgt. John McCluskey, a police spokesman. "He was
> stumbling on the street and brandishing a pistol when the officers arrived
> and witnessed him firing shots," he said. "They challenged him, and he
> turned and fired at them. They returned fire." (Police shoot man to death,
> 1994, 23)

> A man with a carving knife who allegedly lunged at an officer was shot and
> killed Wednesday by police outside a Hancock Park dry cleaners, authorities
> said. . . . Investigators said a 55-year-old man, whose identity was withheld
> pending notification of relatives, argued with the business' owner and
> stabbed the owner's wife in the hand before police arrived. (Police kill man
> who attempted to stab officer, 1992, B8)

> San Diego police have found no evidence of negligence in connection with
> the death of a 14-year-old Mexican boy run over by a U.S. Border Patrol ve-
> hicle in August, and authorities have no plans to prosecute the agent who
> was driving, federal and local officials said Monday.
>   The incident, which occurred just inside U.S. territory in San Diego early
> in the morning of Aug. 20, sparked considerable controversy—and a call by
> the Mexican government for a thorough investigation—after an attorney
> representing the dead boy's family alleged that the agent had been driving
> recklessly.

U.S. Border Patrol officials, who characterized the incident as unfortunate but unavoidable, said immediately afterward that an initial inquiry had uncovered no evidence of wrongdoing by the driver . . . or his partner. (McDonnell 1989)

These simplified news narratives in which officials predominate are sometimes made possible by the marginalization of critical nonofficials, whose perspectives complicate the story about police use of force. Critical nonofficials rarely serve as primary sources of news, though they are sometimes used as secondary sources, appearing not as central characters but in walk-on roles, so to speak.[17] This relative lack of critical voices contributes directly to a lack of systemic claims about policing problems in the news. For example, while 34 percent of *New York Times* items that did cite critical nonofficials also contained systemic perspectives on police brutality, only 8 percent that did not cite critical nonofficials contained systemic claims.[18]

Nowhere is this marginalization of systemic understandings of police brutality more evident than in regard to the complex systemic perspectives developed by many academic experts on police violence. For example, some scholars have located the roots of police violence in a fundamental tension underlying the task of policing. As Skolnick (1966) observes, police are expected both to enforce order and to observe the rule of law. Yet achieving the former often means violating the latter. Police are often implicitly expected to go around or beyond the written rule of law to enforce order and "keep the peace." In fact, police officers are "called upon to test the limits of their legal authority," since they are the law's "chief interpreter" on the street (ibid., 20). Thus, in this view, the practice of policing rests on fundamental dilemmas where conflicting values and police discretion meet. As Chevigny (1995, 141) observes, "The police are asked to keep order and control pariah groups that the public fears; at the same time, the public wants to believe that the police act lawfully. One result is that the police harass those who are 'out of order' and try to make the actions look legal." This fundamental tension underlying the police role is rarely if ever explored in the news.

Similarly, the news rarely acknowledges that the use of force has an expressive as well as an instrumental value to police. As Scheingold (1984, 104) observes, "When the police indulge in expressive violence, their concern is less with the most satisfactory resolution of a particular incident than with teaching the public a lesson." Police utilize force not

only to stop certain kinds of behavior but to express their disapproval
of it. By the same token, many use-of-force incidents originate not from
a suspect's behavior that tangibly threatens officers' physical safety but
from behavior that challenges their authority. While such behavior may
indeed be a prelude to more serious physical threats, "contempt of
cop" is often seen by officers as adequate grounds in and of itself for the
use of physical force against civilians (Chevigny 1969, 1995; Reiss
1971).[19]

Critical academic voices are among the most marginalized in the
news about policing, appearing in only a fraction of police use-of-force
stories.[20] Consequently, more complex causal stories about police brutality are marginalized as well. For example, the notion that police use
force expressively as well as instrumentally so rarely enters the news
that one single example across the entire ten-year period examined here
stands out: a letter to the editor published in the *New York Times* in
March of 1991, in the aftermath of the Rodney King beating. The
writer, a clinical professor of psychology, observed that

> In our society the function of the police is not merely the apprehension but
> also the immediate punishment of wrongdoers. The punitive role of the po-
> lice is not explicitly acknowledged, but it is nevertheless part of the job de-
> scription. . . . As a forensic psychiatrist, . . . I often encounter instances of
> police brutality. A typical case: a husband kills his wife; upon coming to his
> senses he calls the police; the arresting officers beat up the killer and tighten
> the handcuffs more than necessary. . . . Personnel in emergency rooms par-
> ticularly in large cities, commonly see a parade of people who, while in po-
> lice custody, suffered injuries inflicted as punishment by policemen. (Tanay
> 1991, 32)

Stone (1989, 289) observes that complex causal stories are "not very
useful in politics, precisely because they do not offer a single locus of
control, a plausible candidate to take responsibility for a problem, or a
point of leverage to fix a problem." Complex causal theories of police
brutality are perhaps less "useful" in the news arena as well. The causes
of police violence may run deep and extend beyond particular police
departments or particular local political regimes, but the most newsworthy causes are those with more identifiable black hats: racist police
officers, insulated police chiefs, politically compromised prosecutors.
Thus, even systemic claims about police brutality have a way of becoming more individualized, and the systemic causes most likely to be

discussed in the news are those that point to clear perpetrators or, at least, to people clearly responsible for addressing an incipient brutality problem.

STRUCTURAL AND CULTURAL
DETERMINANTS OF POLICING NEWS

Despite the fact that police voices are much more common in the news than those of activists or academics, police generally believe that the news does not fairly represent them. As reviewed in chapter 2, police often view the media with suspicion and express frustration and bitterness over what they see as the media's willingness to sensationalize the use of force without making the public aware of the difficulties and dangers faced by police officers. Activists and other would-be police reformers often feel marginalized in the media arena as well and view the media as partly responsible for systemic and pervasive police brutality.

Do the news media tend to sensationalize police misconduct and provide a platform for police critics, or do they favor police versions of events and marginalize systemic criticisms of policing? The answer, as subsequent chapters will explore, is "both," and that particular conditions determine when one news pattern prevails over the other. In the most typical pattern, as this chapter has demonstrated, the media respond cooperatively to official efforts to control the public definitions of violent police-citizen altercations.

The explanation for this news pattern is relatively straightforward and draws not only upon the research presented here but on a large body of evidence from previous studies of the news: Most news about policing, just as much news about a variety of social issues, is structurally biased in favor of official sources and culturally biased in favor of officially sanctioned claims. The news about police use of force is constructed by news organizations in which a well-established beat system and a norm of "professionalism" encourage journalists to draw primarily on police sources. And, like the audiences they write for, journalists share in a larger cultural discourse of crime control, in which crime is believed to be a rampant problem that we must "crack down" upon. Thus, three factors—police communication strategies, journalistic professionalism on the beat, and a prevailing discourse of crime control—create practical and ideological limitations on what is commonly said about police use of force in the news.

POLICE COMMUNICATION STRATEGIES

In their study of news coverage of the Canadian criminal justice system, Ericson, Baranek, and Chan (1989, 92–93) make an observation that applies equally well to the American scene: that police organizations increasingly "have made an effort to control their environment through a proactive strategy of selectively disclosing knowledge about organizational activities. . . . The police now accept that in relation to a particular incident or activity, a proactive approach to the news media is useful in controlling the version of reality that is transmitted, sustained, and accepted publicly."

Indeed, despite the frustration many police express over media portrayals of policing (see Corrigan 1994), police departments increasingly view the media as an important component of both crime control and police-community relations.[21] Many of today's police chiefs, such as former NYPD commissioner William Bratton, are becoming as media savvy as politicians in Washington, D.C. (see Smith 1996). As one police expert told me, today's police officials generally "don't take a simple-minded view of the media as enemy. They see the media as a tool" (Geller 1997).

Yet most police departments remain protective of information, especially about the use of force, often displaying a "wagons-in-a-circle" public-relations strategy (Katz 1994, 40). Consequently, police communication strategies involve selectively providing and withholding information (Chermak 1995; Ericson, Baranek, and Chan 1989, 1991). Police attempt to control the news about crime and policing by selectively opening their "front regions" to reporters—providing relatively free access to police reports, briefings, and other police-provided information—while closing off "back region" information. "Police and court sources are the primary definers of crime news because they provide the media with enough front-region access to easily satisfy daily story requirements yet protect their own interest by limiting access to back regions" (Chermak 1995, 85). Police provide and withhold information to produce a "unitary account" of their work, especially regarding potentially problematic events. Indeed, the purpose of police communications is to make police actions "seem sensible, proper, and officially authorized" (Wheeler 1986, 15, cited in Ericson, Baranek, and Chan 1989).

With impressive regularity, police present their use of force as a "sensible, proper, and officially authorized" response to a violent world.

The individualizing narratives police provide to reporters create what political scientist Murray Edelman has described as "language categories": symbolic representations of events, issues, and social groups that establish power relationships (Edelman 1977; 1993). By describing those subjected to the use of force as the dangerous and deviant "enemy," and the use of force as an essentially defensive strategy for fighting the enemy, police not only describe things as they see them but establish categorizations for social groups (threatening criminals, dangerous deviants) and for the use of force as a public phenomenon. Police-supplied news narratives thus draw from and help to sustain popular policing myths in which "the world is depicted as rife with crime and deviance, and the police as *the* authority for keeping a lid on it" (Ericson, Baranek, and Chan 1989, 144).

These individualizing narratives are part of ongoing public-relations strategies that police see as crucial to the job of policing. What is at stake, police often believe, is not just their "image" but their ability to do their jobs with a reasonable amount of safety and community cooperation—something that can be rendered difficult when the public does not believe that police use force with restraint. Indeed, a common complaint police make against journalists, activists, and civil rights lawyers—groups they often label "antipolice"—is that they arouse community sentiment against police and make policing more difficult and dangerous.[22] At the same time, police seek to protect their discretion to use force, which they see as an absolutely essential tool of their job; indeed, "the use of force is not a philosophical issue for the policeman. It is not a question of should or whether, but of when and how much" (Rubenstein 1973, 323). By offering individualizing narratives to reporters, police seek to ward off critical examination of "should or whether" and to protect police discretion to decide "when and how much."

The success of these claims in containing the public definitions of the vast majority of use-of-force incidents rests upon police control of information. Police are of course the primary sources of news about policing, and in many instances the police version of events is the only information readily available to reporters.[23] Moreover, police departments often control certain kinds of information about use-of-force incidents quite carefully. For example, the LAPD had a policy in the 1980s of not releasing information on misconduct complaints or the names and histories of officers against whom complaints were lodged unless that officer was already the subject of administrative proceedings (Oswald 1988b).

Similarly, police departments are in the best position to produce statistics on police use of force overall, but they often fail to track or refuse to provide such information to the public, as discussed in chapter 2. What departments do not provide is what reporters cannot easily write about. By controlling this kind of information, departments close off their "back regions" and shut down alternative narrative possibilities to reporters.

Police communication strategies are bolstered by a general (though not absolute) unanimity among police and elected officials on questions of police use of force. While some politicians and political candidates from time to time attempt to "make an issue" out of police brutality, elected officials are generally reluctant to fan the flames of some communities' discontent with the police and to risk the wrath of police unions and their supporters. This difficulty is indicated by the imbalance between the sums some cities pay to settle excessive-force suits and the amount of attention their politicians devote to the subject of brutality. New York City, for example, paid out over $50 million to settle police misconduct suits between 1987 and 1992, a figure equal to $400 per officer. The city of Los Angeles paid at least $20 million to settle excessive-force cases between 1986 and 1990 (Chevigny 1995, 53). Yet during that period, few politicians in New York City or Los Angeles were willing to take on local police departments by publicly talking about a brutality problem—at least until the Rodney King incident made that silence hard to maintain (Chevigny 1995; Davis 1990; Domanick 1994).[24]

MEDIA PROFESSIONALISM

Police communication strategies also succeed because they meet an organizational structure and culture within mainstream journalism, particularly print journalism, that create a favorable climate for police to manage the news. Undergirding the pattern of official dominance of the news is a dominant norm within mainstream news organizations that encourages journalists to allow officials to set the news agenda. This "professionalism" norm, as I will label it, stresses that good journalism transmits legitimate information to the public without actively or intentionally setting the public agenda or amplifying marginal social voices.[25] According to this norm, the first job of the news is to gather information provided by legitimate sources and to convey that information as "neutrally" as possible. As this norm is played out on the crime beat, the news tends to report fairly faithfully the claims of police officials and to construct the definitions of most use-of-force incidents accordingly.

The image of the journalist as a neutral professional who conveys information without slant or bias is a powerful ideal in American culture, although one that the general public often thinks the media fail to achieve.[26] The ideal of journalistic objectivity has been the subject of controversy among journalists as well (Boylan 1986; Schudson 1978, chap. 4). Today's professional journalist is often quite willing to admit that the ideal of objectivity is difficult if not impossible to attain. One tenet of the profession's code of ethics nonetheless remains the obligation to strive for neutrality and objectivity, and their role as "disseminator" has been a favored self-image among journalists since at least the 1970s (Weaver and Wilhoit 1992).

Journalistic neutrality in practice, however, often creates a preponderance of official sources and officially sanctioned ideas in the news. This paradox underlies the "official dominance" model of the news popular among critical media scholars. According to this model, news "objectivity" is bounded by the ideas that are acceptable to the power structures within which news organizations themselves are embedded (Donohue, Tichenor, and Olien 1995; Hallin 1986; Tuchman 1978). This meaning of "objectivity" tells reporters that in a world full of competing sources making competing claims, it is best to report information that can be officially verified and make less use of sources and claims that are most likely to invite charges of bias. "Objectivity" thus becomes reporting "what happened" in a way that is least likely to be criticized by those in power. Since elites are in the best position to create verifiable claims and activities for reporters to report (Bennett 1996; Molotch and Lester 1974) and to create "flak" when news organizations stray too far from "neutrally" reporting those claims and activities (Herman and Chomsky 1988), the "neutral" accounts journalists construct are often biased in favor of official voices and views. Indeed, "for reporters, the most credible information or the hardest data are accounts which come from the 'most competent' news sources, who, in turn, are the bureaucrats and officials recognized as having jurisdiction over the events in question" (Fishman 1980, 94).

The norm of media professionalism also makes journalists hesitant to amplify social conflicts or to independently set the political agenda. Professional reporters are all too aware that, in the words of one journalist, "something [could become] a major issue *because* a large daily newspaper has written about it" (quoted in Molotch 1979, 87). Indeed, local news organizations in particular often act as "guard dogs" of the power structures with which they are linked by their beat systems (Donohue, Tichenor, and Olien 1995). This journalistic deference was expressed concisely by former *New York Times* publisher Adolph Ochs, who once wrote that the *Times* "is not a crusading newspaper. It is impressed with the responsibility of what it prints . . . and, so far as is possible—consistent with honest journalism—attempts to aid and support those who are charged with the responsibility of government" (quoted in Konner 1996, 4).[27]

This norm of professionalism is not the only norm that guides contemporary journalists. Indeed, a common criticism of the mass media today is that they are too willing to stir up trouble for officials by focusing on scandals and controversies (Patterson 1994; Fallows 1997). Later chapters will discuss how competing newsroom norms encourage reporters to produce news that is critical of police and explain under what conditions that is likely to occur. But despite these competing norms and the general tendency of the mainstream media (particularly television) to be more cantankerous and sensationalistic than ever before, the norm of professionalism is still alive and well.

PROFESSIONALISM ON THE CRIME BEAT

The norm of professionalism is enshrined in the beat system, a news-gathering system that places reporters at key institutional listening posts, such as city hall and police precincts, to report what occurs there as "news" (Cook 1994; Tuchman 1978). Reporters working a beat develop regular contacts with the institutionally positioned officials their beat assigns them to, and these contacts provide reporters with many of the raw materials of the daily news. The practices of routine beat journalism "[lead] newsworkers to treat their sources' accounts not as versions of reality but as 'the facts' " (Fishman 1978, 15). Past research has demonstrated the typically symbiotic relationship that exists between reporters and police and underlies the construction of news about policing and crime (Fishman 1980; Ericson, Baranek, and Chan 1989; Chermak 1994). Through their daily contact, reporters often gain a sensitivity for the concerns of police—"an inevitable consequence of long-term socialization through close proximity to police cultures" (Ericson, Baranek, and Chan 1989, 105). Indeed, interviews with reporters working the police beat reveal that they are often sympathetic spokespersons for the police, well aware of the difficulties and dilemmas of police work and of how their own work sometimes adds to those difficulties.

The flip side of this professional deference to officials is a subtle suspicion of grassroots voices. Critical nonofficials, such as activists and minority community leaders, may lack credibility with reporters, both because they lack the imprimatur of being "official" and because they may offer claims that challenge the very officials on whom journalists depend to do their jobs. As Don Jackson, whose videotaped "sting" of Long Beach police created a national stir over police brutality in 1989, has put it, the media "look at whose side you are holding up," and "if it's the little side, you better have all the credibility in the world" (Jackson 1997). Mirroring Jackson's observation, one journalist told me that "plenty of people on the street are willing to say bad things about the police," many of them "drug-related" people who have an interest in undermining police power (Krauss 1996b).[28] Crime beat reporters are wary, in other words, of acting as megaphones for deviants and illegitimate claims against police.

Moreover, people who accuse police of brutality are often non-white, are often relatively poor, and often have criminal records (if nothing else, they often face a resisting arrest charge resulting from their altercation with police). These are not the kinds of people reporters feel most comfortable relying on for "news." Nor are they the audiences for whom many reporters and editors envision producing the news. Former *Los Angeles Times* publisher Otis Chandler said as much when he once commented that "We could make the editorial commitment, the management commitment to cover [poor] communities. But how do we get them to read the *Times*? It's not their kind of newspaper" (quoted in Reeves 1995, 42). When officials are not willing to talk about brutality problems, and news organizations do not see themselves as speaking to the communities most affected by real or perceived brutality, little room is left for critical voices and views about brutality in the news.

It would be misleading to overemphasize the degree of control police achieve over the news or the level of journalistic deference to police. Reporters do not automatically screen out nonofficial voices when reporting on police activities, nor do they reflexively avoid writing negative stories about police. As the data presented above indicate, nonofficials do appear in the news about police use of force relatively often; as later chapters will explore, the claims and activities of nonofficials are often key factors in journalists' decisions about what kind of news to produce about use-of-force incidents. Moreover, reporters have professional incentives to write some stories that reflect quite poorly on police, incentives that are occasionally engaged by cues signaling that a big news story is brewing. The point here is simply that there are hurdles of credibility and legitimacy that nonofficial sources must overcome, hurdles that generally do not exist for official sources. And that means that the kinds of claims nonofficials often wish to make—claims that they or someone they know has been brutalized by police, that brutality is common, that brutality stems from structural flaws in the criminal justice system itself—do not appear as readily in the news as the kinds of claims officials typically make. And as Kaniss (1991, 177) found in interviews with local reporters, "Although most reporters . . . said they would not hold back on a major negative story about one of their chief sources, some did suggest that minor transgressions might be overlooked." This suggests that on a day-to-day basis beat reporters are not necessarily eager to uncover stories that may damage their relationship with key sources.

Indeed, the practical effect of their socialization on the crime beat is a professional orientation in which, as one *New York Times* reporter told me, a "serious" reporter is one who "is not just out to slam the police" (Krauss 1996b). Reporters are keenly aware that claims about police brutality may be untrue. Reporters generally show less skepticism concerning police narratives, however, though they often privately recognize that official narratives are efforts to put the best face possible on potentially problematic events. Nevertheless, the norm of media professionalism as inculcated on the beat creates news that is careful always to tell the police side of the story. Thus, when covering the police, as Chibnall (1977, 142–43) observes, "the notion of 'responsible' reporting . . . entails the promotion of police interests."

Moreover, the beat system and police control of information encourage news organizations to make shrewd calculations about future interactions with police officials when reporting on the use of force. News organizations are loath to endanger their institutionalized relationship with police for the simple reason that crime makes up a considerable chunk of the daily news. Roger Grimsby, former news director of KGO-TV in San Francisco, whose crew filmed police beating a suspect in 1967, has stated this calculation succinctly, on the basis of which he decided to kill the story: "I knew I had a great piece of film. But at the same time I knew that our nighttime crew would not be able to operate effectively without the full cooperation of the San Francisco Police Department. And that film almost certainly would jeopardize our relationship" (quoted in Irwin 1991, 16).

Similar considerations have likely entered into the calculations of the two news organizations examined here. For example, New York Mayor Rudolph Giuliani instituted an official news control system in which the police press office notifies the mayor's office of the stories reporters are working on; the mayor's office may then limit reporters' access to the police department if the mayor disapproves of coverage of the department (Krauss 1996b). A more direct approach was adopted by former LAPD Chief Daryl Gates, who would on occasion try to intimidate reporters and editors. One long-time columnist with the *Los Angeles Times* has said that Gates and his predecessors intimidated the media by complaining so much "that newspaper editors and television news directors began to 'pull back . . . (to) really bend over backward to be 'fair' to the LAPD' " (Bill Boyarsky, quoted in Shaw 1992, A1). One former *Los Angeles Times* reporter claims that Gates tried to intimidate her personally and complained to her editors when she covered a story about LAPD officers seriously vandalizing several South Central apartments during a 1988 drug raid. According to this reporter, such tactics may have worked in the past because "nobody had ever covered them that way before" (Ford 1997).

Intimidation is not the primary means by which police manage news. More typical are standard police communication strategies interacting with journalists' news-gathering routines. Those daily interactions take place within a context of the cultural values and symbols that shape American thinking about crime and crime fighting.

THE CULTURAL DISCOURSE OF CRIME CONTROL

The structural biases that favor police communication strategies are enhanced not only by the culture of professionalism in the newsroom but by the larger cultural milieu in which mainstream news organizations operate: an environment marked by a fearful and punitive discourse of crime control. Crime has become a dominant cultural preoccupation in the United States, reflecting a deep-seated "myth of crime and punishment" that pervades American culture. Americans typically see crime as a problem of the moral failings of weak, deviant individuals and see swift, decisive punishment as the necessary societal response (Scheingold 1984). This discourse, "repeatedly revitalized by the rhetoric of public officials and candidates for elective office, [emphasizes] that crime springs from evil people who thrive upon muggings, robberies, drug abuse, and murders" more than from crimogenic social conditions or inadequate social policies (Edelman 1993, 234). As public fears of crime and officials' willingness to politicize crime have increased, this discourse has intensified. Criminologist Stanley Cohen (1996, 9) has observed that "the political resonance of the . . . 'war on crime' metaphor has become stronger. Many large American cities are routinely described as 'ungovernable' as a result of violence, drugs, and a breakdown of policing and social services. . . . [T]his rhetoric is now taken for granted." Indeed, Cohen argues, "the cult of national security represented by the Soviet threat has given way to a cult of personal insecurity."

Whether or not our national preoccupation with crime has become a "cult," it seems clear that Americans are exposed to more images of crime, violence, and "tough" policing than ever before. Not only do stories about crime saturate the daily news, but "real-life" crime-fighting shows like *Cops* and *LAPD* have become a favorite of networks looking for inexpensive, audience-pleasing fare, with the help of police departments looking for ways to boost their public image. These shows typically feature traffic stops and images of police "break[ing] into every type of home and location to search, confiscate, interrogate, and arrest" (Segal 1993, 50). In these shows, "the heroic, humane cops use justified force to apprehend suspects. One way force is justified is by showing the suspects as irrational, engaging in violence, or resisting arrest. Unknown are the preceding events that might vindicate the suspects' outburst, thereby casting doubt on the police's use of force" (Paletz 1999, 279).

Fictional television shows such as *NYPD Blue*, meanwhile, feature police who routinely use physical coercion to apprehend suspects, intimidate witnesses, and coerce testimony. These shows mimic, in tamer terms, the well-established tradition of the vigilante cop in Hollywood, such as Clint Eastwood's *Dirty Harry* films and Charles Bronson's *Death Wish* series, films in which the protagonists realize that "police procedure is impotent in the face of crime. Only the street-wise cop, understanding the vicious nature of criminals, can deal effectively with them [by] defying any restraints posed by legal or department rules and regulations" (Reiner 1985, 155). These popular culture narratives "[present] police power as the only solution to the major menace of crime."

This cultural discourse of crime control through police power grants considerable leeway to police to act as "primary definers" (Hall et al. 1978) of what levels and uses of force are appropriate in the "war" against crime. Making claims about deviant and threatening individuals who need to be subdued by force is not difficult in this environment. Indeed, poll data suggest that the public is highly supportive of police discretion to use force. Since 1972, over 70 percent of Americans have consistently said they would approve of a police officer striking a male suspect who was attempting to escape from custody.[29]

The discourse of crime control is not the only lens through which Americans may view police use of force. As later chapters will explore, at least one alternative framework also enjoys considerable discursive power: a discourse of civil rights and due process, in which police power is suspect rather than celebrated. This framework became a key factor in news coverage of the Rodney King beating, since the video-taped images of that beating so clearly evoked disturbing images from America's history of racial oppression through the police baton. But in this society preoccupied with crime and crime control, the power of police is more often celebrated in the mainstream media than scrutinized.

When embedded in a cultural environment preoccupied with cracking down on crime, the ambiguity of police use of force confers considerable rhetorical advantages on police. Separating legitimate from illegitimate uses of force can be difficult under any circumstances. But police claims that cast the use of force as "sensible, proper, and officially authorized" are bolstered by a general belief that police officers daily put their lives on the line in dealing with the criminal, the poor, and the deranged and therefore deserve fairly unqualified public support. The news helps to reinforce these ideological boundaries, but it is also subject to them. No less than other members of the public, journalists are often somewhat hesitant to label a use-of-force incident as "brutality" and more hesitant still to seriously suggest that police departments, political regimes, indeed, the criminal justice system itself may be fundamentally flawed—a reluctance heightened by the norm of professionalism and the ties of the beat system that bind reporters to police.

Thus, mainstream notions about the dangers of crime and the necessity of punitive crime control constitute a powerful constraint on news content, somewhat akin to the power of anticommunism in past debates about American foreign policy. News organizations tend to adopt the individualizing narratives offered by police because they "make sense" to their primary audiences—middle-class whites and political elites—who are most fully steeped in mainstream cultural discourses of crime and punishment. Were their audiences primarily lower-strata minorities, systemic understandings of police brutality might emerge more readily in the news (Lawrence 1996b). Editors are well aware that raising questions about police conduct can be bad for business, not just because police can respond by withholding information and producing "flak" but because audiences may not approve. Indeed, "the narrative thread of political news almost always carries within it popular images of good and evil and national fantasies of justice and injustice" (Denton and Woodward 1990, 10). Journalists may believe what television's professional storytellers believe: that "the public wants to see the bad guys get nailed [and] doesn't want to see their heroes with dirt on them" (Lawrence Kubik, executive producer of *Hunter*, quoted in Rohter 1991, 14). The most typical representations of police use-of-force incidents are thus shaped not only by the structure of the beat system and the professional expectation that journalists act "neutrally" and "responsibly" but by a larger culture preoccupied with crime and punishment.

CONCLUSION

This chapter has illustrated the ways in which the news often reflects an officially and culturally sanctioned perspective on police use of force. Instances of police use of force are typically covered in brief episodic news items, relying primarily on official sources and individualizing claims, and pass quickly into and out of the news. Thus, use of force is typically normalized in news that presents it as a necessary and appropriate response to a violent world. The political impact of this kind of news is to keep the questions that some citizens might raise about policing off the news agenda. The news thus often "defines away" policing problems.

The news about police use of force is not always so congenial to police interests, however. Mass-mediated police brutality scandals are in some locales "a familiar urban ritual." Certain cases of alleged brutality become major news stories through which police critics gain prominence (albeit temporary) in the media arena. When police complain of media coverage that sensationalizes the use of force and unfairly criticizes police, it is not the baseline pattern of episodic, normalizing coverage to which they refer but rather those relatively few cases whose public definitions officials fail to control and contain. Understanding the news construction of those events is the task of the following chapters.

FOUR

Setting the Agenda

Rodney King and the Los Angeles Times

As illustrated in chapter 3, most use-of-force incidents reported in the news are successfully contained by official communication strategies. Official claims provide reporters with a news narrative; media professionalism, enshrined in the beat system, encourages journalists to rely on those narratives; and a cultural discourse of crime control discourages coverage that police would call negative.

But sometimes, official news management breaks down, and the public meaning of some use-of-force incidents spins out of official control. Indeed, some incidents become major news events that provide opportunities for critical nonofficials to talk about policing problems. This chapter examines these dynamics by analyzing the most dramatic of these "outlier" cases—the beating of motorist Rodney King.

When a videotape of LAPD officers raining blows on King filled television screens across the country in March 1991, the news pages began to fill with claims that police brutality had long been rampant in Los Angeles. But police misconduct had not been an important issue for the city's premier news organization, the *Los Angeles Times*. In fact, the *Times* had marginalized the issue for years. Yet when the King video was released to a local television news station, the *Times* helped to build the story into a serious crisis for LAPD chief Daryl Gates and played a major role in constructing the brutality problem that would drive Gates from office.

This chapter seeks to explain this apparently schizophrenic behavior on the part of the *Times* and to use the case of the Rodney King beating to build more generalizable propositions about event-driven problem construction. Indeed, the King case thus suggests a phenomenon that extends beyond the issue of brutality: Dramatic news events can upset official control of the news agenda by providing journalists with dramatic story possibilities and a host of cues to pursue politically volatile issues.

This process is a bit more subtle and contingent than might be assumed, however. Three commonplace assumptions about the Rodney King beating miss the subtleties of event-driven problem construction. First, it is commonly assumed that the fact the King incident was filmed is adequate to explain that event's impact on the news. People also often assume that the King video told a clear and unambiguous story of police brutality, a story that needed no journalistic interpretation to point out a policing problem in the LAPD. I argue instead that it was not simply the raw fact of a video that made Rodney King into a defining news event but rather the way in which the video captured the incident. I will also argue, here and in chapter 7, that the King incident was subject to journalistic interpretation. The video did strongly suggest a particular news narrative, but journalists were active in constructing the public meaning of that incident.

It is also commonly assumed that the Rodney King beating single-handedly forced news organizations such as the *Los Angeles Times* to begin addressing the issue of police brutality. I argue instead that the eruption of problem construction in the *Times* in 1991 was a response to a rich set of story cues that licensed journalists to put police brutality front and center on the news agenda. These cues included the images captured on the video, which suggested a different narrative than the LAPD was providing; the rhetorical responses of various officials to the beating, which indicated to reporters that a major political battle between Mayor Tom Bradley and Chief Daryl Gates would soon break out; and the challenge posed to the Gates and Bradley regimes by public reaction to the video and the protests of local activists. Cumulatively, these cues allowed evidence of brutality problems in Los Angeles to become news.

In addition, this case study of the King incident illustrates a dynamic often overlooked in studies of the news: how "accidental" news events can become symbolic weapons in the otherwise limited arsenal of marginalized social groups. The dramatic imagery of the King beating became a vehicle for police critics to enter the news with new force and legitimacy.

POLICE BRUTALITY AS AN EVENT-DRIVEN PROBLEM

The content of the news is often roughly indexed to the activities of political institutions. When officials designate a social condition as a public problem, the news tends to follow suit, and official clashes over an issue license journalists to pursue that debate in the news pages (Bennett 1990). Moreover, surges in media attention to an issue or event often indicate success on the part of officials in problem creation and news management (see Livingston 1994, for example). Indeed, the news about public problems such as terrorism and drug abuse is largely driven by official news-management campaigns, aided and abetted by the media's eagerness to publicize such threats to public order (see Reeves and Campbell 1994; Reinarman and Levine 1988).

But officials rarely wish to "own" the issue of brutality (see Gusfield 1981). Unlike terrorism, crime, or drugs, police brutality offers little symbolic capital to police or elected officials. Nor is brutality generally associated with the kind of routine politics described by the official-dominance model of the news, for it is an issue that political elites and police officials generally wish to keep off the political agenda. Increased media attention to police use of force is usually an indicator not that officials have successfully managed the news but rather that officials have lost control of the news.

News coverage of police brutality, therefore, is territory not fully explained by the official-dominance model of the news. Police brutality appears only sporadically on the political agenda and then almost invariably because of some dramatic case of alleged brutality that spins out of official control—sometimes with truly explosive results.

BRUTALITY IN L.A.

If ever there was a setting in which these dynamics were clear, it is Los Angeles. During the late 1980s and early 1990s, statistical evidence mounted of serious brutality problems in Southern California. For example, the city of Los Angeles paid at least $20 million to settle excessive-force cases between 1986 and 1990, an average of more than $1,300 per officer in 1990—not including payments for other forms of police misconduct (Chevigny 1995, 53). During the 1991–92 fiscal year, the LAPD was the subject of the largest share (over 47 percent) of liability judgments against city agencies (McMillan 1992). Between January 1989 and May 1992, moreover, the county paid over $15 million to settle excessive-force cases against the sheriff's department (Chevigny 1995, 101). Indeed, excessive-force litigation became "a cottage industry" in Los Angeles (ibid., 52), building careers like that of the now-famous Johnnie Cochran.

Yet between 1980 and 1991, the district attorney's office declined to prosecute at least 278 police officers and sheriff's deputies accused of assaulting citizens; of those accused of excessive force, only 13 percent were prosecuted, compared with 77 percent of all civilians arrested for felony assault (Freed 1991). Nor did police officials, district attorneys, or political leaders call attention to the issue of police misconduct. According to local freelance journalist Joe Domanick (1994, 357), "through seventeen years in office and two runs for the governorship," Los Angeles Mayor Tom Bradley "sought to avoid a confrontation" with the LAPD. As City Councilman Zev Yaroslavsky would later say, the LAPD suffered from a "problem of leadership" that extended beyond the police chief: "It wasn't just Daryl Gates. It was the mayor, the police commission, and the city council. . . . There'd been absolutely no interest in investigating police-abuse cases until they became public embarrassments to the leadership." In fact, from 1986 through 1990, the mayor, the city council, and the police commission signed evaluations—written by Gates himself—giving Gates "outstanding" ratings (ibid.).[1] The official silence on police conduct was echoed in regard to the sheriff's department as well. As Chevigny (1995, 54) writes, "The city and the county certainly could have done something about [the large number of excessive-force cases]; they could have insisted that the departments change their tactics to reduce the damages. It is clear, however, that in the last analysis they did not substantially disagree with the sheriff or the chief."

African American activist (and later city councilman) Mark Ridley-Thomas observed late in 1990 that Mayor Bradley "for years" had deployed aides and police commissioners to Los Angeles's African American community to urge blacks to refrain from criticizing Gates and the LAPD. "The fear," according to Ridley-Thomas, "was that a majority white electorate would conveniently forget" that Bradley himself had been an LAPD officer for many years, and would "somehow view him as anti-police or at least soft on crime"—a political kiss of death (Ridley-Thomas 1990, B7). Indeed, Mayor Bradley and other city officials publicly responded to only two cases of alleged police misconduct, other than the Rodney King case, from 1985 through 1991; in neither of those cases did Bradley publicly criticize Chief Gates or the LAPD.[2]

Despite years of personal animosity, Bradley and Gates were united in public silence on the issue of brutality.

Meanwhile, Chief Gates publicly signaled his department's attitude toward the use of force in a series of comments made to reporters. After testifying for the defense in an excessive-force suit in 1988, for example, a case in which a man named Jessie Larez sustained a broken nose during an LAPD raid on his home, Gates said, "How much is a broken nose worth? Given the circumstances in this case . . . I don't think it's worth anything. [Larez] is probably lucky that's all he had broken. . . . People keep asking me, 'Chief, why don't you do something about gang killings? . . . And we do something and then [juries] give $90,000" (Freed 1988, sec. 2, p. 3).[3]

COVERING BRUTALITY BEFORE RODNEY KING

Police brutality may have been a growing concern for some sectors of the city, but critical nonofficials and systemic claims about police brutality were largely marginalized in the pages of the *Los Angeles Times*. Between 1985 and 1990, out of an average of over 70 stories per year about police use of force, an average of eight *Times* stories per year prominently featured systemic claims about police brutality problems.[4] Moreover, from 1985 through 1990, the *Times* produced only four thematic news stories exploring police use of force as an *issue* (in contrast to twenty-three thematic news items that appeared in 1991 after the Rodney King incident), and one of these stories downplayed the existence of policing problems.[5] Two of the other three pieces hinted at problems yet to be constructed: one, in September 1988, reported national experts' criticisms of the tactics of the LAPD's Special Investigations Unit (which became controversial in 1990 after its high-profile slaying of three armed robbers); the other, appearing in May 1990, reported that settling excessive-force cases against the sheriff's department had cost taxpayers millions of dollars. That piece in particular, along with data displayed below, indicates that the issue of police conduct was becoming more visible prior to Rodney King. But as the *Times'* media critic, David Shaw, subsequently observed, "Neither The *Times* nor any other mainstream news organization took a serious look at the pattern of police use of excessive force at the end of the 1980s . . . not even as evidence mounted that the LAPD was increasingly resorting to force, especially in minority communities, and that discipline for such misconduct was minimal" (Shaw 1992, A1).

The *Times'* relative silence on issues of police conduct is illustrated by its coverage of the so-called Dalton Avenue incident. During an August 1988 LAPD drug "sweep," approximately 80 LAPD officers raided four apartments located on Dalton Avenue in South Los Angeles, ripping out walls, carpets, and plumbing, destroying residents' personal belongings, and spray-painting graffiti such as "LAPD Rules" on the walls. They also beat numerous people, according to subsequent civil lawsuits, but four officers were later tried only on vandalism charges (and were acquitted in June 1991, with jurors saying the district attorney had not clearly traced particular acts of destruction to particular officers). In February 1990, the city of Los Angeles settled the residents' civil claims for over $3 million, the largest such settlement to that date.

While the Dalton Avenue incident eventually became an important indicator to the *Times* of a serious police misconduct problem, the *Times'* initial coverage of the case was muted, especially its handling of allegations that police had beaten and humiliated residents. The *Times* did not report the victims' allegations of police beatings, nor their claims that such drug sweeps were motivated by "anti-black animus," until those claims appeared in a lawsuit in late October, two months after the raid.[6] In fact, the *Times* did not quote the Dalton residents directly until January 1989, roughly five months after the incident occurred.[7]

The Dalton Avenue incident gained more news attention than most use-of-force incidents prior to Rodney King. Yet it was not until February 1990, a year and a half after the raid occurred, that the *Times* editorial page began to discuss the Dalton case as an example of problems in the LAPD (cued by the city's record $3 million settlement with the Dalton plaintiffs).[8] In many news and editorial items appearing after the Rodney King beating two and a half years later, the *Times* mentioned the Dalton case as an important early indicator of problems within the LAPD. But at the time it occurred, the Dalton raid was not defined by the *Times* as an indicator that Los Angeles had a police misconduct problem.

COVERING BRUTALITY IN THE
AFTERMATH OF RODNEY KING

In March 1991, the *Times'* coverage of brutality changed dramatically. This shift is illustrated in figure 2, which shows that mentions of police

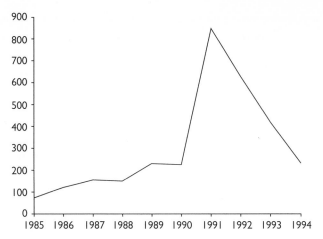

Figure 2.   News Coverage of Police Brutality, *Los Angeles Times*, 1985–94. Source: Data are based on a search of the *Los Angeles Times*, via the Nexis database, for the words "police" and either "brutality" or "excessive force" in close proximity for each year from 1985 to 1994. The data displayed represent the number of items from the local ("metro") desk, the national desk, and the editorial desk.

brutality in the *Times* rose gradually from 1985 through 1990 but increased significantly in 1991. (A smaller increase in coverage is visible in 1989, which reflects the appearance of two other use-of-force incidents, the belated coverage of the Dalton Avenue raid and the video-taped altercation between antibrutality activist Don Jackson and a Long Beach police officer, discussed below.)

This increased media attention to police brutality was accompanied by the increased prominence of nonofficial voices and systemic claims about brutality. Figure 3 shows the relative prominence of nonofficial voices and systemic views in *Los Angeles Times* reporting of police use of force from 1985 through 1994.[9] The data indicate a dramatic increase in the number of nonofficials and systemic claims in 1991; the numbers remain relatively high in 1992, coinciding with the acquittal of the officers charged with abusing King, which touched off the Los Angeles civil disturbances. These effects mirror the trends in mentions of police brutality shown in figure 2.

Indeed, in the weeks after the King incident was first reported, the *Times'* news and editorial pages were filled with systemic claims about police misconduct, many of which placed Chief Gates's leadership and the culture of the LAPD at the heart of the problem. A partial listing of news summaries for March 1991 (see table 2) gives a flavor of the cov-

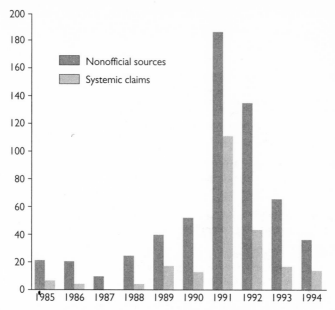

Figure 3. Nonofficial Voices and Systemic Claims in News about Police Use of Force, *Los Angeles Times*, 1985–94. Source: Data are compiled from the *Los Angeles Times* index. Columns indicate the number of index items each year mentioning either nonofficial voices or systemic claims about police brutality.

erage. As those summaries indicate, police brutality suddenly was discussed as a serious public problem.

The *Times'* relative silence about police conduct from 1985 through 1990 confirms the expectations of the official-dominance model of the news. Officials were unwilling to "make an issue" of police misconduct, and so the issue was relatively (though not entirely) absent from the news pages. Yet the explosion of critical news in 1991 suggests the power of accidental news events to open the news gates. In chapter 7 we will consider how print media across the country interpreted the King incident and searched for solutions to a newly designated nationwide brutality problem. Here, we will concentrate on understanding how and why the King beating ushered a host of critical voices into the pages of the *Los Angeles Times*. Three factors appear to have been crucial in moving the problem of brutality to the forefront of the *Times'* agenda: the narrative power of the King video; the official and political responses to the beating; and the intense public reaction it aroused.

TABLE 2.   SELECTED INDEX ENTRIES,
LOS ANGELES TIMES, MARCH 1991

Date	Index entry
March 7	Criminologist Jerome Skolnick argues that the LAPD "has a propensity towards brutality and racism" that only the videotape of the King beating could reveal.
March 8	Columnist Mike Downey recounts the story of two well-known African American athletes manhandled wrongly by the LAPD.
March 10	Rabbi Dov Aharoni argues that the King beating "was racially motivated" and that Los Angeles's African Americans "should be outraged about the pattern of brutality."
March 10	Activist Carol Watson argues that the LAPD "sanctions brutality by enforcing an implicit code of silence regarding misconduct."
March 11	Local residents tell reporters that they are relieved that the officers who beat King have been caught but that they are "aware that any black could become a victim of comparable brutality."
March 15	Lawyer and activist Geoffrey Taylor Gibbs urges that Gates be fired despite his protection as a civil servant.
March 21	Criminologist James Fyfe argues that Los Angeles must make its police department accountable to elected officials in order to stem the department's current wave of brutality. Insulation from politics has allowed the brutality to continue unabated.

THE NARRATIVE POWER OF THE VIDEO

A common assumption is that the King beating had a major impact on the news and political agendas simply because it was filmed and broadcast on television. That assumption is partially but not fully correct. The video was certainly important; police brutality remains a marginalized political issue in part because so much of it occurs out of the public spotlight. But other videotaped cases of alleged brutality in Southern California did not have nearly the same impact on the news.[10] The key to the impact of the King video lies not simply in the fact that the beating was filmed but in the way that film portrayed the altercation and in the way it was used by television stations.

The videotaped version of the altercation began several minutes after the real altercation had begun. During the unfilmed minutes, officers of the California Highway Patrol and the LAPD had pursued King for many miles at high speeds, ordered King and his two passengers out of the car, and handcuffed the passengers. What transpired after King exited the car is disputed, with various participants and witnesses offering competing versions of events. But both prosecution and defense witnesses at the criminal trial of the officers agreed that King refused to lay prone on the pavement, as LAPD officers typically required of suspects, and therefore had not been searched for weapons. Rather, King got on all fours, and then as Officers Laurence Powell and Timothy Wind attempted to handcuff him, King shook them off and rose to his feet. Sergeant Stacy Koon then warned King he would be shot with a Taser if he did not prone out; when King stood up, Koon fired two Taser darts into King, at which time King fell to the ground (Parloff 1992).

The videotape began to roll just as King rose from the ground a second time. The first few seconds are blurred, but King can be seen lunging in the direction of Officer Powell; the prosecution conceded this but argued that King may have been trying to run away. Powell strikes one blow to King with his metal baton and knocks King to the ground.[11] Then Powell hits King with eight to ten additional blows, which are quite blurred and whose impact is partially blocked from the camera's eye by a car, but nonetheless visible.[12] At this point, the video comes into focus, showing both Powell and Officer Timothy Wind striking King, then showing Officer Theodore Briseno grabbing Powell's arm, clearly attempting to stop further blows. But as King continually refuses to remain prone, as the officers claimed, or physically recoils from the pain of the baton's blows, according to others, the blows continue—56 of them in total captured on film.[13] As King finally rolls to his stomach and apparently begins to put his hands behind his back, Officer Briseno steps on King's shoulder, neck, or head (the exact location was disputed), which Briseno claimed was to force King to remain down so that he could be handcuffed. King recoils, at which point Powell and Wind strike King with the final set of blows. Eventually, King assumes a sitting position, and officers swarm to handcuff him. The final moments of the video show a handcuffed King lying alone on his back on the side of the road.

In subsequent weeks, television audiences saw the middle portion of the tape again and again, not the roughly 10-second, blurred portion at the beginning or the portion after which the beating had ceased and King had been handcuffed. This middle portion of the videotape, in particular, undermined the usual official narrative offered to explain and defend the use of force to the public. Indeed, the initial *Times* story on the case opened by claiming that the videotape "captures Los Angeles police officers repeatedly striking a prone, apparently defenseless man" and observed that the video "shows no indication that King attempted to hit or charge the officers" (Tobar and Berger 1991, A1). Rather than inviting the audience to imagine the threat posed to officers and citizens by a dangerous and deviant suspect, as so many news stories about police use of force do, the videotape shifted attention to the actual force used to subdue King, invited the audience to empathize with the recipient of the blows, and encouraged journalists and the public to fill in the blanks with a different—and more politically volatile—narrative.[14]

Police did their best to fill in those blanks themselves. Police sources portrayed King as the aggressor, claiming that King had charged at Officer Laurence Powell and that "King placed his left hand in his pants pocket when he stepped out of the car—a movement that . . . heightened the officers' concern that he had a weapon" (Tobar and Berger 1991, A1). This claim echoed the report filed by Officers Laurence Powell and Timothy Wind that said they struck King only after he knocked one of them aside and charged at them. Recognizing the explosiveness of its imagery, Chief Gates immediately responded to the event by labeling it an aberration, telling reporters that "One incident doesn't indict an entire department. I would hope the public on this one case not make a judgment on the Los Angeles Police Department" (ibid.).

But these efforts were no match for the narrative power of the video. Indeed, a *Los Angeles Times* poll conducted on March 10 found that 52 percent of respondents believed King's version of events (that he had cooperated with police instructions upon exiting his car) versus 15 percent who believed the LAPD's (that King had acted menacingly); among black respondents, 78 percent said they believed King's version (Rohrlich 1991). Moreover, what struck many viewers was not only the level of force used against King but the number of officers on the scene. At least six officers are visible in nearly every frame of the video, with up to 10 to 12 visible at some points, leading viewers to question how King could have posed a serious threat.[15] The film also suggested that this kind of violent altercation was not unusual for Los Angeles police, not something they were uncomfortable with, for the video shows at least three cars driving by as the beating proceeds, one car obviously slowing to watch.[16]

The narrative power of the video also drew greatly from its symbolic evocation of racist oppression in other eras of American history, given the number of officers involved, the vehemence of the blows rained on King, and, of course, the fact that King was black and the officers white. In a way that would perhaps not have been true had King been Asian or Hispanic, the video resonated powerfully with a particularly American understanding of racism. It was, in the words of one observer, "a display of official savagery like nothing the country has seen since Bull Connor" (Ricker 1991, 45).

Finally, the power of the video lay simply in the fact that it made for great television. It was, according to one journalist, "amazing, sit-up-in-your-chair, holy-shit television. . . . the essence of TV: an entire story in pictures" (Domanick 1994, 383–84). The video—usually the 10- or 15-second portion of it that showed the worst of the beating—was "literally . . . beamed around the world almost every five minutes" by CNN (ibid., 384). Worldwide distribution of the video and the heavy play it encouraged shifted the dynamics of news coverage and politics in a way that Schattschneider (1960) would appreciate: as the audience grew, the pressure on officials grew to reconcile their rhetoric with the images on the video.

Heavy publicity also increased the incentives for reporters to interpret that event for their audiences by drawing on critical voices and views. In a dynamic that is common in the aftermath of major news events (Graber 1993, chap. 5), journalists sought not only to convey facts about the event that had suddenly become the talk of the nation but to explain it. Yet as reporters and editors looked for an explanation, the official response to the beating failed to convincingly rebut the narrative suggested by the video. In a reversal of the usual dynamics, the official account needed to overcome doubts sown by a more vivid source of public information.

OFFICIAL RESPONSES TO THE INCIDENT

While the video encouraged reporters to construct a narrative that challenged police accounts of the event, the rhetorical responses of officials further encouraged reporters to construct more critical news coverage. Recall that prior to the King beating, local elected officials rarely publicly challenged the LAPD, and Mayor Bradley had not challenged an LAPD account of any use-of-force incident since at least 1985. But with images from the video filling television screens across the country, Bradley countered Gates's rhetorical strategy—Rodney King as an "aberration"—with a strategy of his own. Breaking the official silence on police conduct, Bradley offered reporters a different definition of the King beating, along with plenty of cues that he would use that event to try to force his long-time nemesis from power.

The day after the video was first aired, Bradley responded to Gates's "aberration" claim by saying that "supervision does, in fact, flow from the top of the department down—through his orders and instructions, through his training. . . . We want to see where there was a breakdown, a departure from established orders and procedures in this case" (Tobar and Berger 1991, A1). Thus, while Bradley coated his barb by implying that the beating was simply a "departure" from normal practice, he also hinted that Gates's leadership of the department would become an issue. The next day, the *Times* reported Bradley's call for "a broad investigation into what he termed a disturbing pattern of local police abuse, particularly against minorities" (Wood and Fiore 1991, A1). Though he did not actually put that call into action for nearly a month, Bradley's definition of the King incident validated a systemic understanding of brutality which the video had suggested to many observers and directly countered Gates's claim that the beating was not part of a pattern.

Over the next two weeks, Bradley's office orchestrated the release of transcripts of police radio communications recorded on the night of the beating. The transcripts, released on March 18, revealed racist banter among various officers and indicated that the officers involved in the beating had made light of it.[17] In a statement to the press, Bradley again challenged Gates's definition of the King beating and offered reporters a systemic problem definition to frame it: "It is no longer possible for any objective person to regard the King beating as an 'aberration,' " he told reporters. "We must face the fact that there appears to be a dangerous trend of racially motivated incidents running through at least some segments of our Police Department." Bradley also announced that the police commission was "examining whether the department's command structure permits these tragic incidents to occur" (Bradley blasts "bigotry" of police officers, 1991, A12). Finally, on April 1, Mayor Bradley publicly proclaimed that Gates should resign and announced the formation of a commission, headed by Warren Christopher, charged with investigating allegations of systematic brutality and racism in the LAPD.[18]

Bradley was not alone in breaking the official silence on brutality. Officials in Los Angeles and across the country subsequently challenged Gates's definition of the King incident, thus legitimizing for reporters a systemic framework in which to place it. One week after the beating became news, the Congressional Black Caucus demanded a federal investigation of what it called a pattern of police abuse of minorities not only in Los Angeles but across the nation; one week later, the Justice Department announced it would broaden its investigation of the LAPD beyond the King beating to examine roughly 100 other allegations of brutality against the department and to review federal brutality complaints overall. On March 23, three California Congressmen, including Henry Waxman, publicly called for Gates's resignation; and on March 28, city councilman Michael Woo became the first local official to go on record calling for Gates to leave the LAPD. At the same time, some politicians, such as state representative Maxine Waters and candidates for the Los Angeles city council, engaged in a variety of maneuvers to capitalize on the growing anti-Gates sentiment. Thus, numerous public officials—the usual primary definers of use-of-force incidents—broke ranks in response to the King video. With elected officials labeling the incident as part of a pattern rather than as an aberration, the difficult terrain of police brutality became easier for journalists to tread. Thus, it was not simply the video but the way that officials responded to it that encouraged the *Times* to construct a systemic problem around Rodney King.

Even so, the *Times* did not wait for official calls for Gates's resignation to bring critical voices and systemic claims into the news. The suddenness of the *Times*' shift in coverage is evidenced by the news summaries listed in table 2, and by the public opinion polls the *Times* conducted in the aftermath of the beating. Only once between 1985 and 1990 had the *Times* published an opinion poll regarding police. But it conducted four such polls in 1991. The first of the 1991 polls (Rohrlich 1991) was conducted on March 7 and 8—two days after the Rodney King beating was first reported. The poll asked Los Angeles residents whether they believed police brutality was commonplace; two-thirds said they believed that it was. The poll also "found widespread belief among Anglos, blacks and Latinos that King was beaten because he was black and that police generally are tougher on blacks and Latinos than they are on Anglos" (ibid., A1). It found that three-fourths of Angelenos favored the establishment of a civilian board to review alleged cases of police misconduct. And it found that one in eight respondents thought that Chief Gates should step down immediately because of the King beating.

What is more significant than the numbers supporting these various propositions is the fact that the *Times* asked such questions, ushering systemic claims about brutality to the center of the media stage. Thus, while officials' responses to the beating helped to legitimize a systemic problem definition around Rodney King, officials did not control that problem definition. Rather, a complex interaction ensued between the video, the officials, and the *Times*.[19] The video pushed the *Times* to take up the possibility of a systemic problem within the LAPD while pushing Bradley to take up political arms against Daryl Gates. Bradley then provided reporters with cues that the King beating would become the pretext for a major political battle—a prospect that became more clear with each of Bradley's news conferences and as public pressure from around the city and the nation continued to build. For reporters, each of Bradley's announcements became the next move in a positioning of forces that might lead to truly big news—the attempted removal of Chief Gates from the LAPD—that would fully legitimate journalistic attention to the issue of police conduct.

The *Times*' critical reaction to the King beating should not be overstated. Just as in the Dalton case, the *Times* was initially somewhat hesitant to define the King beating as an indicator of a serious policing problem, especially a problem that might extend beyond the leadership of the controversial Daryl Gates. For example, in the first month following the beating, the *Times* published five news items exploring the impact of the King beating on police morale and police-community relations while it published only two pieces exploring the issue of excessive force. Moreover, these pieces broached the notion of a systemic policing problem quite gingerly. The first thematic story, appearing roughly two weeks after the beating occurred, focused mainly on describing the LAPD's training program and policies regarding the use of force. Police officials were quoted first and at length, defending the department's training and emphasizing the danger posed by suspects to officers rather than the danger some officers might pose to the public:

> "We have to stay consistent (in our training)," said Sgt. Fred Nichols, officer in charge of physical training and self-defense at the Police Academy. "The area of use of force is what gets our officers in trouble. . . . If an officer fails to employ the baton aggressively . . . somebody could take your weapon away from you and blow you away." (Tobar 1991, A1)

The second thematic news item was more critical. It explored the mentality that could allow police officers to stand by and observe the King beating without intervening. It noted that the sight of officers standing passively by did not come as a surprise to experts in group behavior, who "say the beating of Rodney G. King is a case of 'us versus them,' typifying the tendency of tightly knit groups to divide the world into opposing camps, to devalue and dehumanize outsiders and, under certain conditions, to commit terrible violence against them" (Scott 1991, A1). The article failed, however, to explore whether the problem of officer solidarity in brutality is amenable to political reform or community control. It was represented as primarily an individual and moral, rather than a political, problem: " 'People change as a result of their own actions,' [according to social psychologist Ervin Staub]. 'People who engage in helping behavior frequently become more helpful. People who engage in aggression that is not checked by others frequently become more aggressive.' "

Thus, the *Times* awaited further cues before more assertively defining a brutality problem. Not until after Mayor Bradley called for Gates's resignation, nearly one month after the beating, did the *Times* engage in more independent exploration of police misconduct. Pushing them toward that position were the increasingly angry voices of local activists and other citizens.

CITIZEN REACTION

The way that George Holliday's video portrayed police use of force was crucial to the problem definition that began immediately to take hold in the news, and the response of Mayor Bradley and other officials further legitimized the construction of a systemic policing problem. But these factors were bolstered by the efforts of local activists to use the King beating to illustrate arguments about an endemic brutality problem. As Bradley and Gates circled one another, reporters had another story line to follow: the efforts of activists to bring about Gates's departure. With officials providing hints of a future showdown, critical nonofficials stepped into the breach to become primary news sources.

Immediately after the video was first aired, assorted local activists swung into action, mobilizing the African American community in particular around a systemic problem definition. They asserted, in contrast to Gates's individualizing claim, that the King beating was symptomatic of racist brutality fostered by an ugly police subculture that was encouraged, or at least tolerated, by Gates himself.

As African American activists took to the streets, the local chapter of the ACLU spearheaded a broader public campaign to force Gates from office. The first volley was fired with an op-ed piece published in the

Los Angeles Times on March 7 written by the local ACLU director, Ramona Ripston, who argued:

> We can't allow Daryl Gates to draw a circle around the 10 men who were present at the beating and pretend that the problem has been taken care of. The brutality that was exhibited Sunday is part of a much larger problem of leadership gone awry.
>
> After years of controversy, after years of multimillion-dollar hospital and trauma bills being paid out to victims of police misconduct, there is only one answer to the problem facing Los Angeles today. In the interest of the department and the city, the time has come for Chief Gates to step aside.

The same day, the ACLU joined other local activist groups at a news conference to publicize their problem definition. Two days later, hundreds of protesters gathered at LAPD headquarters at Parker Center to demand Gates's resignation; they promised to demonstrate every weekend until Gates was gone. There, activists such as Jose De Sosa, the rally's organizer and president of the San Fernando Valley chapter of the NAACP, challenged Gates's definition of the King beating, asserting that "This is the type of thing that occurs under the cover of darkness throughout our city" (Stohlberg 1991a, B1).

The following week, the local ACLU announced a "multilevel campaign" to increase the pressure on Gates. The campaign began with a full-page paid advertisement in the *Times* and six other local newspapers under the headline, "Who Do You Call When the Gang Wears Blue Uniforms?" It invited readers to clip out, sign, and mail a letter calling on Gates to step down. Two days later, with more than 200 letters arrayed before them, the ACLU and other civil rights groups held a press conference announcing Operation Overhaul, a campaign to "end police brutality" and push Gates out of office. They issued a call for a blue-ribbon panel to conduct an independent review of the LAPD. The pressure on Gates and Bradley grew as notable activists from around the country got involved. On March 16, Jesse Jackson joined the chorus calling for Gates's departure while also calling on Mayor Bradley to speak out "more clearly and decisively" on the King beating; on March 29, New York's Al Sharpton led several hundred protesters in a march from City Hall to Parker Center. But the pressure came not only from activists but from the general public, as hundreds of letters and phone calls poured into the LAPD, the *Times*, and the offices of local politicians. By March 24, roughly three weeks after the video was first aired, the *Los Angeles Times* had received 1,749 letters, 1,359 of which were critical of the LAPD (The numbers, 1991).

Citizen reaction to the King beating thus created dramatic action for reporters to follow—a broad-based and vociferous campaign that presented real political challenges to both Gates and Bradley. Indeed, as one *Times* reporter told me, the citizen reaction virtually "became the story," as community leaders challenged the LAPD's explanation of the event and demanded better answers (Newton 1997). This reaction was crucial to the problem definition that emerged in the pages of the *Times*, for it popularized the notion that the LAPD had a brutality problem that went beyond one or two rogue cops. Thus, it was not the video or the activities of activists alone that drove the news agenda but the dramatic admixture of gripping imagery, forceful citizen claims, and the likelihood of political upheaval.

ACTIVISTS AND ACCIDENTAL EVENTS

This dynamic in which news events and activism coincide is suggested by the academic literature on social movements and the media, but in a way that does not fully account for the role of accidental events. Scholars have recognized that an important variable determining activists' entrance into the news is their ability to offer reporters something newsworthy to report. Generally speaking, this means that activists must provide reporters not just with ideas or arguments but with events. As Ryan (1991, 247) observes, "[Since] news downplays history and context, . . . challengers have difficulty getting coverage for an alternative historical explanation or for an analysis of the incremental development of a chronic problem. . . . [Instead,] the mainstream media want the issue packaged in terms of a current event."

The general conclusion of this literature is that activists are in a double bind: they must create unusual and dramatic events to gain news attention, but in so doing they encourage reporters to focus on the unusual or even bizarre aspects of the event and its participants rather than on the claims the group wishes to publicize (Entman and Rojecki 1993; Gitlin 1980; Ryan 1991). The classic example is the political demonstration during which activists march, chant, wear unusual clothing, make dramatic charges against political regimes, stage guerrilla theater, burn effigies, et cetera—providing reporters with stories that are indeed dramatic but chiefly because of the participants' "weird" behavior. In seeking to entice reporters, therefore, activists often sow the seeds of their own marginalization.

What has been less explored is an alternative dynamic in which dramatic news events not staged by activists help them to publicize their claims.[20] While staged events may or may not provide "good news" to journalists, "accidental" events can create openings for news that focuses not only on activists themselves but on their claims.

As Bennett and Lawrence (1995) found regarding the journey of the infamous garbage barge *Mobro* in 1987, dramatic, unsettling news events can provide journalists with story material while encouraging them to seek out sources who can contextualize those events. Moreover, such events can pique news organizations' interest in the public problems suggested by the event. In the case of the *Mobro*, "ideas from the environmental movement were picked up and legitimized in the mainstream media" (33). As news organizations turned to environmental activist groups and concerned officials to comment on the barge's significance, recycling emerged in the news as a legitimized policy response to a newly important problem of garbage. Thus, "events play an important role in whether—and when—social movement concerns are legitimized by mainstream media gatekeepers" (35).

Sometimes, therefore, activists and other critical nonofficials can ride dramatic events not of their own making into the news—and perhaps without losing as much control over their message. As Wolfsfeld (1997, 81) observes:

> Political and non-political events sometimes change the rules of entrance to the [media] arena. A nuclear accident can serve as a cultural explosion that opens that arena to a plethora of antinuclear challengers who under normal circumstances would be left out. When a doctor is killed for carrying out abortions, journalists look for activists from both pro-choice and pro-life movements to react to the event. When the threat of war hangs in the air, the value of peace group sources rises.

Indeed, "critical events . . . change the political context [and] change in context creates news pegs as journalists look for sources and stories linked to that event" (103).

That the Rodney King beating provided just such an opportunity for antibrutality activists in southern California is suggested by the data in figure 4. The figure shows the number of news and editorial items in which various antibrutality organizations were mentioned in the *Los Angeles Times* across the ten-year period examined here, according to a search of the Nexis database. Antibrutality groups, particularly the ACLU and NAACP, clearly benefited, in terms of media exposure, from the Rodney King beating. While they were not the only voices framing

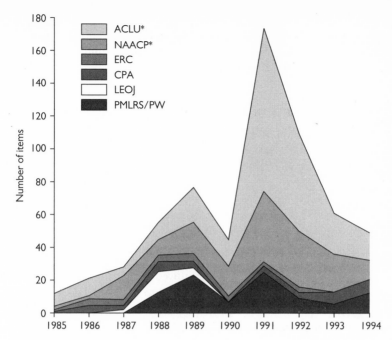

Figure 4. Coverage of Antibrutality Activist Groups, *Los Angeles Times*, 1985–94. Source: Data are based on a search of the Nexis database for all news and editorial items mentioning each group.

Note: Most groups included here focus exclusively or primarily upon police misconduct and so were located on Nexis simply by name. The NAACP* and ACLU* focus on a variety of issues in addition to police misconduct, and so references to these groups were located by searching for their names in close proximity to the words "police" and "brutality," "excessive force," or "misconduct."

Legend: ACLU: American Civil Liberties Union; CPA: Coalition for Police Accountability; ERC: Equal Rights Congress; LEOJ: Law Enforcement Officers for Justice; NAACP: National Association for the Advancement of Colored People; PMLRS/PW: Police Misconduct Lawyers Referral Service, which became Police Watch in 1991.

the King incident in the news, they did play a prominent role in shaping its public definition.[21]

The data in figure 4 show a smaller spike in media attention to these activist groups in 1989. This is especially true of the Police Misconduct Lawyers Referral Service (later renamed Police Watch), which gained virtually as much news coverage in 1989 as in 1991. The increased attention to PMLRS even before the King beating was no mere coincidence, for in 1989 that group helped to build its own vehicle into the news: a videotaped "sting" of Long Beach police. We turn to a brief examination of this case before concluding this chapter, for it prompts some useful propositions about the power and the limits of news events as vehicles for designating public problems.

DON JACKSON AND THE CREATION OF "ACCIDENTAL" EVENTS

In January 1989, Don Jackson, an African American policeman on leave from the Long Beach police force and a member of PMLRS, invited the local NBC affiliate to film him as he drove through Long Beach in an old rental car and shabby clothes.[22] Jackson believed that African Americans were routinely subject to brutal and arbitrary treatment by police throughout southern California and the nation, and he hoped to illustrate that argument with a filmed "sting." Jackson's car was stopped by Long Beach police, and as hidden cameras whirred, an altercation ensued in which a white officer, spewing a string of obscenities, grabbed Jackson and pushed him into a plate glass store front, shattering the glass. The image was replayed on local and national television, even appearing on *The Today Show.*

The Jackson case became the second most-mentioned case of alleged brutality to be reported in the *Times* during the ten-year period examined here. It was mentioned in nearly 200 *Los Angeles Times* pieces between 1989 and 1991 (coincidentally, the trial of the officer accused of abusing Jackson began one day after Rodney King was beaten by LAPD officers). Indeed, 24 percent of all 1989 *Times* articles about police use of force were about Jackson's case, far more than any other single case that year. Riding the sting into the news, Jackson and likeminded activists gained a voice in both news pieces and editorials. Jackson was quoted in 42 news stories, and the *Times* published five of his op-eds and letters to the editor, all of which offered his view of police brutality as a serious systemic problem rooted in societal racism and an insular police subculture. As noted above, the event created an opening not only for Jackson but for other members of the PMLRS to enter the news.

But despite the apparent similarities of the Don Jackson and Rodney King incidents, the latter had a much more significant effect on the amount and type of reporting about police brutality in the *Los Angeles Times.* Both were dramatic videotaped news events that seemingly illustrated the claim that minorities are routinely subjected to arbitrary and violent treatment by police. Yet the Rodney King beating influenced the news representation of police use of force in ways that Don Jackson's altercation with police did not. Why?

Several contextual differences between the two cases undoubtedly contributed to their different treatment in the news. While the King beating involved institutions central to the *Times'* political turf (the LAPD and the mayor's office) in a major political showdown, the Jackson incident involved the smaller and more peripheral government of Long Beach and promised few future political news pegs for journalists.[23]

Furthermore, Jackson's treatment was at the hands of a single officer. While apparently brutal, that treatment paled in comparison to the specter of more than 20 police officers surrounding King while four beat and kicked him repeatedly. In fact, Jackson's videotaped altercation did not suggest systemic framings of police use of force quite as clearly as Jackson asserted. In fact, the incident could be easily explained in terms of the common officially sanctioned framing of police use of force. As the president of the Long Beach Officers Association put it, "Mr. Jackson's motives are apparent to any human being. If you go looking for trouble, you find it" (Woodyard 1989, sec. 2, p. 1). In other words, the video suggested that the officer manhandled Jackson because Jackson prompted him to—a charge Jackson for obvious reasons had trouble defending himself against.

This points to a subtler difference of *origins* lurking beneath the more obvious differences between the two videos. The Don Jackson case was an attempt by activists to *create* a brutality event to ride into the news—a nonaccidental accidental event, so to speak.[24] Jackson collaborated with other antibrutality activists in the PMLRS and with the local NBC affiliate in taping his "sting," and had worked for months to capture just this kind of police behavior on film. Thus, the camera showed an altercation that was not completely spontaneous. King, in contrast, had no hand in capturing his own beating on film, while the man who did was generally thought to have no ulterior motive. These differences in origin and in what the camera recorded created different connections with the usual news discourse about police brutality. For Jackson could be said to have "asked for it" in a way that King had not.

Consequently, despite its considerable success in bringing brutality to the headlines, Jackson's video also met with considerable critical media scrutiny that ultimately may have kept it from becoming even bigger news. Journalistic discomfort with the Jackson video surfaced almost immediately, as the local station that participated in the "sting" was put on the defensive by accusations that it had overstepped the bounds of objective journalism. Indeed, four out of the seven *Los Angeles Times* editorials dealing with the Jackson event actually focused on criticizing or defending KNBC's role in the sting.

Moreover, Jackson himself was the focus of as much or more attention than were his claims of systematic police mistreatment of minorities. This is especially notable in a lengthy *Los Angeles Times* piece describing Jackson's "heady days" in the limelight. The 2400-word article claimed Jackson "has seized the moment by the throat. He has plans, major plans, for his crusade and for himself." It raised questions about Jackson's motives, describing his financial difficulties prior to the taped altercation and his much-improved prospects as a new-found favorite son of civil rights organizations. This piece echoed the theme of an earlier *Los Angeles Times* profile of Jackson, which introduced its subject by saying, "Jackson's tactics have been debated from the opinion pages of newspapers to the Los Angeles barber shop he uses. Some have questioned his actions, while others have asked: Who is Don Jackson and what is he trying to prove?" (Rainey 1989a, 1).

Thus, while Jackson's video won a hearing for his views, he also was subjected to the same kinds of marginalization often experienced by other grass roots activists who attempt to stage events to capture media attention and put their concerns before the public. Jackson himself became the focus of news reporting, edging out the claims he was making about race, policing, and brutality. His case suggests that the possibility of activists intentionally creating symbolically resonant news events is limited by news organizations' reluctance to be "used" by nonofficials to push particular problems and framings of problems onto the public agenda (see Gans 1979, 122, and Molotch and Lester 1974, 108).

CONCLUSION

According to the official-dominance model of the news, the news agenda generally follows institutional agendas, and the treatment of public issues in the news is roughly indexed to the treatment of those issues by officials. Officials act as primary definers of issues and events, and news is anchored in established news beats and the routine political communication strategies of officials. Only when a policy issue is highly contested in official circles, or when officials fight among themselves to compete for control of the news narrative, will the news reflect a broad range of debate on that issue. And when nonofficials, especially activists, try to set the news and the institutional agendas, they often falter against the structural and cultural determinants of routine news.

The news about police use of force is usually structured around official claims, as chapter 3 illustrated, and yet it sometimes spins out of official control to consider the possible systemic roots of police brutality, as this chapter has illustrated. Some dramatic "accidental events" can encourage journalists to open the news gates to more critical voices and views. Of course, the news is unlikely to seriously construct a public problem unless some official action offers journalists license to do so. Even while it opened the door to critical voices and their claims of systemic brutality, the *Los Angeles Times* refrained from a full thematic exploration of police brutality until it was clear that the issue would bring real political challenges to the LAPD and the mayor. But the case of Rodney King does suggest that official control of problems in the news is tenuous and incomplete. For even though journalists have incentives to write from the officially provided narrative, they also have incentives to focus on events that conform to their notions of "newsworthiness." Moreover, official responses to accidental news events have to contend with the narratives suggested by those events. Official responses that are too far afield of the narrative suggested by an event, such as Gates's "aberration" claim, have trouble reasserting control over the news.

This argument raises a crucial question: How commonly do officials lose control? Clearly, relatively few events so dramatically affect the news agenda as did the Rodney King beating. Yet while such events arise only rarely, the same dynamics that shaped coverage of that event might shape coverage of other events as well. As explored in the next chapter, the shifting frames in the news reflect the shifting availability of the "story cues" that make some instances of police use of force into major news events.

FIVE

Making Big News

Story Cues and Critical
Coverage of Policing

Which police use-of-force incidents become major news stories, and how do they differ from those that do not? Over 500 cases of police use of force were reported in the *New York Times* and the *Los Angeles Times* between 1985 and 1994, but only a handful of these became major, highly controversial news stories. This presents a puzzle, because the details of many of these incidents are similarly ambiguous and could be construed as equally disturbing. Given the inherent ambiguity of many use-of-force incidents, news organizations must decide which are more newsworthy than others and which, if any, are indicators of policing problems. Why do some of these incidents prompt more critical news than others?

Chapter 4 identified three conditions that helped to make the Rodney King beating a major news event in the *Los Angeles Times*: the narrative power of the video that captured (a portion of) the event; the willingness of Mayor Tom Bradley to publicly challenge the LAPD's definition of the event, which foreshadowed a future power struggle between Bradley and LAPD chief Daryl Gates; and the efforts of local activists to step into that breach to become primary definers of the King beating—efforts that were greatly aided by the first two conditions. The narrative suggested by the video was crucial to how that incident broke out of officials' usual news containment strategies, while the reactions of officials and the public to the video gave reporters at the *Los Angeles Times* ongoing news pegs on which to hang more critical reporting.

The contextual factors that influenced news coverage of the King case provide the starting point for the more systematic analysis presented in this chapter, which examines the varying news coverage given to a large number of use-of-force incidents. In this chapter, I develop a typology of "critical story cues" that influence how use-of-force incidents are represented in the news. Critical story cues, I argue, signal to journalists that a "good story" about police misconduct is at hand and enable and encourage journalists to tell stories that diverge from official claims about police use of force. These story cues create openings in the news for critical societal voices who depict police brutality as a systemic problem. They arise out of the immediate details of particular events and from subsequent official and citizen reaction to them. Evidence for the importance of critical story cues rests upon the scholarly literature on the construction of the news and is developed by analyzing 552 use-of-force incidents reported in the *New York Times* and the *Los Angeles Times* and supported by open-ended interviews conducted with crime reporters from both newspapers.

This analysis begins by theorizing the underlying journalistic norms guiding news-gathering and news-writing decisions that make critical story cues work.[1] We saw in chapter 3 how one normative order, which I labeled media professionalism, shapes journalists' decisions about how to cover the subject of police use of force. Media professionalism is closely tied to a standard set of routine news-gathering practices, especially the beat system, which puts journalists in close contact with police sources and sensitizes them to police perspectives on the use of force. According to the media-professionalism norm, journalists should transmit legitimate information to the public without actively or intentionally setting the public agenda or unduly amplifying social conflict or marginalized social voices. As this norm is played out on the crime beat, the news tends fairly faithfully to report the claims of police officials and often marginalizes concerns about police conduct.

But if certain story developments can trigger more critical news coverage, this suggests that journalistic norms other than professionalism are at work. Accordingly, this chapter begins by describing two other sets of norms and incentives operating in the newsroom: media commercialism and media reformism. Commercialism and reformism encourage journalists to see good news possibilities in stories that are dramatic and involve official wrongdoing. Thus, while media professionalism encourages journalists to grant officials the power to define issues and events in the news, media commercialism and reformism can encourage journalists to give critical attention to issues and events that police and elected officials would rather leave unexplored.

COMPETING JOURNALISTIC NORMS

Professionalism is in many ways the predominant journalistic normative order in most news organizations, enshrined as it is in the beat system and journalistic understandings of "objectivity." But it is not the only normative order in the newsroom. As Weaver and Wilhoit (1992) have found in their surveys of journalists, news organizations strive to adhere to multiple models of what constitutes good journalism and "good news."[2]

News organizations are driven to get the news: to identify what happened today that will be important and interesting for audiences. But what constitutes good news depends on journalistic norms governing what "news" is. The official-dominance model of the news rests on the fact that journalists often act as professional conveyors of information provided by legitimated official sources. But mainstream news organizations also act as commercial storytellers and monitors of social and political transgressions.

COMMERCIALISM: THE NEWS AS STORYTELLING

Despite the predominance of the professional norm of neutral information-conveyance, news organizations are in the business, fundamentally, of storytelling. The news tells us, through stories, who we are as a people and keeps us apprised, through stories, of the events and issues that shape, challenge, and threaten us. In more prosaic terms, journalists are—indeed, must be—daily crafters of stories that editors, audiences, and other reporters find interesting.

Journalists are not always entirely comfortable with their storytelling role, even in the context of the increasing commercialization of the news media. Many do not think of themselves as "entertainers," as Glasser and Ettema's interviews with investigative journalists revealed, and less than 20 percent of journalists in Weaver and Wilhoit's survey identified "being entertaining" as an important goal (1992). As one reporter put it, "I guess I don't consider myself a story-teller . . . I consider myself a gatherer of facts" (quoted in Weaver and Wilhoit 1992, 23).

Yet a number of observers within and outside of the profession have expressed fears that crude forms of media commercialism—the increasing emphasis on ratings, drama, and entertainment—may be crowding out norms associated with professionalism (Bagdikian 1992; Kurtz 1993; Lehrer 1999; McChesney 1999; Underwood 1993). Meanwhile, in a more subtle form, the notion of journalism as storytelling has long been embedded within the same journalistic culture that claims to value neutral information-conveyance (Darnton 1975; Schudson 1978). Indeed, journalists have been storytellers longer than they have been objective professionals (Ettema and Glasser 1988, 8; Schudson 1978). This tradition remains vital to the profession today, even though in practice many journalists may disavow the storytelling dimensions of their work (Roeh 1989). There is little doubt that the reporter who wins the respect of his or her colleagues will have, among other things, a well-developed sense of how to recognize and tell compelling stories. As Patterson (1994, 80) observes, tightly structured stories built around clear themes and narratives have increasingly become the norm not only in television but in print reporting. Indeed, a concern with "production values" focuses journalists' attention on "fashioning a quality story from the material they receive. A story's quality is judged by the 'play' it receives in the news" (Cook 1996, 473).

Thus, while media professionalism encourages journalists to convey information in a neutral and responsible manner, media commercialism encourages journalists to structure that information to hold audience attention. According to the logic of commercialized news, good journalism is good storytelling; the more compelling the stories, the better the product (Cornfield 1992, 48). In its cruder forms, this journalistic normative order produces many news characteristics bemoaned by critical scholars: dramatization, personalization, and news full of dramatic "moments" that pack emotional punch (Bennett 1996).

As storytellers, news organizations also seek "serialization." They try to recognize events that will develop into longer-running stories. Serialized news stories are valued because they facilitate the routine production of the news and because they sustain audience attention (Chermak 1994). At a deeper level, as Cook (1996, 474) observes, reporters see daily news events as "episodes of larger continuing sagas that carry their own 'meta-messages'. . . . [F]or news to be produced routinely, journalists must be able to visualize events as part of a larger, broader story line and must move the plot along from one episode to the next."

Consequently, what looks to news organizations like material for "good news" depends not only upon its status on institutional agendas, as the official-dominance model of the news holds, but upon its narrative possibilities—that is, upon journalists' perceptions of what audiences find interesting and on the possibilities for "serialization" it offers.

REFORMISM: THE NEWS AS MONITOR OF TRANSGRESSIONS

Journalists' recognition of dramatic story lines is shaped not just by professional and commercial imperatives but by a reformist ideal that sprung from roots in the penny press and the Progressive movement and was nurtured—some would say warped—in the hothouse politics of the 1960s and 1970s. A powerful and controversial cultural ideal of the press as an adversary of government and a force for reform—journalists as the "watchdogs" of democracy—reflects this third journalistic normative order.

According to the popularized version of this ideal, journalism is a crucial means of exposing misconduct, injustice, and hypocrisy and of exercising countervailing power against political and economic elites. Reporters are expected to take a skeptical stance toward official claims and to identify problems stemming from government failure or political malfeasance. This ideal, highly resonant in our popular culture, "is a celebration of the notion that the public interest is best served by a continuing rivalry between the press and the powerful" (Glasser and Ettema 1989, 3). While the resonance of this ideal may have faded since its Watergate heyday, it still constitutes one component of contemporary journalistic culture (Glasser and Ettema 1989; Miraldi 1990; Protess et al. 1991). According to Weaver and Wilhoit's (1992) survey, while only 20 percent of journalists today believe that "being an adversary of government" is an "extremely important" aspect of their work, a majority believe that "investigating government claims" is one of the two most important activities of their profession—the other being speedy information-conveyance.

The belief in journalistic adversarialism has been taken more seriously by journalists than by scholars and has been subjected to fairly withering academic critique.[3] But the watchdog ideal is nonetheless useful for understanding journalistic culture, for it hints at a more fundamental orientation of the news as a monitor of transgressions. As many scholars have observed, the news is preoccupied with order and disorder; indeed, a basic thrust of the news media's construction of reality is toward "representing order" (Ericson, Baranek, and Chan 1991). News organizations habitually monitor the socially defined boundaries of acceptable and expected political and social behavior, and they define transgressions of those boundaries as "news." The news "focuses upon what is out of place: the deviant, equivocal, and unpredictable," offers a "social discourse of procedural propriety," and thus "articulates public morality" (ibid., 3–7). The prime targets of this surveillance are elites and public institutions. As one top news executive told Gans (1979, 149), the role of journalists is to report "when things go awry, when institutions are not functioning normally."

Shaped by historical roots in muckraking and Progressivism, media reformism emphasizes journalism's role not only in identifying transgressions but in bringing about redress and reform. The media's constant surveillance of the political scene yields a common pattern in the daily news: stories in which problems of elite incompetence, malfeasance, or failure are identified and in which elites are pressured to fix those problems, atone for transgressions, and restore "normalcy." Thus, the media are often fixed upon exposing incompetence and scandal and subtly emphasize a continual need for reform. Highly commercial media, particularly television, may emphasize scandal more than reform. But other news organizations, particularly high-quality daily newspapers, often seek "to improve the American system by pointing out its shortcomings" (Protess et al. 1991, 11). Thus, the news "reinforces and relegitimates dominant national and societal values by publicizing and helping to punish those who deviate from the values" (Gans 1979, 293).

COMPETING NORMS AND THE NEWS ABOUT BRUTALITY

Commercialism and reformism often work together to challenge official efforts to control the news. News organizations see good news possibilities in events that promise dramatic storytelling and indicate brewing problems stemming from official transgressions. Of course, these competing norms do not guarantee that news organizations will always construct news that challenges official claims. Commercialism can dovetail nicely with official efforts to manage the news, such as in the case of most crime reporting: As news organizations have discovered, crime sells, and much crime news is premised on police-supplied images of police and crime fighting (Ericson, Baranek, and Chan 1991; Reeves and Campbell 1994). Sometimes, commercialism works against reformism, encouraging news organizations to be cautious and conservative in their coverage of issues such as police conduct. As one former television reporter has put it, "If you're in the TV news racket, your principal goal is to be loved, and it is self-destructive to give viewers unsettling informa-tion, particularly to tell viewers that their confidence in their police might be misplaced" (Wayne Satz, quoted in Irwin 1991, 15).

Yet commercialism and reformism also create incentives to tell stories that are damaging to official efforts at news control. Much investigative print journalism, for example, reflects both reformist and commercial considerations. As Kaniss (1991, 88) observes, "Investigative journal-ism is valued at metropolitan newspapers both because of professional respect for uncovering wrongdoing as well as economic interests that recognize the value of impressing audiences with successful crusading." For other examples of the blending of commercialism and reformism, one need look no further than the weekly television newsmagazine shows, which are both popular with audiences and explicitly reformist in their orientation; the narrative thread of such programs often in-volves rooting out political or business behavior that does not comport with the law or public norms. This dovetailing of commercial and re-formist impulses in large part explains the growing "tabloidization" of the mainstream media, which focuses ever more obsessively on events such as the O. J. Simpson murder trial or the Monica Lewinsky scandal.

Dramatic cases of alleged police brutality can arouse reporters' com-mercial and reformist instincts. Such stories provide high drama, with im-ages (occasionally captured on film) of officially perpetrated violence and nearly inevitable questions of guilt, truth, and justice. Police brutality makes for "good news" because it represents a basic transgression of so-cial and political norms and upsets standard assumptions about the po-lice as upholders of the law. As *Los Angeles Times* media critic Howard Rosenberg commented on the Rodney King case, "violence by criminals against police is dog biting man. We expect this of criminals precisely be-cause they are criminals. Police beating [someone] is man biting dog. It's a case of the good guys—the ones sworn to protect the public and whose integrity is crucial to civilized society—becoming the bad guys" (Rosen-berg 1991, F1). As another *Los Angeles Times* reporter explained to me, a use-of-force incident is newsworthy if it indicates wrongdoing on the part of the officer, and it is particularly newsworthy if it indicates some systemic problem beyond the incident itself (Newton 1997).

This reformist urge to identify problems, together with the dramatic appeal of some brutality stories, provides an opening for voices and views normally marginalized in the news to be ushered to center stage, as antibrutality activists were in the wake of the King beating. When media commercialism and reformism are strongly engaged by a breaking news story, nonofficial groups can actually become primary definers of news events. In such circumstances, journalists' professional suspicion of grassroots voices competes with journalists' interest in crafting dramatic and commercially competitive news stories that uncover official transgressions.

The key questions are, when are commercialism and reformism engaged? Which events win news coverage that challenges official efforts at news control, and why? In order to answer these questions, we begin by examining further a phenomenon first introduced in chapter 3: the correlation between the amount and type of news coverage that various use-of-force incidents receive. Those events that journalists find the most newsworthy are also the events that open the news gates to critical societal voices and views. Put simply, the more coverage, the more critical coverage. I then examine what differentiates these highly newsworthy events from less newsworthy events, which reveals what arouses media commercialism and reformism in the news about policing.

HIGH-PROFILE INCIDENTS AND CRITICAL NEWS

To begin to understand this relationship between newsworthiness and critical coverage, recall from chapter 3 that very few use-of-force incidents gain more than fleeting news coverage. Most cases of police use of force reported in the news are the subject of only one or two stories before they disappear from the news pages.

The more coverage an incident receives, however, the more likely it will also be the subject of more critical news coverage.[4] Figure 5 reports differences in coverage across the three groups of use-of-force incidents examined in chapter 3: those mentioned in only one or two news articles ("low-profile" incidents), those mentioned in between 3 and 10 articles ("mid-profile" incidents), and those mentioned in more than 10 articles ("high-profile" incidents). The data show that the more coverage an incident receives, the more likely it is to appear in articles that prominently feature critical nonofficial voices and systemic claims about police brutality. In the *New York Times*, for example, only 16 percent of incidents that appeared and disappeared from the news quickly were also marked by prominent coverage of nonofficial voices, and only 13 percent were the subject of prominent systemic claims. Yet eight out of nine high-profile cases in that paper prominently featured critical nonofficials, and all nine cases were the subject of systemic claims.[5]

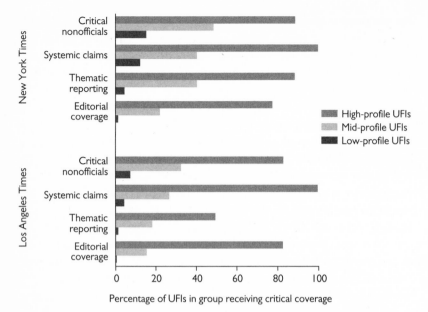

Figure 5. Relationship between Amount and Type of Coverage of Use-of-Force Incidents (UFIs), *New York Times* and *Los Angeles Times*, 1985–94. Source: Data are compiled from the *New York Times* and *Los Angeles Times* indexes. One-way analysis of variance indicates that the differences between groups regarding each indicator of critical news coverage are statistically significant (p < .05).

Furthermore, the more coverage a case receives, the more likely it is to be the subject of "thematic" news (Iyengar 1991) and of editorials.[6] Thematic news items and editorials are important indicators of potential problem construction in the news. Whereas episodic news stories focus on the details of particular events, thematic reporting examines broader social phenomena and places events in the context of some rising trend or troubling social condition. Editorials often explicitly offer particular problem definitions to contextualize news events and often suggest particular remedies.

Figure 5 shows a positive association between the newsworthiness of various incidents and their appearance in these news formats. In the *Los Angeles Times*, for example, only 2 percent of low-profile cases were the subject of thematic news reporting, compared with 27 percent of mid-profile cases and all of the high-profile cases. Similarly, only 1 percent of low-profile cases were mentioned in editorial items, whereas 50 percent of high-profile cases were the subject of editorials.

Coverage of high-profile use-of-force incidents is also more likely to make reference to other use-of-force incidents, thus extending beyond a strictly episodic focus. While coverage of only 26 percent of low-profile cases in the *New York Times* linked those incidents with other use-of-force incidents, 80 percent of mid-profile and 100 percent of high-profile cases were so linked. Similar associations are found in the *Los Angeles Times*: 23 percent of low-profile cases were linked with other events, compared with 75 percent of mid-profile and 100 percent of high-profile events.[7] With increased attention to one incident, therefore, comes increased attention to other incidents, an implicit (and sometimes explicit) challenge to common official claims that use-of-force incidents should be viewed in isolation as purely random and occasional occurrences.

THE JOURNALISTIC CONSTRUCTION OF HIGH-PROFILE INCIDENTS

Thus, a small percentage of use-of-force incidents become closely watched and highly controversial in the news pages. Before offering an explanation for the variable news coverage granted to different events, I will consider an important question that the critical reader will already have asked: Don't different use-of-force incidents essentially get the coverage they deserve? It could be, in other words, that the coverage meted out to various incidents essentially mirrors the reality of each situation, so that the cases that become big stories are the cases in which officers are clearly guilty of overstepping the line between appropriate and excessive force.

This proposition, while appealing on its face, overlooks the inherently ambiguous nature of most use-of-force incidents. These incidents are often at least potentially problematic for officials because different observers and participants may view them in different ways, as discussed in chapter 2. Moreover, the objective truth of any incident, to the degree that it exists, is difficult to know before legal proceedings have sorted through all the evidence and is often never settled definitively.[8] Indeed, some of the highest-profile incidents analyzed here led to criminal trials (indicating that there was some reason to suspect the officers' behavior), yet the officers were ultimately vindicated (indicating either than the officers acted appropriately or that the prosecution could not overcome the considerable obstacles to convicting police officers of excessive force).[9]

This fundamental ambiguity alerts us to a basic fact about the news: journalists construct versions of events and draw upon the claims of various sources to do so. The real question is not whether the news represents the truth about police use of force but whose truth it does represent. The status of most use-of-force incidents as either appropriate or excessive depends greatly upon who is asked to define those events.

The fact of ambiguity is further demonstrated with regard to the videotaping of use-of-force incidents.[10] Videotapes do not necessarily provide objective renderings of events or irrefutable evidence of excessive force. Videotaped accounts are often as murky and inconclusive as the verbal accounts offered by eyewitnesses.[11] While many observers saw the Rodney King video as incontrovertible evidence of excessive force, it was ultimately understood by a Simi Valley jury to show aggression not by police but on the part of Rodney King. Moreover, not all videos have the same narrative power, as the analysis of the Don Jackson case in the previous chapter suggested, and reporters may view videotapes with skepticism. For example, in 1992 *Los Angeles Times* media critic Howard Rosenberg criticized a local television station's broadcast of a video showing a Santa Cruz county sheriff's deputy swinging a baton and kicking at a prone white man (Rosenberg 1992). Rosenberg noted that the suspect, George Nichols, who was under suspicion of child molestation, was later found to be innocent of that charge; but he complained that the video was not newsworthy, precisely because Nichols was resisting arrest. Comparing this video to the infamous Rodney King video, Rosenberg argued:

> In contrast, George Holliday's videotape of the King incident is quite shocking. Unlike that video, in which King at times appears to be helpless on the ground while being clobbered by baton-wielding police officers, Nichols can be clearly seen sitting and moving around while being shouted at and then struck by [deputy Todd] Liberty. Based solely on what the video shows, Liberty appeared to be acting properly in using the level of force that he did. . . . One could conclude from the videotape that Nichols could have avoided being hit by cooperating with Liberty and settling the molestation allegation later.

This example brings us full circle to the question with which we began: Don't use-of-force incidents get the coverage they deserve? My argument is that the coverage these events get depends upon what evidence and allegations are made available to reporters, upon what claims reporters avail themselves of, and upon what reporters decide about the merits of competing information and claims. Those deci-

sions are based on reporters' sense of whether an incident has really involved officer wrongdoing—as one reporter explained, whether an officer has made "a mistake of the head, not of the heart" (Krauss
1996b). But this yields news that is still at least one step removed from
simply mirroring reality: reporters attempt to make sense of highly ambiguous events that, as one reporter put it, "almost invariably come
down to the word of a complainant versus the word of an officer"
(Shaw 1992, A1).

A second question follows from similar premises. The data above
show a strong association between the newsworthiness of incidents and
the prominence of critical voices and views about police brutality in the
news. But should those voices and views be treated as independent or as
dependent variables? The systemic claims that sometimes appear in the
news could be independent variables driving more critical coverage, or
they could be dependent variables reflecting choices that journalists
make about what to include in the news. I submit that they need to be
thought of as both.

Given the norms of professionalism and objectivity that guide their
work, journalists are unlikely to construct critical discourse about police brutality in the absence of sources providing them with critical
claims.[12] But the very "existence" of critical perspectives on policing is
to some degree dependent on whether reporters look for them. If a reporter covers a use-of-force incident without consulting any sources
other than police, she is unlikely to write a story that includes challenging discourse about the issue of police use of force. Moreover, systemic
claims about police brutality in the real world do not simply rise and
fall in response to discrete events. The persistence of complaints about
police behavior in certain communities across the country, the fact that
allegations of brutality have continued to spark urban unrest for many
decades, and the persistent racial divide in public attitudes toward the
police all suggest that systemic views of police brutality are best seen
not as a phenomenon that varies with news events but as a constant of
the political environment in which many reporters work. The question
is, when do reporters decide to include those perspectives in the news?
These journalistic choices are particularly evident in reporters' sporadic
use of academic experts on police misconduct, for they are equally
"available" to journalists at all times but are only occasionally included
in the news.

Ultimately, to assume that news coverage simply reflects the objective reality of events overlooks the fundamentally ambiguous nature of

police use of force, as well as the role of journalistic choices in constructing the news. The task here is to uncover those choices and to understand how ambiguous events come to be represented in particular ways in the news. I argue that the variations in news coverage across different events stems in large part from the "critical story cues" journalists recognize in some events.

STORY CUES AND "GOOD NEWS"

Critical story cues indicate to journalists that there is a dramatic, interesting, commercially appealing story to tell about official wrongdoing or the transgression of public norms. Story cues offer reporters "good news" possibilities by providing the raw materials of interesting, dramatic news narratives pegged to developments on the current political scene. Story cues also indicate that an event may develop into a "continuing saga" (Cook 1996). They thus encourage news narratives that are not dominated solely by official claims and, by engaging the journalistic norms that compete with media professionalism, encourage news that is more critical of police. Media professionalism does not disappear at such moments, however. The story cues that most news organizations are most likely to respond the most strongly to are those that "license" journalists to challenge official claims while allowing them to remain (or appear to be) responsible and objective.

Journalists often find their first critical story cues in the accounts of witnesses, family members, or other sources who come forward to publicly contradict or challenge the official version of a use-of-force incident. They find stronger cues when a coroner's report categorizes a police-involved death as a homicide or when legal proceedings are initiated against police officers. The racial identities of the officer and the suspect are also an indicator of newsworthiness, for white-on-black police brutality evokes a particularly troubling possibility of official wrongdoing.

Subsequent story cues can indicate that an event will have political ramifications, making the story even more newsworthy. When officials and citizens respond publicly to a use-of-force incident, this signals that a police conduct issue may be developing on the political agenda and licenses news organizations to examine that issue. Strong citizen reaction to a use-of-force incident signals that a political challenge may be brewing for local officials. When officials respond to an incident by making public pronouncements or official visits, by initiating special investigations, or by reforming police policies, they signal to journalists that the issue of brutality is fair game for news coverage.

The importance of what I call critical story cues has been suggested, using different terminology, by other studies of the news. Herbert Gans (1979), for example, discusses the role of "availability" and "suitability" in journalistic decisions about what to cover and how. Similar considerations are at work in the cues identified here: the news about police use of force reflects the sources and claims that are available to reporters (or that reporters avail themselves of) and reflects journalists' assessments of how easily an event can be transformed into a compelling story that still meets professional criteria of objectivity. Both Chermak (1995) and Best (1999) find that victims drive news coverage of crime. According to Chermak (1995, 88), victims who offer reporters colorful, emotional sound bites largely determine which crimes become news stories, and "as the newsworthiness of a story increases, so does the media's reliance on sources outside of their established criminal justice contacts." Similarly, victims of alleged brutality, their families, and witnesses often provide the crucial impetus for a brutality story, and the range of voices increases with additional story cues. And Cook (1996, 52–57) argues that journalists identify key news sources and developments as those that contribute to a news story by moving political processes forward. Similarly, as we will see below, legal proceedings, citizen activism, and official concessionary responses alert journalists that a good political story is unfolding and can make critical nonofficials more newsworthy as they become key political players whose moves "advance the story."

The relationship between cues and coverage is also suggested by the responses of journalists whom I asked, "What makes a use-of-force incident newsworthy?" Most responses journalists gave to this question fell into the categories of cues outlined here, and many of their responses are reported below. They spoke of the willingness of victims, families, or witnesses to challenge the police version of events (or the presence of videotape that seems to call the police version into question), and the availability of physical evidence (such as serious injuries sustained by the suspect) that calls official claims into question. They all mentioned the race of the suspect and the officer as an important determinant of newsworthiness. And they mentioned the political context— such as previous use-of-force incidents that had already become controversial or the public response that followed a particular incident—as important indicators of newsworthiness. Though journalists do not use the same abstract terminology, they do rely on the contextual factors identified here to decide how to cover use-of-force incidents.

Finally, the relationship between cues and coverage is suggested by a systematic analysis of ten years of news coverage of hundreds of use-of-force incidents. In the remainder of this chapter, I describe each cue in more detail and present data that suggest their importance in driving news coverage of police use of force.[13]

COMPETING ACCOUNTS

Perhaps the most important initial cues encouraging journalists to depart from official narratives about use-of-force incidents are evidence and sources that provide competing accounts of those events. Sources and evidence that challenge official narratives give journalists storytelling possibilities. Most use-of-force incidents disappear quickly from the news because there are no such narrative possibilities to sustain them. Officially provided narratives that individualize the use of force offer little that lends itself to storytelling, as one reporter explained to me (Whitely 1996). Indeed, many news reports about police using force could be summed up neatly by the headline, "Bad Guys Lose, Cops Win"—not a recipe for sustained media attention. As another reporter put it, "If you have a weapon on the street and a cop tells you to drop it and you don't, there's nothing to say" (Kocieniewski 1997). The available facts of such incidents seem to clearly vindicate the officers involved, rendering them largely uninteresting as news.

Use-of-force incidents that win sustained attention in the news generally do so because reporters become aware of either physical evidence or witness allegations that raise doubts about official claims. Based on the physical evidence and witnesses' accounts that they gather, reporters decide whether a use-of-force incident is really a "story." One *Los Angeles Times* reporter, for example, told me that a lawyer had recently contacted him with a story about a client, an African American, being stopped by LAPD officers and made to "prone out" on the pavement. This, the reporter said, was hardly a story, since such things happen frequently. He had been intrigued, however, by the story possibilities when he learned that the man was a prison guard on his way home from work, a fact that made the officers' behavior seem more questionable. But, the reporter said, he also learned that the man was carrying a gun in the front seat of his car, which "made you think that maybe the police were right" (Newton 1997). Ultimately, the reporter decided this was not a story.

The competing accounts offered by witnesses to an incident and by the family and friends of the person subjected to the use of force play a crucial role in determining how newsworthy the incident is perceived to be by journalists. As one *New York Times* reporter told me, families generally drive police brutality stories, and if the family isn't talking, reporters are left with no story to tell (Blumenthal 1996). When these sources tell reporters that a particular instance of police use of force was excessive, they are suggesting that the simple script "Cops Win" is inadequate. Indeed, all reporters I interviewed said that a basic news-gathering technique when covering a police-civilian altercation is to troll for alternative narratives by attempting to interview family members, friends, neighbors, witnesses, and other potential sources; according to one *New York Times* reporter, "that's Reporting 101" (Krauss 1996b). And, as another reporter put it, the information gleaned from these sources determines how far the story goes. If victims, families, or other witnesses provide a scenario that raises questions about police behavior, then it's a story (Kocieniewski 1997).

Consequently, the initial news about high-profile incidents often follows a script in which the police version of events is contrasted with the version provided by the alleged victims, their families, and witnesses. The lead paragraphs of a *Los Angeles Times* item reporting on the death of three armed robbers in February 1990 provide an example of this standard competing-accounts script:

> To his family and friends, Herbert Burgos was a responsible, intelligent man who rose through the ranks of McDonald's employees from a humble cook to the position of store manager at one of the chain's franchises.
>
> Even now, days after Burgos, 27, was killed by police after he robbed a McDonald's in Sunland, framed diplomas and certificates from the fast-food company line one wall of his Venice duplex.
>
> Burgos left McDonald's last year and enrolled full time at a Hollywood business school. His English teacher there, David Thomas, said: "He was probably the nicest person we've known at this school. I can't see anyone of his caliber deserving to be shot in the back."
>
> Los Angeles police know Burgos as a very different man. They say he and his brother-in-law, Jesus Arango—also a former McDonald's employee—used their knowledge of the fast-food business to direct a ring that may have robbed at least nine other local fast-food restaurants since August. (Tobar and Connelly 1990, B1)

Competing accounts are not always available, either because there are no witnesses to a police-civilian altercation, or because all witnesses agree that police acted rightfully, or because no witnesses are willing to publicly challenge the police (see Chevigny 1969; Muir 1977). At the same time, while the families or friends of people wounded or killed by police may privately believe that police actions were excessive or even brutal, unless they are willing to publicize their beliefs, reporters may see little grounds for media attention. This is illustrated by the case of Eneea Moldovan, a 20-year-old Romanian immigrant and junior pre-medical student at the State University of Stony Brook, who was shot to death by a Suffolk County police officer in December 1994. Moldovan was pursued by police after he and two friends attempted to buy clothing with a stolen credit card. After pursuing Moldovan through the mall with his gun drawn, police officer Thomas Tatarian apprehended Moldovan in the parking lot. Tatarian's gun discharged, killing Moldovan with a single bullet wound to the neck.

The seemingly out-of-proportion death of an unarmed college student with no prior criminal record might have become a focus for critical media attention. But the case was mentioned only three times in the *New York Times*, in large part, it appears, because Moldovan's family was rather unwilling to engage in rhetorical struggle with police officials via the media. Moldovan's father told reporters, "Even if something was wrong with a credit card, you can't kill a 20-year-old boy because he was running. . . . I don't know why they don't shoot him in the leg or something." But Moldovan's sister, according to the *Times*, "declined to discuss the police account of the shooting. 'We don't want any publicity,' she said. 'Let them think what they want to think' " (McQuiston 1994a, B1). Moldovan's family was never mentioned in the *Times* again, and in two subsequent stories the public definition of the incident was quickly contained by official claims. Even though tests showed that Tatarian's gun did not misfire, the *Times* reported that Moldovan died "because of either mechanical or human error" (McQuiston 1994b, B4).

LEGAL PROCEEDINGS

Although competing accounts are necessary to the early development of a police brutality story, not all competing accounts carry equal weight. Competing accounts that become the basis for grand jury investigations and criminal or civil trials are likely to be deemed especially newsworthy. Legal proceedings give strong "legs" to a story, signaling the possibility of a steady supply of story developments and heightening the drama of accusations against police. Legal proceedings also offer news organizations stories that are legitimized by their appearance in official institutions, which appeals to media professionalism; news organizations hesitant to unduly amplify challenging claims about police brutality are likely to find cases already being processed by the legal system the best ones to publicize.

For these reasons, cases of alleged brutality that are processed by the legal system make for bigger stories than cases that are disposed of exclusively by administrative proceedings within police departments, while cases that officials deem unworthy even of administrative proceedings are likely to drop out of the news quickly. By the same token, once legal proceedings have come to an end—once the DA or jury has spoken—news organizations are unlikely to find any further story to tell.

But as with competing accounts, legal proceedings do not by themselves guarantee that an incident will become a major news story. Even trials of police officers charged with excessive force are unlikely to generate media attention if the event that precipitated them was not considered newsworthy.[14] This suggests that contextual cues other than competing accounts and legal proceedings encourage journalists to see better story possibilities in some events than in others.

ANOMALOUS OR PATTERNED EVENTS

Some use-of-force incidents seem more newsworthy to journalists either because the police behavior seems especially egregious or because it suggests a pattern of police misconduct. Some incidents are so unusual or apparently egregious that they pique journalists' storytelling interest while arousing reformist alarms about transgressions of "normal" behavior. One simple measure of egregiousness, for many reporters, is whether a suspect died in an altercation with police. As one reporter told me, the only incidents that really get reported are "shootings or chokings"—fatal or near-fatal uses of force, especially those that seem inappropriate given the circumstances (Krauss 1996b).

Some incidents, on the other hand, are particularly newsworthy precisely because they look a great deal like other events, suggesting an underlying pattern or trend. When one dramatic incident occurs shortly after another, bears strong resemblance to another case, or enters a political context that has been shaped by a previous high-profile police-brutality case, journalists consider themselves invited to construct a linkage, to contextualize recent cases by reference to previous ones. Such linkages provide thematic context for news stories that deviate from official, individualizing narratives. As one *New York Times* reporter told me, "the same event can be a big story or a negligible story" depending on what else is going on. If reporters are "sensitized by previous incidents," the newsworthiness of subsequent cases increases "because it seems to be part of a pattern" (Blumenthal 1996). This echoes Fishman's (1978) observation regarding the construction of "crime waves": journalists' search for such thematic hooks can encourage them to link events that may or may not really be connected.[15] This "patterning" of police misconduct in the news can lay a foundation for the construction of policing problems.[16]

Both kinds of cues appeared on the New York scene in 1985, for example, when a series of young men came forward claiming that NYPD officers had tortured them with electric stun guns in order to obtain confessions of drug selling. The "stun gun cases" became very big news—indeed, between 1985 and 1994, collectively they garnered attention in the *New York Times* second only to that of the Rodney King case. What provided the "hook" that first piqued journalistic interest was the apparently anomalous, even egregious, nature of the force used, which the victims described as "torture": police used the then relatively new "stun gun," which jolts the subject with up to 50,000 volts of electricity and can burn and permanently scar the skin. The police treatment of the first and most prominent victim, Mark Davidson, also seemed out of proportion to the crime he supposedly committed: selling $10 worth of marijuana (Davidson was subsequently acquitted). Though Davidson also alleged that police slammed his head into a wall and punched him in the eye, these details were only briefly mentioned in most reports on the case and eventually dropped out of the coverage altogether. What was interesting—from the perspective of media commercialism and reformism—was the more out-of-the-ordinary brutality of the stun gun, along with the appearance of a clear pattern linking the cases. As other victims stepped forward to tell similar stories of torture and forced confessions, a major news event was created.

Another example of patterned events is found in a series of police shootings in New York City in 1990.[17] On January 31, Louis Liranso, 17 years old and unarmed, was shot in the back by an officer who was arresting him after a violent street fight with a neighbor. Four days later, Jose Lebron, 14 years old and unarmed, was shot by an officer pursuing him as a robbery suspect. The two shootings occurred five blocks apart. Two days later, 13-year-old Robert Cole was shot and killed in a different neighborhood after he allegedly refused to drop a handgun. *New*

York Times reporters immediately linked these events, and nearly every *Times* story on each incident mentioned the others. One day after Lebron's death was reported, the lead paragraphs of the news story established a pattern underlying the shootings, saying, "Since Saturday, two unarmed Hispanic youths in the Bushwick section of Brooklyn have been killed by officers who apparently thought the youths were reaching for weapons" (McKinley 1990a, B3); the story reporting the third death opened with the observation that this case "was the third shooting of a teenager in six days" (James 1990, 31). In response to this concurrence of similar events, the *Times* also engaged in some thematic exploration of the phenomenon of police use of deadly force in a piece headlined " 'Tough Call' for Police on When to Fire." The piece did not seriously challenge police policies; indeed, it concluded with a police captain's observation that "It's a tough call. [A police officer] may have to make a decision: Do I want to go home to see my wife and family tonight?" (McKinley 1990a, B3). But the theme of the piece was rare nevertheless and arguably might not have appeared in response to any one of these shootings alone. Thus, events that seem either highly anomalous (such as the torture of suspects with stun guns) or highly coincidental (such as a rapid series of police shootings) offer journalists narrative cues that can trigger more critical reporting.

RACE

A factor that makes use-of-force incidents particularly newsworthy is when they involve suspects who are racial or ethnic minorities. The frequent appearance of such incidents in the news, demonstrated in quantitative data below, in part simply reflects the statistical reality that police use more force more often against minorities than against whites (Chevigny 1995; Geller and Scott 1992). But race offers a story cue of its own that engages the norm of media reformism. When racial minorities accuse police officers of abuse, a well-known news script is invoked. That script harks back to earlier periods in American history and raises the specter of continuing racism in a supposedly more progressive era.

Accusations of police abuse by minorities are particularly interesting to journalists on the lookout for dramatic stories of official wrongdoing and transgressions of widely shared norms. Indeed, all the reporters I interviewed said that the racial dynamics of a case are an important determinant of its newsworthiness. As one reporter told me, race "adds a level of controversy" (Blumenthal 1996) which adds

to the story's interest as news. Another said that a use-of-force incident is more newsworthy to him if there appears to be racial animus
motivating the police officer, because "we're supposed to have equal
application of justice no matter your color or where you live" (Kocieniewski 1997).

Race is not only a powerful story cue on its own; it is likely to trigger
other story cues. Given the long history of mistrust of the police in many
minority communities, reporters may be even more likely than usual to
find people willing to challenge the police version of events in those
communities. Many organized antibrutality and civil rights groups are
particularly active in minority communities, which means that serious
citizen activism in the wake of use-of-force incidents against minorities
is more likely. Moreover, some urban minority communities are key
constituencies in local electoral politics and have a history of urban unrest set off by police use of force. In these settings, official concessionary
responses to a controversial use-of-force incident are also more likely.

CITIZEN ACTION

Occasionally, citizens respond to a use-of-force incident by engaging in
public activism: holding special meetings with officials or with the press,
flooding officials with letters or phone calls, staging marches or demonstrations, or, sometimes, engaging in violence. Public demonstrations, civil
unrest, or other expressions of public outrage make for "good news" in
their own right while also signaling to journalists future story possibilities:
How will officials respond? Will order be restored? Will justice be served?

Such visible public controversy not only appeals to reporters looking
for stories about conflict but also licenses news organizations to pursue
the controversy, even if officials are less than willing to "make an issue"
of police brutality. Citizen reactions tell news organizations that police
conduct matters to at least some segment of the public. This can be crucial to engaging the reformism norm because reporters and editors have
little interest in exposing an issue that they perceive their audiences don't
care about—one reason the Los Angeles media were hesitant to cover police misconduct in the years before the King beating. As one deputy man-
aging editor of the *Los Angeles Daily News* has said, audience disinterest
in the issue was made clear by the lack of public reaction to the paper's investigative report in October 1990 on questionable shootings by the Los
Angeles County Sheriff's Department. "You can't beat people to death
with a story unless they care," said the editor (Ron Kaye, quoted in Shaw

1992, A1). This sentiment has been echoed by a *Los Angeles Times* reporter who covered the LAPD throughout the 1980s. Though he was "a firm believer in the journalist as quasi-public servant and the notion of the newspaper as watchdog," he said, "I'd bark and nobody would listen" (David Freed, quoted in Shaw 1992, A1). Indeed, citizen action engages all three journalistic norms, creating a convergence among norms that are often contradictory. Not only does it validate the reformist impulse, but it signals that news about police brutality will be welcome with audiences (the commercialism norm) and that the issue is a "real" one that journalists are not unilaterally placing on the agenda (the professionalism norm).

Citizen action is often unable on its own to induce news organizations to produce critical news about police brutality. Indeed, as numerous academic studies have shown, the mainstream media often tend to be dismissive of grassroots political action (Entman and Rojecki 1993; Gitlin 1980; Ryan 1991). But citizen activism in combination with other contextual factors can offer journalists a cue to usher critical voices and views onto center stage. Especially when activism is violent, is widespread, or poses a serious political challenge to officials, citizens become "players" in the political game, as the African American community did in the aftermath of the King beating by breaking a tacit agreement with the Bradley administration not to criticize the LAPD.[18] News organizations that do not normally draw upon such groups may see them, in these circumstances, as more legitimate news sources.

Thus, citizen action can play important direct and indirect roles in the construction of news about brutality. First, for marginalized discourse to appear in the news, journalists must have such discourse available to them. Second, when citizen action is particularly intense, and especially if officials respond or seem likely to respond to it, journalists see a bigger story in the making. In these circumstances, journalists' interest in—and comfort with—publicizing critical claims about police brutality is likely to increase.

OFFICIAL CONCESSIONARY RESPONSES

Finally, the way in which officials respond to a use-of-force incident, particularly when public reaction is intense, provides clear story cues to journalists. In response to controversial or potentially controversial use-of-force incidents, police and other officials sometimes employ concessionary communications strategies by staging public appearances, making public promises, and announcing reforms. The chief of police may announce a change in department policy governing the subduing of violent suspects, for example, or (in a highly unusual response) the mayor may visit the family of a person killed by police. Meanwhile, officials in other quarters may respond as well—the FBI may launch its own investigation of a case, for example, or a local legislator may initiate an independent investigation or a policy change. All of these concessionary responses signal that officials have recognized (if not validated) citizen grievances about police. Such responses cue journalists that a major news story may be at hand, a story that satisfies all journalistic norms— professionalism, commercialism, and reformism—simultaneously.

ANALYSIS OF CUES AND COVERAGE IN THE *NEW YORK TIMES* AND *LOS ANGELES TIMES*

Figure 6 displays data derived from coding the full text of news coverage of a randomly selected sample of 114 use-of-force incidents reported in the *New York Times* and *Los Angeles Times* between 1985 and 1994. All news and editorial coverage that mentioned each of these incidents was coded for evidence of the critical story cues outlined above: whether "competing accounts" of victims or witnesses were reported; whether a district attorney's investigation, grand jury investigation, criminal trial, or civil suit was reported; whether the suspect was identified as a racial or ethnic minority; whether citizen activism (peaceful or violent) in response to the incident was reported; and whether official concessionary responses of the sort described above were reported. Given the difficulties in determining what constitutes either an "anomalous" or a "patterned" event, those cues are not included in the quantitative analysis presented here. The data indicate a positive association between the reporting of these various story cues and the amount of news coverage granted to different use-of-force incidents.[19]

For example, 63 percent of the low-profile *New York Times* incidents were met with competing accounts, while 77 percent of mid-profile and 100 percent of high-profile incidents generated competing accounts that challenged official versions of the event. Similarly, 50 percent of all low-profile UFIs reported in the *Times* led to reported legal proceedings, compared with 73 percent of mid-profile and 100 percent of high-profile incidents. The relatively high number of low-profile incidents marked by competing accounts and legal proceedings suggests (as do my interviews with reporters) that competing accounts and legal

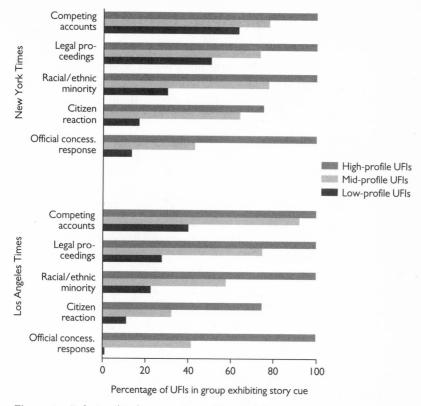

Figure 6. Relationship between Story Cues and Amount of News Coverage of Use-of-Force Incidents (UFIs), *New York Times* and *Los Angeles Times*, 1985–94. Source: Data are derived from coding the full text of news coverage of a randomly selected sample of 114 use-of-force incidents reported in the *New York Times* and the *Los Angeles Times*. Each set of three bars corresponds to one story cue, and the length of each bar corresponds to the percentage of cases in that group that exhibited the story cue. Differences across the three groups of UFIs are statistically significant (mid- and high-profile cases are different from low-profile cases, p < .05) for the *Los Angeles Times* data regarding competing accounts and legal proceedings and for both newspapers regarding the racial identity of suspects, citizen reaction, and official concessionary responses.

proceedings are a baseline condition for many incidents to gain news coverage at all. It also suggests that these cues alone cannot explain why some cases of police use of force become major news stories.[20] The data indicate that the greatest differences in coverage are associated with the political cues of citizen and official reactions.

STORY CUES AND THE OFFICIAL-DOMINANCE MODEL OF THE NEWS

The official-dominance model of the news would predict that how officials react to a controversial event is crucial in determining how that event is defined in the news and what problems, if any, are constructed around it. If officials begin talking about police misconduct, the model would predict, then journalists will index news coverage to that debate (Bennett 1990). Thus, police-brutality problems will "exist" when officials acknowledge they exist.

The analysis presented here suggests that that model is correct yet somewhat incomplete. It is true that official responses offer a powerful cue to journalists looking for "legitimate" stories to tell. Official concessionary responses can legitimize news attention to what is otherwise a difficult subject to broach. Yet when officials speak or act on the issue of brutality, they are usually responding to a context created by dramatic news events yielding other rich story cues. Still, official action remains for journalists the most powerful indicator of a story's newsworthiness. For example, while citizen action encourages critical news coverage, official concessionary responses together with citizen action provide a much stronger cue than does citizen action alone.[21]

The evidence presented here nevertheless suggests that a combination of additional story cues typically brings an event into the news and keeps it there to become the focus of critical news coverage. The cumulative influence of these story cues is suggested by the fact that all the high-profile incidents involved minority victims who offered (or on whose behalf were offered) competing accounts of their treatment by police, and all these incidents led to legal proceedings; in a large majority of those cases, moreover, citizen activism in response to the incidents was reported. What initially drives journalistic attention, it appears, is a combination of promising narrative cues that at some point are joined by citizen and official responses. Thus, once an incident piques journalistic interest and is perceived by reporters as something more than a routine low-profile event, officials face challenges in winning the struggle over meaning that ensues.

CONCLUSION

Story cues cannot fully explain everything about the relative newsworthiness of use-of-force incidents. A certain amount of variability is due, for instance, to differences among individual reporters, editors, and news organizations. The quantitative data presented above also cannot capture the chronological relationships among various cues and how the timing of these cues may affect the way a news story unfolds. Careful qualitative analysis of a smaller number of cases is necessary to further tease out these complex and contingent relationships—a task for the next chapter.

Yet as the data reported in this chapter demonstrate, a theoretical connection can be drawn between the brief and uncritical reporting given to most use-of-force incidents and the much more critical coverage spawned by the Rodney King beating and other high-profile use-of-force incidents. What links these opposite poles of news is a continuum of cues and contexts. With a strong combination of story cues, news organizations see the raw materials both for good storytelling and for problem defining. These cues signal to journalists the possibility of telling what Gans (1979, 52–53) calls "social and moral disorder stories" and encourage journalists to bring critical voices and claims to the foreground of the news. The variation in coverage across incidents suggests not only the importance of story cues but the underlying tension among competing journalistic norms: those that emphasize telling the police side of the story and those that emphasize getting a dramatic and significant news story.

Thus, official control of the news about policing is incomplete and imperfect, a fact that lies at the heart of common official complaints about the media. From the perspective of many police officials and rank-and-file officers, the news is far too willing to make police look bad by "sensationalizing" allegations of brutality (Corrigan 1994). Reporters, especially those working the police beat, are also aware that "getting the story" sometimes creates public perceptions based on dramatic events that may not be representative of the behavior of most police most of the time. As *Los Angeles Times* reporter David Rosenzweig told a fellow reporter, "I'm sure there's not a day that goes by that some cop isn't risking his or her life to save some kid or whatever, and I don't know that that's adequately reported." Over time, he said, that imbalance creates "a false image of the department" (Shaw 1992, A1). And as a *New York Times* reporter told me, while the police version of events may dominate in initial stories about a case of alleged brutality, "as the story plays out," the news "often makes the police look very bad" (Krauss 1996b). It is to these event-driven dynamics of problem definition in the news that we now turn.

SIX

Struggling for Definition

Policing Problems in the New York Times

Previous chapters have argued that the news about police use of force is generally contained by a combination of routine police communication strategies, the routines and culture of mainstream journalism, and a larger political culture preoccupied with fighting crime. These factors create practical and ideological constraints on what is said in the news. But some use-of-force incidents become occasions for more critical news reporting. An important key to understanding which events become big news lies in the narrative possibilities provided by the contextual cues available to journalists.

This chapter closely examines news coverage of three high-profile use-of-force incidents in New York. Occurring within a period of a few years, these were the most controversial and intensely covered local incidents in the pages of the *New York Times* in the early 1990s.[1] These three deaths in police custody—Federico Pereira in February 1991, Jose Garcia in July 1992, and Ernest Sayon in April 1994—provide an opportunity to see how the same news organization may construct public problems differently as contexts and story cues shift. These cases are also particularly revealing because they coincided chronologically with increased national attention to police brutality and police-community relations in the wake of the Rodney King beating. They also coincided with efforts of local and federal officials to examine and reform policing in New York. In July 1992, for example, when Jose Garcia's death occurred, a federal investigation was being conducted of drug-related police corruption in the 34th precinct, where Garcia was killed; in September of that year, the Mollen Commission, appointed by Mayor David Dinkins, began its investigation into allegations of widespread police corruption in the NYPD and issued its report just over two months after Sayon died in the custody of an NYPD drug-fighting unit. These investigations would reveal not only significant drug corruption but police brutality routinely visited on drug dealers and suspected drug dealers as well.[2] Meanwhile, Dinkins successfully fought for the establishment of an all-civilian review board to oversee the complaints process against police, which became the subject of intense controversy during the election of November 1992, in which Dinkins lost his seat to Rudolph Giuliani. This context provided fertile ground for the construction—and the warding off—of brutality problems in the news.

As we will see, the problems the *New York Times* constructed around the deaths of Pereira, Garcia, and Sayon were shifting and at times inconsistent. Despite a political backdrop suggesting that some grounds existed for concern about the quality of policing in New York, the policing problems constructed in the *Times* in the early 1990s were tentative and highly mutable.

News coverage repeatedly opened and shut down again, becoming more or less critical of the NYPD with the story cues that journalists responded to.[3] These case studies illuminate the clash of forces that contribute to occasional eruptions of the issue of brutality in the news, and often to the ultimate containment of policing problems. The story possibilities provided by cues such as competing accounts and citizen activism create openings for more critical news coverage of police brutality. But media professionalism continues, in the midst of struggles over meaning, to grant officials privileged access to the news, and the cultural discourse of crime control continues to establish limits on what can be publicly said about crime and policing. Officials are therefore often able, over time, to reassert control over the definitions of events in the news, while a larger script often begins to unfold in the news: a ritual of normalization in which problems are identified but then handed off to officials to resolve.

Ultimately, the ability of police brutality to achieve lasting recognition as a public problem is seriously constrained by this combination of factors. In a sense, the claims of competing sources and the available contextual story cues are the variables in how news about policing is constructed, while the practical and ideological constraints of media professionalism and the widely shared ideology of crime control are the constants. While events and story cues can therefore open the news to critical voices and views, their time in the media spotlight and their long-term impact on the news about police use of force are often rather limited.

WHAT REALLY HAPPENED TO FEDERICO PEREIRA?

Federico Pereira died in police custody in February 1991 after police discovered him sleeping in a stolen car in Queens. Officials claimed that Pereira violently resisted arrest before succumbing to "cocaine psychosis." The police-union lawyer representing the officers who were later charged with Pereira's death described Pereira to reporters as a "maniac" who "caused his own death"; the officers who subdued him, he claimed, were "facing the possibility of jail time for an act that deserves an award" (Fried 1991a, A1). Roughly two weeks after the Rodney King beating became national news, police authorities announced that the initial investigation of Pereira's death had been seriously inadequate because it had relied only on the testimony of the officers on the scene. Alleged witnesses surfaced after the initial investigation had exonerated the officers of wrongdoing; these witnesses claimed they saw the victim punched, kicked, and choked in a "camel clutch" hold in which an officer sat on Pereira's back and pulled his head back by the neck. The medical examiner's report, though it showed no evidence of blows to Pereira's body and found cocaine in his system, ruled the death a homicide. As a result, in a highly unusual development, five officers were arraigned on murder charges in mid-March. But in June, Queens District Attorney John Santucci resigned, and his successor, Richard Brown, sought and received a dismissal of charges against four of the officers; the remaining officer, Anthony Paparella, was tried before a judge in 1992 and found not guilty.

Federico Pereira was mentioned in over 30 *New York Times* news and editorial pieces, making it the biggest police use-of-force story since the "stun gun cases" of 1985 (see chapter 5). Eleven of those items appeared in the first 10 days after the Pereira story broke in the *Times*, and it is during that ten-day period that the struggle over the meaning of Pereira's death largely played out. The *Times'* early interest in the case appears to have been driven largely by a strong set of story cues: the appearance of witnesses who claimed to have seen police brutalizing Pereira; the NYPD's decision to reinvestigate the case; the highly unusual indictment of the officers on murder charges; and perhaps most important, the chronological proximity and external similarities of

Pereira's death with the Rodney King beating. The importance of these cues is suggested by the fact that Pereira died several weeks before King was beaten but only became news in the pages of the *Times* after the King video filled television screens and the officers were charged with murder.[4]

New York Times coverage of the Pereira case was fairly critical at the outset, and the *Times* tentatively used the case to suggest the possibility of policing problems within the NYPD. In its initial coverage, the *Times* repeatedly linked Pereira's death to Rodney King and to other brutality cases in New York and contextualized it with systemic claims about police brutality. The article that announced the officers' indictment, for example, claimed that "The charges . . . are the latest in a string of accusations of brutality to be made against New York City officers in recent years"—a "string" of incidents that had not previously been linked in the pages of the *Times*. The piece provided a brief overview of the 14 cases in the previous decade of on-duty NYPD officers charged with killing suspects. It also described the Pereira case as occurring "at a time when the prevalence of police brutality is being debated nationwide" because of the King incident, suggesting that the implications of the case ranged beyond the confines of the case itself (Fried 1991a, A1).

Early coverage also alluded to a possible racial dynamic in Pereira's death, as the Pereira family and civil rights activists attempted to frame the death in terms of racist police abuse. Though these claims were mostly relegated to brief, unelaborated paraphrases that did not become the central focus of the story, the lead paragraphs of one news item appearing on the first day the story broke focused on how the family "portrayed the death as part of a pattern of killings of Hispanic residents at the hands of police" (Navarro 1991, B6). The notion that racial motivation might underlie Pereira's death was never given a great deal of attention in the *Times*, however. For instance, the National Congress for Puerto Rican Rights, a group that worked with the Pereira family to try to define Pereira's death as a symbol of police racism, appeared in only two early stories on the case. A year after Pereira died, the story reporting the acquittal of the officer on trial for his death opened by noting that the case had "once again raised questions about the treatment of black and Hispanic residents by the New York police" (Fried 1992a, B3). But even a diligent reader of the *Times* may not have learned this, for only two other stories, out of a total of 34 items discussing the Pereira case, mentioned the notion that race might have some connection to his death.

Ironically, in its reporting on the Rodney King beating, the *Times* did consider another policing problem that was being raised by police critics in New York as well as Los Angeles: the problem of poor civilian oversight of police. Several editorials and thematic news items that appeared on the heels of the officers' indictment in the Pereira case prominently featured these critics' claims. An op-ed piece by Norman Siegel of the New York Civil Liberties Union, for example, suggested a series of reforms to address brutality in New York, especially the creation of an all-civilian oversight board (the existing board was partially composed of NYPD employees). That solution was examined in a thematic news item appearing the next day entitled "Police Attacks: Hard Crimes to Uncover, Let Alone Stop" (Bishop 1991). While the piece cast a skeptical eye on the benefits of all-civilian review, it did quote at length various critical nonofficials: Siegel, Karol Heppe of the Police Misconduct Lawyers Referral Service in Los Angeles, and academic experts Jerome Skolnick and Samuel Walker. Another thematic piece three days later examined the reported drop in brutality complaints against the NYPD since 1985 and again featured Siegel's problem definition. "What these numbers reflect," Siegel argued, "is the growing cynicism of New Yorkers. More and more New Yorkers, mostly people of color and poor people, have lost confidence and faith in the [existing review] board" (McKinley 1991b, A1).

This problem definition was ratified by the *Times'* editors three days later with regard to the LAPD but not necessarily with regard to the NYPD. The editors argued, "If it hadn't been for an alert witness with a videocam, the infamous police beating in Los Angeles might never have come to light. That adds weight to the already strong argument for expanding civilian oversight of big city police departments" (How to police the police, 1991, 18). While noting that police officials had legitimate reasons to oppose the strengthening of civilian review, the editors reasoned that "It shouldn't be all that difficult to create a review panel capable of reassuring the public while respecting the needs of police." But the editors did not talk directly about the Pereira case or its implications for the NYPD. In fact, by this point the *Times'* coverage of the Pereira case was taking a decisive turn toward containment. After the brief opening of critical news coverage, the public definition of Pereira's death was being contained, at least in the pages of the *Times*, by official communication strategies that effectively focused the *Times'* attention on problems with its story cues, not problems with the NYPD.

GAINING CONTROL OF THE NARRATIVE:
OFFICIAL STRATEGIES

After its briefly critical initial reporting, the *Times'* coverage of Pereira became highly episodic and largely confined to untangling how exactly his death had occurred. In pursuing this line of reporting, the *Times* followed the lead suggested by Daniel Sullivan, the chief of inspectional services for the NYPD. The day after the officers were charged with Pereira's death, Sullivan publicly questioned the credibility of the witnesses upon whose testimony the indictments were in part based. Sullivan told reporters he had trouble understanding why the three teenage witnesses had not come forward immediately and as a group, since they claimed to have seen the event together.[5] Police investigators also raised questions about witness credibility by telling reporters that they were investigating the witnesses' personal relationships with Pereira. Meanwhile, Police Commissioner Lee Brown reiterated to reporters that the medical examiner's report revealed "no medical evidence" of the beating the witnesses claimed to have seen (Fried 1991b, 25). The *Times* also followed the lead of Philip Caruso, president of the NYPD officers' union, the Patrolmen's Benevolent Association. Caruso complained to reporters that NYPD officers were "demoralized" because "they feel that public sentiment is swinging against them. They need public support in order to do their jobs" (Blumenthal 1991b, 21). Thus, police communication strategies implicitly denied that excessive force had occurred in the Pereira case, explicitly challenged the credibility of the evidence against the officers, and explicitly invoked the discourse of crime control.

Meanwhile, Commissioner Brown's official response to the incident helped initially to increase the newsworthiness of the Pereira case but simultaneously to contain its public definition. One day after the Pereira story first broke in the *Times*, he announced to reporters that in future cases of deaths in custody, fuller investigations would be required. He also promised an internal investigation of the precinct where Pereira died. Finally, Brown announced an order to police officers facing violently resisting suspects to call in special police units trained in the nonlethal use of force.[6] Brown thus signaled for reporters the importance of the Pereira case but also signaled that any problems it might represent were now under control.

In response to this solid official front, just one day after the *Times* had appeared poised to make a problem out of Pereira, its critical stance began to dissolve. Within five days, the *Times* published its first and only editorial on the case (Police brutality, public trust, 1991). Noting that the officers' indictments "invite comparisons with the videotaped brutality of Los Angeles police," the editors asserted that "Although the facts in the New York case remain murky, one thing is already clear: Police Commissioner Lee Brown has responded more vigorously to the possible brutality than did Chief Daryl Gates in Los Angeles." The editors conceded that the Pereira case "is more serious than the police beating in Los Angeles," because the victim died, but asserted that "it is also more ambiguous. With no videotape, it remains for the court to sort out evidence on the extent of police brutality."[7] The editors then placed the Pereira case in a firmly individualizing frame:

> Police are human; while the stresses of the streets don't excuse a lapse of control, they often do explain it. There may be no way for any big-city department to guarantee professional conduct from all officers at all times. . . . Surely most of the public understands that, and resists judging an entire police force on the basis of occasional failures.

Thus, in language remarkably similar to that Daryl Gates was using to defend the LAPD, the *Times* relieved the NYPD leadership of responsibility for controlling the actions of "all officers at all times." Taking official responses as its most important cues, the *Times* foreclosed the possibility of leadership problems in the NYPD similar to those it was simultaneously acknowledging in regard to the LAPD and in "other big-city police departments."

RECONSTRUCTING A DEATH IN CUSTODY

In response to official strategies, the *Times* did more than applaud Brown's superior handling of the Pereira case—it worked to untangle the competing accounts of Pereira's death. While witness accounts initially helped to make the story newsworthy, they soon virtually became the story. A few days after the story broke, the *Times* reported that,

> unlike the Los Angeles case, the Queens incident has left no footage of Mr. Pereira's last moments. Instead, his death has ensnarled the three [alleged witnesses], all with minor criminal records, and the police in a thicket of seemingly irreconcilable accounts. At the heart of the dispute is a single question: Is this a case of murder by the police or an incident in which legitimate restraint had fatal results? (Gonzalez 1991, 1)

Indeed, in the bulk of its subsequent reporting on Pereira, the "single question" that the case raised in the *Times* was what really happened on the night of Pereira's death, not any possible connections between Pereira and larger policing problems. In the first week following the arraignment, the *Times* published two lengthy news pieces (1,629 and a whopping 2,867 words, respectively) that attempted to sort through the contradictions in testimony and evidence in which the case had become "ensnarled." In so doing, the *Times* played a decisive role in constructing the public definition of Pereira's death not only in the media arena but in the legal arena as well.

The medical evidence in the Pereira case was ambiguous. The medical examiner's report found no evidence of blows to Pereira's body; it indicated that Pereira had a "moderate" amount of cocaine in his system when he died but that he "was not in the throes of cocaine reaction" when he died (McKinley 1991a, B6). Police officials and defense lawyers asserted that the autopsy undermined the accounts of the witnesses who claimed to have seen Pereira being kicked and beaten as well as choked. The verity of the official claim depended on how the autopsy evidence was interpreted, for the medical examiner insisted that, despite the presence of cocaine, Pereira had died from asphyxiation.

The *Times* sought to adjudicate these competing claims by submitting copies of the autopsy report to four medical experts and asking them to evaluate whose claims the report better supported. In a lengthy story appearing two weeks after the officers' indictment, the *Times* reported the experts' assessments. Though all four experts agreed that the evidence was consistent with, or could be interpreted as consistent with, the prosecution's case, the *Times* emphasized their disagreement: two experts believed that the evidence could also be consistent with "cocaine psychosis" or "cocaine toxic delirium." In such a condition, former medical examiner claimed, "their body temperature rises and they can die—they just stop breathing" (Dr. Joseph Davis, quoted in Fried 1991c, sec. 4, p. 18). (The *Times* also noted that Dr. Davis had "helped to popularize the concept of cocaine psychosis" [ibid.].)[8] The implication of these differing assessments, according to the *Times*, was that "the medical evidence may be inconclusive and probably will be sharply questioned at the officers' trial" (ibid.). In fact, the effect of this information was more dramatic: three months later, the new prosecutor announced he would seek dismissal of the charges against four of the officers and cited the *Times* story as a key element prompting his reexamination of the case (Fried 1991d).

Meanwhile, as it diligently pursued evidence that Pereira had died from drug abuse, the *Times* produced comparatively little thematic reporting on policing issues. Of 34 *Times* news and editorial items mentioning Pereira by name, none utilized his death as an occasion for seriously questioning the structure and practices of policing in the NYPD. Instead, the *Times* explored NYPD officers' reactions to the "specter of brutality" haunting the public mind. Emphasizing the theme launched by Officer Caruso several days before, the *Times* reported that demoralized police officers were struggling against misguided public perceptions and second-guessing of their work. The only other thematic piece mentioning Pereira by name appeared after Officer Paparella was acquitted in March 1992. The story described the Pereira case as "typical" of a "steady stream of cases across the country in which people with drugs in their systems suddenly die during or shortly after their arrests, sparking sometimes emotional and widely publicized disputes over whether police brutality or a drug-poisoned physiology killed them" (Fried 1992b).

JOSE GARCIA AND THE PROBLEMS OF WASHINGTON HEIGHTS

In July 1992, Jose Garcia, an immigrant from the Dominican Republic, was shot by police officer Michael O'Keefe in the lobby of a Washington Heights apartment building. Police claimed that Garcia was carrying a concealed gun and that he struggled violently with Officer O'Keefe, though they declined to say whether Garcia actually threatened O'Keefe with the gun. Neighborhood residents claimed to have seen O'Keefe push Garcia into the building and then beat and shoot him. Days of serious unrest followed the shooting, during which many civilians and police officers were injured, and one man fell from a rooftop to his death under disputed circumstances (some witnesses claimed police had pushed him). This occurred just two months after civil unrest had broken out in Los Angeles and around the country in response to the verdict in the criminal trial of the officers charged with beating Rodney King—unrest that had seemingly bypassed New York. In September 1992, Officer O'Keefe was acquitted by a grand jury, which uncovered serious discrepancies in the witnesses' accounts of Garcia's death, as well as evidence that Garcia and the alleged witnesses were involved in the drug trade in Washington Heights.

Officials employed similar communications strategies to contain the news about Jose Garcia as they had in the Pereira case, and problems with witnesses' accounts similarly diverted the *Times'* attention away from possible policing problems in the NYPD. But some dynamics in the two cases were quite different, especially the presence of a powerful political cue: the violent reaction of Washington Heights residents to the shooting. This reaction gave rise to more critical reporting than in the Pereira case. Nevertheless, the struggle over meaning was short-lived, and a nascent systemic problem definition was soon effaced by an officially supported problem definition. The death of Jose Garcia ultimately came to signify, in the pages of the *Times*, that Washington Heights was suffering from a drug infestation, not a policing problem.

A DEATH AND A PROTEST

Peaceful protests as well as looting and violence in the heavily Domini-can Washington Heights area lasted nearly one week after the shooting of Garcia. The unrest evoked strong associations with the recent unrest in Los Angeles over police brutality, indicated by the fact that the Los Angeles disturbances were mentioned in eight out of 35 stories men-tioning Garcia.[9] The unrest also presented a serious political challenge for local officials, particularly because it came just one week before the Democratic national convention was to be held in New York. Mayor David Dinkins responded immediately by sending Deputy Mayor Fritz Alexander to meet with community leaders and with the Garcia family; the next day, in a move that would become highly controversial, Dink-ins himself repeated these visits, pleading with one crowd, "Justice we will have, but peace I beg you for" (Dao 1992b, A1). As the unrest wore on, Dinkins and Police Commissioner Lee Brown continued visit-ing the neighborhood, meeting with residents and appealing for calm.

The Garcia case provided powerful story cues to journalists: a police shooting met with civil unrest, just two months after the King trial and the Los Angeles riots and an unusually concessionary official response. The Garcia story immediately became big news; 35 news and editorial items in the *Times* mentioned the Garcia case directly, and 17 of those items appeared in the first week of coverage. As the unrest touched off a series of articles about Washington Heights, it gave its residents a mo-mentary chance to designate policing problems in the news, particularly in five thematic news items exploring Washington Heights, its residents, and its problems. Thus, in the first week's coverage it was not uncom-mon to read quotations from residents such as, "We're in the United States, but we still lack a lot. We are marginalized" (Gonzalez 1992, 1), or "They shot [Garcia] like a dog, but worse than a dog. Because Americans, they respect their dogs, but they don't respect their Dominicans" (Dao 1992b, A1).

Jose Garcia's death therefore came to symbolize problems plaguing Washington Heights. What exactly those problems were constituted the heart of a struggle over meaning. Two problems were initially linked to the case, but only one emerged victorious.

PROBLEM DEFINITION I: POLICE AND RACE

Initially, the shooting was designated by some sources as signifying that a predominantly white suburban police force policing a predominantly minority urban community had created tensions that were boiling over. This problem definition was advanced not only by Washington Heights residents but by at least two local officials as well. One early news story observed, for example, that many residents "said they viewed the shooting of Mr. Garcia as symptomatic of simmering tensions between the police and the local immigrant community" (Dao 1992a, A1). In this story, Guillermo Linares, the city councilman representing Washington Heights and a leader of peaceful protest marches in response to the Garcia shooting, argued that "There is definitely a problem with the police here. We have a situation where the overwhelming number of officers come from outside the community, outside the city." A subsequent story also cited Dennis DeLeon, New York City's human rights commissioner, who claimed, in the words of the reporter, that "there had long been reports of police mistreatment of residents of the area, but in some cases, people held their anger rather than report[ing] it to authorities" (Gonzalez 1992, 1).

Most notable was a thematic news story exploring police-community relations in Washington Heights, which boldly began,

> Beyond the question of Officer Michael O'Keefe's guilt or innocence in the killing of a young Dominican man last week, the clashes between the police and Hispanic residents in Washington Heights have exposed a fundamental tension found in precincts in many parts of the city. The core of the trouble is that white officers from suburban neighborhoods continue to dominate the police force, despite gains for minorities in recent years through recruitment drives. The State Legislature has stymied efforts to require officers to live in the city. (McKinley 1992, B6)

The story went on to explain that David Dinkins, "like many mayors before him," had pushed for requirements that officers policing the city live in the city but that a legislature highly sensitive to police-union demands had frustrated such reforms. The first quotation to appear in this story was from Ruben Franco, president of the Puerto Rican Legal Defense Fund, who asserted that in areas such as Washington Heights, "The police are seen as outsiders who are there as a force to maintain the peace, to keep the natives down."

Thus, the unrest in Washington Heights allowed residents, activists, and a few low-level officials to become primary definers of Garcia's death and to frame a policing problem in systemic terms. But their problem definition was quickly challenged by another problem definition more congenial to police interests.

PROBLEM DEFINITION 2: DRUGS

Another definition of Garcia's death emerged simultaneously: that Washington Heights' drug problem was the real problem. This argument first appeared in a brief thematic news item examining the community of Washington Heights, which it described as "increasingly torn apart by the fear and violence that the drug trade has spawned" (Bennet 1992, B4). This problem definition was bolstered by the communications strategies employed by police. Police told reporters that, in the reporters' words, "drug dealers, realizing that the actions of officers are being widely scrutinized now, are taking advantage of the situation to foment unrest and thereby have the streets to themselves" (Wolff 1992, B2).

The next day, an editorial notably titled "It's Not the Rodney King Case" (1992) expanded on this theme. Taking their cues from the rhetorical strategies employed by police, the *Times'* editors began by noting that the Washington Heights disturbances create "the quick impression of more police brutality in yet another poor community." Yet the story, the editors claimed, "is much more complicated," because "Washington Heights has in recent years evolved into a booming drug marketplace that imposes enormous stress on police and law-abiding residents alike." Describing Dominicans, especially those hailing from the town of San Francisco de Marcoris, as running "an unofficial bracero program" of drug smuggling and dealing in Washington Heights, the editors argued that

> Thriving drug markets create special problems for the police. Frustrated officers may react with overly aggressive tactics that abuse the law-abiding. At the same time the money creates a powerful corruption hazard, to which some officers all too willingly succumb.

Thus the people of the community clearly have reason for concern. But it's dangerous to focus on possible police misconduct to the exclusion of the larger problem. It is not because of police abuse that Washington Heights last year led the city in murders, most of them drug-related.

The editors then presented what the death of Jose Garcia—and the Washington Heights unrest—really signified:

While the extent of Mr. Garcia's drug involvement isn't clear, he, too, came from San Francisco de Marcoris. He was shot in a building on West 162d Street, in the heart of the drug bazaar. Law enforcement officials say the drug gangs, stung by recent arrests, are helping to foment the protest violence, hoping public reaction will further demoralize the police and cause them to back away from drug investigations.

From this point on, the question of Garcia's involvement in the Dominican drug trade became the focal point of *Times* reporting on this case.[10] The larger implications of his death were construed in terms of the scourge of drugs, thus placing around the case a frame that excluded the structure of the police force as part of the problem. In no subsequent reporting was the problem of suburban officers policing the inner city raised. Meanwhile, the view that Garcia's death and the unrest that followed it were symptomatic of police insensitivity and racism, or the notion that drug corruption and brutality might somehow be connected in the Garcia case, arose sporadically but did not become the focus of reporting.

CLOSING IN ON MEANING

This struggle between two competing frames indicates that the definition of Garcia's death was initially quite unsettled in the pages of the *Times*. Indeed, even two days after the editorial cited above appeared, the *Times* published a lengthy report probing the background and character of both Garcia and Officer O'Keefe, raising questions not only about Garcia's drug involvement but about O'Keefe's record of aggressive policing (Gonzalez and Fritsch 1992). The story offered sympathetic descriptions of Garcia from his friends and family and noted that "some young men on the street said [Officer O'Keefe] harassed and hit them without provocation, and one former drug dealer says the officer shook him down for drugs and money" (1). The *Times* also quoted a Legal Aid study that found Officer O'Keefe had made "an unusually high number of improper arrests." These assertions were backed up, in the story, by court records indicating that many of O'Keefe's arrests had been dismissed before trial and that one judge had found O'Keefe had "no objective, credible reason" for stopping a suspect in one dismissed case.

But one day after the *Times'* editorial page had endorsed the drug-problem definition, Police Commissioner Lee Brown announced an official response to the Washington Heights situation that steered attention away from race, drug corruption, and brutality. Brown announced that the NYPD would split the 34th precinct, in which Washington Heights was located, in order to improve police coverage of the troubled community. At the same time, Brown denied the problem of community resentment against police perceived as outsiders. "I have been up there myself, I have walked the streets, and we don't have a community that is hostile," he told reporters (Dao 1992c, 28).

Meanwhile, other developments gave reporters a more appealing story to pursue. For within a few days, a serious political conflict broke out as the police officers' union (the PBA) began an offensive against Mayor Dinkins that would ultimately help to push Dinkins from office in the November 1992 elections. The campaign capitalized on many police officers' resentment of Dinkins's support for the establishment of an all-civilian police review board and his role in stopping the state legislature from replacing police officers' standard-issue revolvers with more powerful semiautomatic weapons. The PBA attack, first launched in a full-page ad in the *New York Post*, claimed that, by visiting the Garcia family, Dinkins had treated Garcia like "a martyr" and thus encouraged the violence in Washington Heights. The PBA also focused attention on a medical examiner's report showing cocaine in Garcia's system, which, the PBA claimed, validated the official claims about Garcia's death. Two days later, Officer O'Keefe testified to the Manhattan district attorney that he shot Garcia after Garcia pulled a gun on him—a clearer, more exculpating narrative than police had previously supplied.

This combination of developments closed what remained of the initial struggle over the meaning of Garcia's death. The *Times* published no further thematic or editorial coverage other than a series of letters to the editor that argued over whether Dinkins's response to the Washington Heights unrest had been appropriate, until the editors responded to Officer O'Keefe's acquittal in September. On its editorial page, the *Times* firmly individualized Garcia's death and again emphasized that the King and Garcia cases were not connected. "A grand jury's refusal to indict New York City police officer Michael O'Keefe . . . carries a simple, sobering message," the editors intoned: "Don't jump to conclusions about police brutality" (The lesson of Washington Heights, 1992, sec. 4, p. 20). As for the unrest and the complaints the *Times* itself had uncovered about police conduct in Washington Heights, the editors dismissed these as disingenuous:

> So what were the Washington Heights riots all about? At the time, law enforcement officials speculated that drug gangs hoped to exploit the Garcia case to force a police retreat. [District Attorney] Morgenthau's investigation and the grand jury's good judgment greatly reduce the chances of that. They also teach something to people everywhere: the importance of caution and restraint when the next such incident occurs.

A "Week in Review" piece subsequently closed the Garcia story by observing that "Jose Garcia was no Rodney King" (Sullivan 1992, sec. 4, p. 2).

THE GARCIA EPILOGUE

The Garcia case might have then disappeared from the news but for a subsequent event that brought it back in a new light. The PBA offensive against Dinkins was joined by mayoral candidate Rudolph Giuliani, who charged in a *New York Times* editorial in August 1992 that "the Mayor's calculated response to Jose Garcia's death led the public and the media to conclude that the shooting had been unjustified" (Giuliani 1992, A27). The week after O'Keefe's acquittal, Giuliani spoke at a city hall rally of 10,000 police officers protesting the Dinkins administration's policies. The rally turned into a chaotic public demonstration, with hundreds of police officers reportedly trampling cars and blocking traffic on the Brooklyn Bridge, and some accused of yelling racial slurs at passersby.

The demonstration put the Garcia case on page 1 once more and prompted a thematic news piece (McFadden 1992) in which minority police officers echoed the problem definition asserted by many Washington Heights residents in the immediate aftermath of Garcia's death: that NYPD officers from largely white suburbs did not understand or respect the inner-city communities they served. According to one black officer, these white officers "get assigned to a field precinct like Harlem and . . . it's culture shock because they've never seen so many black people in all their lives. And they're scared. It has to do with inbred prejudice" (1). And a Hispanic officer claimed, "I think the Police Department has to address the training of the police who come on the job. I think we have to hold the police accountable for the way they deal with all communities."

DRUGS, POLICE, AND THE DEATH OF ERNEST SAYON

On April 29, 1994, Ernest Sayon, Brooklyn-born son of Liberian immigrants who was known by police and neighbors as a low-level drug dealer, died as police arrested him in front of a Park Hill apartment complex in the Clifton area of Staten Island. Initial reports held that Sayon died of head injuries sustained during the arrest, though police were unable or unwilling to explain how those injuries occurred, other than to claim that Sayon had struggled with Officer Donald Brown when Brown had attempted to detain him.

Many neighborhood residents claimed to have witnessed police officers beating Sayon. They immediately staged protests, marching through the streets of Clifton and around the NYPD's 120th precinct. Unlike the protests following Jose Garcia's death, these protests were mostly peaceful, though riot police were called onto the scene and a few unidentified shots were fired. But the protests were challenging to officials nonetheless. Mayor Rudolph Giuliani broadcast an appeal for calm via radio on the evening of Sayon's death; in a veiled reference to the Garcia case, he pleaded, "We've been through situations like this in this city before—where what appears one way at first turns out to be another way a little bit later. So it would be a shame if anybody jumped to conclusions here before at least there was an opportunity to have a full and complete investigation" (Hernandez 1994, 25).

As in the Garcia case, these political cues immediately signaled to the *Times* that the Sayon story was highly newsworthy (11 stories appeared on the case in the first week after Sayon's death, out of a total of 38 stories appearing over the course of the year), and reporters were deployed to Clifton who gathered residents' comments on crime, policing, and race. And as in the Garcia case, this reporting marked the beginning of a pitched battle in the pages of the *Times* to frame Sayon's death, a competition between problem definitions involving either aggressive policing or the scourge of drugs. But in contrast to either the Pereira or Garcia cases, further narrative cues tipped the battle in favor of Clifton residents' systemic claims about police racism and misconduct.

STRUGGLING TO DEFINE A DEATH

The strong citizen reaction to Sayon's death provided an opening for residents of Sayon's neighborhood to become (momentarily, at least) primary definers of his death. Thus, not only those who saw drugs as the problem but those who saw the police as a problem were relatively successful in getting their messages heard in the early coverage.[11] For instance, the first thematic piece about the case, appearing one day after Sayon's death was reported, explored the "schism . . . reflected in Park Hill residents' views of the police":

> Some said they welcomed officers because they would do anything to rid their streets of increasingly aggressive drug dealers. Others said they saw the police as an occupying force charged with making sure the ills of Clifton do not spill over into white neighborhoods. "Police officers would rather have us here than in the white sections," said Tislam Thompson. (Levy 1994, 52)[12]

Another thematic piece appearing on the following day used the comments of two area residents to present the "Two Views of Police Presence in Clifton" (Bragg 1994, B3). One resident, Willie Barrett, favored "a strong police presence in his neighborhood, to reclaim it." The other, Robert Collins, "knows that drugs are sold on the sidewalk, but it is a stifling police presence he resents more, he says, because in their zeal the officers ignore basic human rights." The story explored Mr. Collins's critique, and brought in other neighborhood voices that echoed it:

> "The drugs are just an excuse for what happened" [to Ernest Sayon] and have been an excuse for a police presence that has made even the innocents feel like criminals, said Mr. Collins. "The police have used heavy-handed tactics" in dealing with people of the community, he said. "There is a feeling that the community is being surrounded."

Another resident put the point directly: " 'Yes, there is a drug infestation,' she said, standing under a tree painted red, yellow and green to honor Mr. Sayon. 'But does that give you the right to kill people?' "

Subsequent events would allow this question to become a focal point of *Times* coverage. Two days after Sayon's death, news media received a videotape that had been shot by a resident of the apartment complex where Sayon was arrested. It showed a handcuffed man named Dannis Dublin being struck and thrown onto the hood of a police car by police officers. The resident claimed that she had videotaped the incident, which occurred two weeks before Sayon's death, because of the frequency of such incidents in the area; the Sayon family's lawyer claimed that the same officers involved in Sayon's death were shown on the video. The next day, after viewing the Dublin video, Mayor Giuliani vowed an investigation into both incidents and told reporters, "When we say [we support] aggressive police activity, we mean aggressive police activity within the constraints of the Constitution" (Wolff 1994b, B1).

Two days later, an ambulance driver told police investigators that police officers had not allowed him to care for Ernest Sayon as he lay bleeding on the pavement after being subdued. Police officials also revealed that one past excessive-force charge against Officer Brown, out of seven complaints lodged against him, had been upheld. Together, these events provided story cues that suggested not only officer wrongdoing but perhaps even a pattern of police misconduct in Staten Island.

The day that the Dublin video was released, Police Commissioner William Bratton held a press conference in which he attempted to reassert official control over the news narrative. Bratton vowed that drug sweeps would continue in Staten Island, and he suggested a different theme for contextualizing Sayon's death: the difficulties of aggressive policing against drugs. The police, Bratton said, are "between a rock and a hard place," because "you don't go in trying to take back those places without being tough, without being assertive" (Wolff 1994a, B3).

Yet Bratton's efforts to regain control were only partially successful. While the *Times* did convey his claims to the public, residents' notions about local police misconduct were also prominently featured. In an editorial, the *Times* forged a middle line between the competing claims advanced by Commissioner Bratton and Park Hill residents:

> Both incidents took place in the same neighborhood, a part of Staten Island overrun with drug dealers. Indeed, many people who live in and around the Park Hill area want regular drug sweeps and ever tougher policing; some point out that both men in these two cases had arrest records. But others argue, rightly, that even the existence of an arrest record wouldn't justify the use of excessive force. (Tough cops, not brutal cops, 1994, A26)

Thus, in response to a different constellation of cues, the *Times* applied a measuring rod to the use of force against Sayon and Dublin that it had not applied in either the Pereira or Garcia cases: that the legitimacy of police use of force cannot be judged entirely or even primarily by reference to the suspect's prior criminal record or involvement in the drug trade.

FURTHER CUES: AUTOPSIES AND ACTIVISM

Subsequent cues kept the Sayon story in the news and encouraged further development of a systemic framing of police misconduct. One week after Sayon died, the *Times* reported that a private autopsy com-

missioned by the Sayon family concluded that he had died from asphyxiation and found no drugs in his system. The official medical examiner's autopsy, released four days later, validated those findings. It
categorized Sayon's death as a homicide, concluding that Sayon had
died while handcuffed and prone, finding deep bruises in Sayon's back
like those that would be made from a knee.

The official autopsy triggered another *Times* news item that registered residents' reactions to Sayon's death. Its lead paragraphs observed
that some Park Hill residents believed that "such a use of force was too
typical for there to be a margin of sympathy for the officers" (Sexton
1994, B4). According to one resident, "I don't have any sympathy for
these cops, like they were trying to do their job and got carried away. I
know them. They do it every day." According to another, "People in the
projects are usually too scared to speak out about much, and to see
how the people have come together and come forward for this means
that it must have been felt by an awful lot of folks."

Fueled by the autopsies' results, the New York Civil Liberties Union
(NYCLU) appealed to Governor Mario Cuomo for a special prosecutor
to investigate the case. The NYCLU offered a different kind of systemic
claim to frame the problem, claiming that prosecutors' routine reliance
on police for evidence in the cases they must try creates a disincentive to
prosecute brutality cases. The NYCLU also claimed that the Staten Island
district attorney, who was running for reelection at the time, had a particularly strong motivation not to prosecute the officers who arrested Sayon.

As did the autopsy, this activism cued further critical coverage in the
Times. The day after the NYCLU letter was sent, the *Times* published
an op-ed piece by writer Russ Baker that offered an even farther-
reaching systemic problem definition. Baker linked Sayon's death with
the current NYPD corruption scandals (a connection very few news
items had made), arguing that "corruption and brutality can't be tack-
led without a wholesale shift in the way the Police Department does
business" (Baker 1994, A25). Baker urged Commissioner Bratton to
improve officer accountability by fighting the power of the PBA; change
hiring practices to screen applicants with "histories of antisocial behavior"; and reform management practices, improve officer training, and
track problem officers. Explicitly addressing the individualizing claims
so often made about the use of force, Baker asserted, "It's impossible to
overestimate the need for a real transformation—as against the cosmetic 'few bad apples' approach that has so long characterized the official response to internal rot."

(PARTIALLY) REASSERTING CONTROL:
THE OFFICIAL RESPONSE

Thus, nearly two weeks after Sayon had died, the public definition of his death remained unsettled and challenging to officials. The narrative cues arising from witness testimony, the Dublin video, and the medical evidence, along with the political cues of the angry citizen reaction and the NYCLU's appeal to the governor, allowed the tentative construction of policing problems in the news. Officials were at a disadvantage in this struggle over meaning, for the autopsies partially foreclosed the rhetorical strategies used with such success in the Pereira and Garcia cases. While officials could and did emphasize Sayon's criminal record, they could not as easily claim that his death was drug-related.

The official response to these challenges was to link Sayon to a problem not of overly aggressive officers but of undertrained officers—undertrained in uses of force, that is. One day after Baker's critical op-ed piece appeared, the *Times* reported that Commissioner Bratton was reported to be forming a departmental task force to retool the department's policies for handling violent prisoners. Bratton framed the problem carefully: since the NYPD had banned the use of choke holds the previous year, he claimed, officers had not been adequately prepared to employ alternative uses of force. Stressing that he was concerned primarily with officers sustaining injuries while making arrests, Bratton told reporters, "I don't think [the level of violence in police work] has as much to do with police assertiveness or aggressiveness as just, we now have a society where it's become the norm to resist arrest" (James 1994, B1). Bratton thus sought to contain the problem construction in the news by offering reforms that fit an individualizing frame, defining the problem as one of resistance-prone suspects, not violence-prone officers. A *Times* editorial the next day praised Bratton's action and adopted this frame:

> Mr. Bratton rightly asks: Have police officers been adequately trained in alternate techniques for restraining violent suspects? The answer is apparently no. That is a serious deficiency because, as the Commissioner noted, in a too-violent city, it has become commonplace for suspects to resist arrest. (Mr. Bratton's wise policing, 1994, A30)

However, the effects of the powerful combination of cues that drove the story into prominence lingered. Ultimately, unlike the problem definitions in the vast majority of reported cases of use of force, the public definition of Sayon's death remained highly unsettled as coverage of the case continued, sporadically, for many months. This unsettled meaning was noticeable in the connections the *Times* drew between race and the criminal-justice system as the grand jury investigation wore on over the summer. Following the claims of the Sayon family and Park Hill residents, the *Times* on several occasions raised the question of whether blacks accusing police of crimes can get justice. When Officer Brown was eventually acquitted in December 1994, reporters returned to Park Hill to again gather residents' reactions. They found a bitter conviction that "a grand jury from a predominantly white middle-class community would [never] indict police officers for slaying a black man" (Krauss 1994b, 27). And a thematic piece appearing the day after the acquittal explored how and why juries typically back police officers when considering charges of excessive force. The piece consulted the views of several critical nonofficials, such as law professor Randolph Scott-McLaughlin, who argued,

> Cops have a better chance of being struck by lightning than they do of being indicted and convicted on brutality charges. . . . The prosecutors who present the cases must rely on police officers to investigate other cases that they prosecute. In effect, prosecuting a police officer for them is like going against a family member. (Holloway 1994, 54)

Thus, more than the deaths of either Federico Pereira or Jose Garcia, the death of Ernest Sayon became the centerpiece of a much larger social struggle to define or deny a police-brutality problem. The intensity of the struggle is reflected in two op-ed pieces the *Times* published after Sayon's death. In one, entitled "Blue Plague," African American author Jill Nelson wrote,

> Many black and Latino people neither trust nor respect the police, much as we'd like to. Often, society acts as if this attitude springs from some genetic, parental, or cultural deficiency. But why would we respect them when they so often abuse their authority and so often have no respect for the people they are paid to serve and protect? (Nelson 1994, A27)

A week later, in a piece entitled "Black America's Silent Majority," journalist Hugh Pearson answered by invoking the cultural discourse of crime control:

> Yes, police brutality is a serious problem and an inexcusable abuse of power. But blacks should bear in mind that it is not their greatest threat: they have more to fear from their own community. There is a much more common scenario in urban life than that of racist police on a rampage: a law-abiding black man or woman is senselessly murdered by a black male youth. (Pearson 1994, A23)

THE POLITICS OF DEFINING EVENTS

These case studies illustrate how contextual cues and communications strategies influence the definitions of events and problems in the news. In each case, the *Times*' coverage shifted in response to the rhetorical strategies of sources, particularly police officials, and in response to emerging story cues. The effects of official rhetorical strategies are particularly clear in helping to contain the public definitions of each event, while the effects of story cues are particularly clear in the different coverage given to each case. The public definition of the death of Ernest Sayon remained more unsettled for a longer period of time than was true of either Federico Pereira or Jose Garcia—an effect, at least in part, of the contextual developments that encouraged more critical reporting in that case.

That the public definitions of news events draw from available cues and communications strategies points to their socially constructed nature. The definitions of these deaths in custody had as much to do with the narrative and political cues available to journalists and the content of the communications strategies employed by their sources as with any objective facts of the police-citizen altercations themselves. All three men had criminal records and a history of involvement with drugs; all three died under disputed circumstances; and in each case, the officers were ultimately exonerated of any wrongdoing. Yet each death was assigned a particular set of definitions in the pages of the *Times*, and each was linked, at least momentarily, with different kinds of policing problems.

Consequently, news coverage of police misconduct was situational, contingent, even schizophrenic. A problem raised at least obliquely on the *Times*' editorial page after Pereira's death, for example, was one of inadequate civilian control of the police, yet that issue was never raised in regard to Garcia's death, though it occurred just one year later—a year in which arguably not much greater civilian control of the NYPD had been established. The alleged problem of a suburban white police force was raised, suppressed, then raised again after the shooting of Garcia. Moreover, the *Times* did not measure these deaths by the same standards, defending police aggressiveness against suspected drug dealer Jose Garcia but questioning that aggressiveness against known drug dealer Ernest Sayon.

News coverage also shifted across these cases because official responses designed to ward off critical news coverage, ironically, increased the newsworthiness of these incidents. As officials attempted to regain control of the news with concessionary strategies, they inadvertently provided a license to journalists concerned about independently amplifying social conflict and setting the political agenda. This dynamic was visible when Mayor Dinkins appealed for calm in Washington Heights and when Mayor Giuliani responded to the Dannis Dublin video.

Yet as these case studies show, police communications strategies can regain control of the news by presenting a unified front and questioning the credibility of competing accounts (as in the Pereira case) and by assertively providing reporters with individualizing accounts of officers compelled to use force against drug-induced or drug-motivated violence (as in all three cases). Officials can also regain dominance by reframing apparent problems of police aggressiveness as problems of inadequate policing and inadequate means of using force (as in Brown's move to split the Washington Heights precinct and Bratton's move to increase the range of coercive tactics available to officers). Police strategies can also engage reporters' strong sense of professionalism, as when NYPD officials argued in the aftermath of Pereira's death that critical news reporting only undermined officer morale and undercut police effectiveness.

Moreover, reporters' professional unease with amplifying "antipolice" voices contributed to the way these struggles played out. When police officials claimed that the unrest in response to Garcia's death did not reflect legitimate grievances about police conduct but rather the efforts of drug dealers to push the police out of Washington Heights, the *Times* endorsed that problem definition. In fact, the *Times* editors virtually proclaimed that Jose Garcia was a drug dealer (and therefore must have deserved his treatment by police) before such information had been established by official investigations. Coverage of the Sayon case took Park Hill residents' claims more seriously but often explicitly or implicitly labeled them as "antipolice" sentiments.

MEDIA PROFESSIONALISM
AND THE RITUAL OF NORMALIZATION

That official claims and strategies are often successful in regaining control of event-driven news stems from the structural and cultural biases of news production. While news organizations are often driven to publicize dramatic events that will hold audience attention and to raise questions about the legal and moral transgressions of those in power, they are generally not eager to fundamentally challenge the power structures to which they are linked by their beat systems, by their norm of professionalism, and by the power of larger cultural ideas about crime and crime fighting. Thus, event-driven struggles over meaning often constitute "an uneven contest on a tilted playing field" (Gamson 1992a, 382).

The ability of officials to regain control of the news, most clearly seen in the cases of Pereira and Garcia, seems to be part of a ritual of normalization. The same official responses that can license the news to acknowledge policing problems can also begin to shut down critical openings in the news. This helps to explain why the initial news coverage of these events was the most critical, raising questions and suggesting problems that later dropped out of the coverage after officials performed a rhetorical ritual of acknowledging some sort of problem or impropriety and promising a reform that allegedly would address that problem. Similar dynamics were visible in the aftermath of the Rodney King beating. An important difference between the King case and the New York cases examined here, however, is that Mayor Bradley's actions were more than a cosmetic or merely rhetorical response to the King beating. Having helped sow the seeds of a systemic problem definition, Bradley's public challenge to Chief Gates then licensed the *Los Angeles Times* to treat policing problems within the LAPD much more seriously than the *New York Times* did the cases analyzed here.

In the pages of the *New York Times*, the official rhetorical rites were generally rewarded with an editorial praising the official action and approving the official problem definition. For example, in the single *Times* editorial regarding the Pereira case, the editors argued that

> Chief Gates . . . ought to remain under pressure. Though Mr. Gates denounced the beating, he termed it an aberration, despite recent growth in brutality complaints. And he did little to alter either assignments or procedures. . . . [But Commissioner Brown's promised reforms] send appropriate messages—of intolerance for brutality, of soul-searching and of strict accountability. (Police brutality, public trust, 1991, A16)

The intriguing aspect of this editorial is the importance it places on the rhetorical responses of officials to troubling news events. Gates is criticized for using inappropriate rhetoric—calling the beating an aberration and promising no reforms—while Brown is praised for "sending appropriate messages" by implicitly conceding some police impropriety and promising reforms.

Thus, it appears from these case studies that when abundant story cues are available, news organizations are likely to define a use-of-force incident as a sign of a possible policing problem but then to hand the problem off to officials; the ritual is generally concluded when officials respond "appropriately." As Bennett (1996, 41) observes of the news in general, the outcome of the standard news script about policing problems is "almost always the same: Some official action wins out, the day is saved, and the story ends with a return to 'normal.' " And as Bennett also observes, when officials aren't forthcoming with compelling responses, news organizations may prod them to return things to normal:

> Official responses to the . . . crises and problems of society tell us that things will return to "normal" again, if only we will trust those officials to act in our interest. And when officials are unable to establish the right tone of normalcy, journalists are ever-ready to raise the question of alarm ("Should we be alarmed about this?")—a question sure to trigger an outpouring of reassurance from officials eager to seem in charge. (ibid.)

Moreover, critical news about police brutality is seriously constrained by strong cultural limitations. To a greater degree than claims about political issues such as taxes, abortion, or environmental protection, claims about systemic police brutality bump up against strong cultural boundaries on what can be said in public. To suggest that a particular community—or, especially, the nation as a whole—has a systemic brutality problem is to raise a host of serious and difficult questions about crime, justice, and, often, race. These are questions not easily dealt with in the media arena, or in other political arenas. Even when the news expands to grapple with these questions, it often simultaneously begins shutting down. The urge to normalize such troubling questions overtakes the urge to explore and exploit the symbolic meanings of the dramatic news events that raise them.

CONCLUSION

The constraints and story cues identified here cannot fully account for every aspect of news coverage of the deaths of Pereira, Garcia, and Sayon. It is possible, for example, that the general political context varied across these three cases in ways that affected news coverage but are difficult to measure. In keeping with what we know about how major news organizations tend to cover politics, news coverage of these events was probably driven in part by the perceived political strength of key players such as the mayor and the police commissioner. For example, the Pereira affair occurred within a year after Lee Brown assumed command of the NYPD. At that point, Brown enjoyed a good relationship with Mayor Dinkins, and his "community policing" reforms were being praised in the pages of the *Times*. So perhaps a kind of honeymoon effect depressed critical coverage of Pereira's death. Ernest Sayon died while William Bratton was still a relatively new police commissioner—and one who was quite media savvy (see Smith 1996). But Sayon also died while the NYPD was under investigation by the Mollen Commission. The *Times* offered very little coverage of the Mollen Commission's findings and linked the commission's investigation with Sayon's death only very rarely and obliquely. Yet the political backdrop of decreased public confidence in the police brought about by the Mollen investigation may have encouraged more critical reporting of the Sayon case than it might otherwise have received.

Moreover, there are limits to the generalizations that can be drawn from these case studies. These cases all draw from the same newspaper over a short period of time, illustrating roughly the same point in the history of the particular relationship of the *New York Times* with the New York Police Department. To the degree that that relationship is significantly more or less cooperative than the typical police–news organization relationship, the findings presented here are less generalizable.[13]

These case studies do suggest the usefulness of key variables and constants in understanding the shifting definitions of dramatic news events. What remains is to decide what these moments of tentative and incomplete problem construction really represent. In one view, the events examined in this chapter are anomalies, and the openings in the news they engendered are so fleeting as to be inconsequential. After all, the larger story revealed here seems to be that such openings in the news are usually limited, short-lived, and sooner or later contained (more or less) by official rhetorical strategies and the various practical and ideological constraints on news content. But from another perspective, these high-profile events are those that are most likely to linger in the public mind. Indeed, when police complain of media coverage that sensationalizes allegations of police brutality, or when writers such as Jon Katz of *New York* magazine wonder if media coverage of police brutality has become "easy prey for lawyers and spokespeople now fully adept at the art of racial media manipulation" (Katz 1994, 39), it is major news events like the deaths of Pereira, Garcia, and Sayon to which they probably refer. These occasional openings in the news, moreover, illuminate the underlying factors that drive the construction of public problems in the news. Like solar eclipses, high-profile events that engender critical coverage of policing come along rarely but are no less worth studying simply because they are rare.

In comparison to the cases analyzed in this chapter, the case of Rodney King created a rather sizable and long-lasting critical opening in the news. Spurred by the video and the political conflict it engendered, news organizations across the country defined that event as a clear and unambiguous case of excessive force and defined the problem underlying it as one of poor police management and a hostile and racist police subculture. We now turn to the construction and impact of that "news icon."

SEVEN

Interpreting Rodney King

Police Brutality in the National Media Arena

On March 4, 1991, Attorney General Richard Thornburgh convened a "summit" on "Law Enforcement Responses to Violent Crime." Basking in the afterglow of the recently concluded Persian Gulf War and looking for a domestic agenda in which to invest his political capital, President Bush had seized upon the issue of crime, and the summit unveiled his administration's domestic crime initiatives. Over 650 law enforcement officials from across the country attended the summit, including LAPD Chief Daryl Gates. In his keynote address, Thornburgh urged police to attack crime in the United States much as the United States had attacked its enemies in the Gulf, urging law enforcement to wage "the fight against violent crime" with "the same command and control, the same ingenuity and certainty" as "the weapons that turned back the ruthless and violent intrusion by Saddam Hussein's forces" (quoted in Skolnick and Fyfe 1993, 113–14). President Bush also spoke at the summit; among other comments, Bush praised Daryl Gates as an "all American hero" (Balz 1991, A4).

One day earlier, unbeknownst to those gathered at the summit, black motorist Rodney King had been pursued at high speed by officers of the California Highway Patrol and the LAPD. When King finally pulled over and exited his car, he had been violently subdued by LAPD officers. And a resident had captured part of the episode on video.

One day after Thornburgh's keynote address, footage of what was quickly becoming known as the Rodney King beating filled television screens across the nation. Within two weeks, echoing the insistent demands of citizens in Los Angeles and beyond and the attempts of local and federal officials to appear responsive, the news pages would fill with critical assessments of the LAPD, the leadership of Daryl Gates, and the prevalence of police brutality across the country. Within one month, Mayor Tom Bradley would call for Gates to resign the position he had held since 1978, and the news would amplify voices repudiating the crime-attack model of policing represented by the LAPD. By the next year, Gates would be gone, and the LAPD, joined by police departments across the country, would at least rhetorically embrace a style known as community policing.

FROM ACCIDENTS TO ICONS

This vignette captures a key phenomenon of interest in this study: how some dramatic and spontaneous news events can become the centerpieces of refigured public conversations about public problems. Some "accidental events" can present serious challenges to dominant ways of framing issues in the news, temporarily upsetting official control of the news and encouraging journalists to bring voices and views that are usually marginalized to the center of the media arena. The deaths in police custody in New York analyzed in the previous chapter are examples, on a smaller and more limited scale, of this phenomenon. Some accidental events are so vivid, widely publicized, and controversial that they set off prolonged political and rhetorical struggle in the national arena. These events crystallize deep political and cultural concerns and often remain etched in the nation's public memory long after they occur. These memorable "news icons" shape many of the political debates of our time.

News icons arise when dramatic, unexpected events prove irresistible to news organizations both because their imagery is so compelling and because the cultural and political tensions they raise are profound and troubling (Bennett and Lawrence 1995, 23). They facilitate the processes of problem definition by encouraging journalists to identify public problems and by providing certain groups with powerful symbolic weaponry with which to wage struggles over meaning in the media arena. And they become thinking tools for officials, journalists, and the public to define public problems in new ways.

For example, the street corner assassination of an alleged Viet Cong captive by a Vietnamese officer during the Tet offensive became a widely disseminated image associated with a host of doubts about the Vietnam War. The image was so newsworthy not only because it captured a powerfully dramatic moment but because it crystallized concerns that events in Vietnam did not reflect the values for which the war presumably was being fought (Bennett and Lawrence 1995, 24). Similarly, the grounding of the *Exxon Valdez* entered the pantheon of defining events in American consciousness because it crystallized deep cultural conflicts over the exploitation of natural resources in America's "unspoiled" West (Lawrence and Birkland 1999).

News icons also encourage news organizations to resolve cultural and political tensions by identifying solutions for the public problems they raise. Thus, for example, the 1987 journey of the garbage barge *Mobro* from its Long Island home to countless foreign ports, all of which refused its cargo, became an occasion for news organizations to raise questions about American consumption and waste and to point to a "new" problem of garbage. Moreover, in the barge's wake, news organizations increased their attention to the "new" solution of recycling (Bennett and Lawrence 1995). These examples indicate that dramatic news events can serve as centerpieces of problem definition and invite discussion of solutions, in the process "mainstreaming" marginalized ideas and facilitating social change.

Similarly, when George Holliday's video camera captured images of LAPD officers raining kicks and blows on a prone African American man, a news icon was born. The event challenged Americans' beliefs about policing, the war on crime, the protections offered by due process rights, and the prevalence of racism in contemporary American society. This chapter analyzes national news coverage of the King beating and the issue of police brutality in selected print media from across the country: the *Atlanta Journal and Constitution, Chicago Tribune, Los Angeles Times, Newsday* (New York), *New York Times, San Francisco Chronicle, St. Louis Post-Dispatch, St. Petersburg Times, Seattle Times, USA Today, Washington Post, Newsweek, Time*, and *U.S. News and World Report*.[1] It describes how the King beating was interpreted in the mainstream print media, explores how the struggle over meaning engendered by the King beating played out, and explains how particular problem definitions subsequently emerged in the news. As we will see, the policy discourse driven by the King event was marked by a vigorous struggle to define what the King incident really symbolized.

Several factors generally keep police brutality from becoming recognized as a public problem, especially on a national scale: the fact that American policing is highly localized; the inherent ambiguity of most use-of-force incidents; the lack of statistical data that could definitively establish whether police brutality is indeed patterned and widespread; the geographical and cultural distance between some communities that experience an ambivalent relationship with police and the rest of the public; and the discourse of crime control, which focuses attention on the threat of crime and grants police greater discretion in fighting it. In addition, a journalistic norm of professionalism encourages journalists in most circumstances to defer to official claims designed to ward off policing problems.

To a significant degree, news reporting in the aftermath of the King beating overcame these obstacles. The beating was widely interpreted in the national media as an unambiguous case of excessive force, and reporters defined it by drawing upon the claims of police critics and minority leaders who portrayed police brutality as a widespread problem stemming from deep roots in American racism, politics, and the criminal justice system. Moreover, journalists linked Rodney King not only with a contemporary pattern of police misconduct but with a historical pattern of police abuse of minorities, drawing upon the King beating's strong symbolic associations with past moments in the history of American struggles over civil rights. In making salient a dimension of policing that is usually obscured by the discourse of crime control, news organizations thus evoked larger cultural tensions associated with race, civil rights, and progress. But the critical voices to which journalists turned to contextualize the King beating did not decisively win the battle to define police brutality as a serious public problem, in part because journalists could not come by statistical "proof" of a pattern of brutality.

Out of this prolonged and unresolved struggle over problem definition emerged one putative solution: community policing. The King incident and its violent aftermath in Los Angeles in 1992 helped to popularize the notion of community policing and to redefine it as a solution not only for the crime problem but for a newly perceived police misconduct problem. Neither problem nor solution was completely new, but both were rediscovered and reinterpreted in the wake of Rodney King. In fact, that the beating was widely interpreted in the national

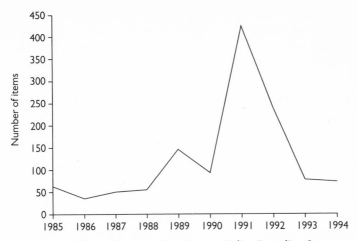

Figure 7. News Coverage Focusing on Police Brutality, Selected National Print Media, 1985–94. Source: Data are compiled from the Nexis database of news and editorial items published in the *Chicago Tribune, Los Angeles Times, New York
Times, Washington Post, Newsweek, U.S. News and World Report*, and *Time*. "Number of items" equals all items appearing
in these newspapers and newsmagazines that mentioned police
brutality or excessive force at least three times.

media as an indicator of a past problem that had resurfaced was crucial
to the "new" solution that was joined to it.

ESCAPING CONTAINMENT

On March 3, 1991, motorist Rodney King was stopped by officers of
the LAPD who allegedly had pursued him at speeds over 100 mph. The
officers ordered him out of the car and in the ensuing altercation shot
him with Taser darts, kicked him repeatedly, and struck him with batons 56 times—blows that were recorded on videotape by area resident
George Holliday. After attempting to file a formal complaint with the
LAPD, Holliday turned his videotape over to the local news station
KTLA for $500. It first aired locally on March 5; within 48 hours, it
had been aired around the world.

In a classic example of event-driven policy discourse, the Rodney
King beating boosted the attention of news organizations around the
country to police brutality. News organizations not only reported on
the King case itself, repeatedly airing key moments from the video, but
produced more coverage that focused on the larger issue of police brutality. This is illustrated in figure 7, which shows a dramatic increase in

1991 in news and editorial items across the country that focused on the issue of excessive force.[2]

Some idea of the content of this reporting can be gained by examining the headlines. Table 3 shows selected headlines that appeared in March through May 1991 in newspapers and newsmagazines across the country. They illustrate how the news not only examined police brutality as a serious public problem but foregrounded questions about the systemic factors that might create and sustain brutality: institutionalized racism; a police subculture in which an "us-against-them" mentality can thrive; and the unwillingness of local prosecutors and federal law enforcement agencies to pursue allegations of brutality. Judging from these headlines, it appears that the news took the Rodney King beating as indicative of a larger problem in the LAPD—and beyond. I turn first to explaining how that problem definition arose so speedily and powerfully.

CONSTRUCTING A PROBLEM OF POLICE ABUSE

In a *Los Angeles Times* poll reported just days after Holliday's video first aired, two-thirds of Los Angeles residents reported they believed that police brutality was common in their city (Rohrlich 1991). This finding contrasted with a *Times* poll taken just the year before, that had found that, although nearly one-half of African Americans believed there was a "fair amount" of police brutality in Los Angeles, the public in general was satisfied with police performance. Similarly, based on a Gallup poll it commissioned, New York *Newsday* reported in 1991 that

> the public's perception that New York police use excessive force is increasing. . . . In March, 1,010 New Yorkers were asked whether the police department uses too much force, and 43 percent said yes; 44 percent disagreed. When asked the same question in July, 1989, just 29 percent said too much force was used and 60 percent disagreed. (Kocieniewski and Levitt 1991, 6)

These local patterns were seemingly repeated at the national level. A *New York Times*/CBS poll conducted in early April 1991 found that "slightly more than two-thirds of a national sample of respondents said that when they hear of an allegation of police brutality, they feel the charge is 'very likely' or 'fairly likely' to be justified" (Holmes 1991, A16). Moreover, 51 percent said they believed that police in large cities are generally tougher on blacks than on whites, and 53 percent of black respondents agreed that the police in their community "rough up people unnecessarily" after arresting them.

Part of the power of Holliday's video thus seems to have been to per-

TABLE 3. SELECTED HEADLINES, NATIONAL
NEWSPAPERS, MARCH–MAY 1991

Newspaper	Date	Headline	Type
Los Angeles Times	March 7	It's not just a few rotten apples	op-ed
New York Times	March 7	Tape of beating by police revives charges of racism	news
Washington Post	March 8	Police beatings called chronic problem	news
New York Times	March 10	An "aberration" or police business as usual?	news analysis
Los Angeles Times	March 13	Police abuse: Fronting for the haves	column
Seattle Times	March 16	Police brutality—at last, federal concern over patterns of violence	editorial
Atlanta Constitution	March 18	L.A. beating video prompts closer look at claims of police brutality	news
Atlanta Constitution	March 19	It's clear that L.A. beating was not an isolated event	column
USA Today	March 20	Fighting a mentality of "us against them"	news
Newsday	March 21	"Brutality, I think, is a reality"	news
Chicago Tribune	March 24	Police brutality: How widespread is it?	news
Washington Post	March 24	Can the violence in L.A. teach us why cops lose control?	news
Seattle Times	April 1	Civil-rights cases often hit dead end—Justice Dept., FBI investigate fewer than half of complaints	news
Los Angeles Times	April 4	Has the videotape of the King beating exposed a dirty little secret?	news
Washington Post	April 5	Police inspire trust, fear; mixed views played out in neighborhood	news
New York Times	April 5	Police brutality is not the norm	op-ed

TABLE 3 *(continued)*

Newspaper	Date	Headline	Type
Los Angeles Times	April 7	Heavy collateral damage in war on crime?	op-ed
Chicago Tribune	April 14	When is a tough police-man a brutal policeman?	news
Los Angeles Times	April 14	Cracks in government: King fallout shows a structural problem in key L.A. office	editorial
Washington Post	April 28	The difficult task of policing the police	news
Newsday	April 30	Cop brutality settlements cost city millions in '90	news
Los Angeles Times	May 15	City's imbalance is unmasked	editorial
St. Petersburg Times	May 19	Changes sought in policing the police	news
Los Angeles Times	May 19	Racial disparities seen in complaints to LAPD	news
St. Petersburg Times	May 24	Meaningful dialogue needed between police, community	editorial

suade many Americans that the King incident was not an "aberration," as LAPD Chief Daryl Gates had claimed. As one poll respondent told a *New York Times* reporter, until he saw the video, "I knew it happened, but I figured it was behind the scenes and less frequent than it probably really is. . . . It is not until you see it like that do you really believe it" (Holmes 1991, A16). Of course, it is difficult to know to what degree this widespread public reaction reflected long-standing beliefs among some segments of the public and to what degree it was a response simply to the video. Neither can we know to what degree responses to the video were shaped by the way the video was described and contextualized by reporters, columnists, and editorialists. Put more simply, we cannot know if news organizations simply echoed or actively shaped public beliefs that the King beating symbolized a common problem of police misconduct.

But it is clear that news organizations across the country were quick to highlight claims of widespread and patterned brutality as a way of contextualizing the King beating. As the following sections will argue, this way of framing Rodney King grew out of the way the video por-

trayed the event, the subsequent story developments that strongly suggested a pattern underlying it, the claims of police critics and black
leaders who were ushered in to explain it, and the symbolic associations
of Holliday's video images with iconic images of the past.

THE VIDEO AS A COMPELLING COMPETING ACCOUNT

Holliday's video mattered greatly to the problem definitions that arose
around Rodney King. It provided irresistible news opportunities to
news organizations across the country, particularly television broad-
casters, and thus created a national audience riveted on a phenomenon
most would never personally witness or experience. But the video
would not have had the same impact if the film had not begun rolling
and come into focus precisely when it did, or had it not captured such
clear images of batons and boots repeatedly striking King's body. The
video made for good television precisely because of what it emphasized
and deemphasized. The in-focus frames were both the most dramatic
and the most damning to the officers, while the early, unfocused
frames, which might have raised questions about King's behavior, were
difficult to see and interpret and were usually not shown on television.
As Goldberg (1991, 256) recounts, television stations

> other than CNN seldom, if ever, showed the tape in its entirety. . . . What the
> networks showed repeatedly was five- or ten-second clips showing the po-
> lice raining blows on King as he lay on the ground. The public, having seen
> those same horrifying actions over and over, tended to believe that it had
> seen the full tape, or at least all that mattered.

Thus, the videotape truncated the chain of events leading to King's altercation with police and effectively undermined the usual official narratives offered to legitimize and rationalize the use of force (see chapter
4). It constituted, in other words, a highly dramatic and compelling
competing account that was instantly more newsworthy than any de-
scription of the event the LAPD could offer.

The particular story the video seemed to tell encouraged journalists
and their audiences to evaluate King's altercation with the LAPD independently of official claims about it. In fact, reporters often took the
unusual step of unequivocally describing King as the victim of an un-
provoked assault. A nationwide newspaper sample of news and editorial items that mentioned the King beating in their lead paragraphs
from March through May 1991 illustrates this point: 48 percent of
these items described that event in ways that cast King as the victim and

the LAPD officers as the aggressors, often in quite dramatic terms. King was described as a "victim of a brutal beating," as "unarmed" or "unresisting" or "defenseless"; the attack was described as "brutal" or "savage," a "vicious assault," a "case of blatant brutality." These assessments were offered not only in the editorial pages. Half (49 percent) of these depictions appeared in the news pages, and the majority (62 percent) of these news-page descriptions were offered in journalists' own words, not in phrases they attributed to their sources.[3] On March 13, for example, *USA Today* matter of factly reported that "A grand jury is questioning witnesses in connection with the savage beating and kicking of black motorist Rodney King, 25, by three white police officers" (Stewart 1991, A3). Similarly, on March 14 the *New York Times* reported that "The [Los Angeles] Police Commission . . . is scheduled to hold a public meeting with [Gates] on Thursday to discuss the March 3 beating of an unarmed, unresisting black motorist by white officers" (Reinhold 1991a, 17). New York *Newsday* even claimed that the video showed police "kicking and clubbing suspect Rodney King as he lay on the ground, handcuffed" (Bessent and Tayler 1991).

These descriptions may seem unremarkable because they undoubtedly seem accurate to many readers. But they are remarkable, for they signal a profound shift from the usual reporting of police use of force examined in earlier chapters. Moreover, it is important to remember that these journalistic depictions of the video were interpretations. As the nation subsequently learned, the video did not necessarily speak for itself and could be made to look very different under the direction of skilled lawyers. Moreover, though the LAPD's treatment of King was undeniably harsh, it is not necessarily clear from the video whether King was unarmed or unresisting, especially initially, and King was not handcuffed and searched until after the segment of the altercation that was usually shown on television. These points (together with the defense team's tactic of "deconstructing" the video by breaking it into individual frames) helped the Simi Valley jury to decide that the officers had, on the whole, behaved appropriately (Parloff 1992).[4]

In short, such unequivocal statements by journalists regarding a use-of-force incident are exceedingly rare; over the ten-year period covered in this study, I found no other use-of-force incident about which statements such as these were made by reporters in the news pages. Indeed, the King video was widely viewed by news organizations as so unambiguous that the lead paragraphs of a *Newsday* article could proclaim: "So unequivocal was the evidence, [the beating] was quickly seen not just as a convincing chronicle of the police assault on King, but as a defining symbol of police brutality" (Wilson 1991, 49).[5]

Thus, the way the video portrayed the King-LAPD altercation licensed journalists to start their storytelling from a point that most use-of-force incidents never reach: an assumed certainty about police misconduct. Moreover, the large number of officers at the scene beyond the four directly involved in the altercation, none of whom appeared to intervene, suggested strongly to viewers that this scene was somehow business as usual. As one police expert put it bluntly in an op-ed piece, "in the Rodney G. King videotape . . . we see officers who had to be confident that their colleagues would remain silent and that their department would reject any citizen's account of their conduct" (Fyfe 1991, B7).

ADDITIONAL STORY CUES

The video also set in motion political dynamics that provided abundant additional story cues to news organizations, all in a relatively short period of time. First, strong and widespread citizen reaction to the King beating echoed at the highest levels of government. Members of the Congressional Black Caucus demanded a federal investigation of brutality complaints across the country, bringing to the official agenda the claim that police brutality is widespread in minority and urban communities. John Conyers, Democrat from Michigan and a member of the CBC, also opened congressional hearings on police brutality two weeks after the video was first aired. And prominent politicians such as Sen. Joseph Biden began calling for Gates to resign, signaling that, to at least some degree, officials endorsed a systemic problem definition arising from Gates's leadership of the LAPD.[6]

Furthermore, a succession of story developments in mid- to late March kept the case in the news and opened news gates across the country to more in-depth coverage of the issue of brutality: the announcement that indictments would be sought against four officers involved in the beating; the opening of the Justice Department's nationwide probe of brutality complaints; and the release of the patrol-car radio transcripts, which revealed LAPD officers using racial slurs and making light of their treatment of King and others. The transcripts in particular strongly suggested that the beating of King was not an isolated aberration. One message recorded from the patrol car of Officers Powell and Wind said, "I haven't beaten anyone this bad in a long time." In response came the message, "Oh not again. Why for you do that . . . I thought you agreed to chill out for a while" (Wood and Stohlberg 1991, A1).

What is significant about these numerous and provocative story cues is the license they provided to news organizations to focus critical attention on the issue of police misconduct. The release of the LAPD transcripts in particular triggered a spate of in-depth news articles about police brutality—something the video alone did not accomplish. Indeed, the bulk of in-depth news items in the national media appeared during a six-week period after the transcripts first became news, from March 19 through the end of April 1991. Before the release of the transcripts, however, newspapers across the country did not examine the King story or the issue of police brutality at length.[7] Thus it was these additional story cues, and not simply the video itself, that prompted news organizations to begin constructing a brutality problem around Rodney King.

DRAWING UPON CRITICAL CLAIMS

The strong imagery of the video, the initiation of legal proceedings, and the additional evidence of brutality throughout the LAPD opened the national news gates to voices critical of the LAPD and of policing in general. Critical perspectives were offered not just by activists, but by black elected officials. Representative Conyers portrayed police brutality as a widespread threat to public order, telling reporters that "a culture of violence . . . has swept many police departments" and arguing that "If we cannot protect citizens against the kind of videotaped violence that occurred in Los Angeles that night, then we are a nation in jeopardy" (Campbell 1991, 16; L.A. police beating prompts U.S. study, 1991). His claim was echoed by other black members of Congress, such as Edolphus Towns of New York, Maxine Waters of California, and Don Edwards, also of California, who told reporters that police brutality against minorities was an epidemic, that incidents such as the King beating were "the order of the day in Los Angeles," and that the King beating was "symbolic of what is happening around the country" (Johnston 1991). And when he released the damning radio transcripts, Mayor Bradley announced that "It is no longer possible for any objective person to regard the King beating as an 'aberration' " (Bradley blasts "bigotry" of police officers, 1991, A12).

Even before they were licensed by black officials' comments, however, journalists from around the country drew directly from antibrutality activists and community groups in Los Angeles and beyond to define the King incident. The *New York Times* led this charge in the lead paragraph of its very first story about the incident:

> A two-minute amateur videotape of the beating of a black motorist by a group of police officers has jarred Los Angeles and revived charges that the police department has failed to confront an alleged pattern of police brutality and official abuse of minorities among its officers. (Mydans 1991a, A1)

The article amplified the claims of civil rights organizations who saw a "pattern of violence and racial abuse among Los Angeles law-enforcement agencies." It included comments from a spokeswoman of the Police Misconduct Lawyers Referral Service, saying, "I must tell you that we receive complaints in this office of that kind of conduct on a weekly basis, if not on a daily basis. . . . The difference this time is that there was somebody there to videotape it. That's the only difference." And the *Times* did not stop at the LAPD but also pointed out that

> The Los Angeles County Sheriff's office has also been accused of violence and racial discrimination. In one pending case the NAACP Legal Defense and Educational Fund said deputies in the Lynwood station had engaged in 40 documented incidents of "shooting, killing, brutality, terrorism, house-trashing and other acts of lawlessness." (ibid.)

Shortly thereafter, in a front page news analysis, the *Times* asserted that "A number of points have heightened the sense that the beating was far from the aberration claimed by Police Chief Daryl F. Gates" (Mydans 1991b, A1). Drawing upon the *Los Angeles Times* opinion poll described above, the fact that the video showed the officers beating King "with impunity," and the fact that "court records depict a history of similar cases in Los Angeles, some of which seem to differ from the beating of Mr. King primarily in that there was no camera to record them," the *Times* portrayed the King beating as a strong indicator of serious policing problems in Los Angeles.

This amplification of voices that are usually muffled in the news was not unique to the *New York Times*. As figure 8 indicates, coverage of certain civil rights organizations and claims about the systemic nature of police brutality increased dramatically in 1991 over previous years across the national media.[8] As critical groups' framing of the King beating caught on in the national media, the notion that police brutality is

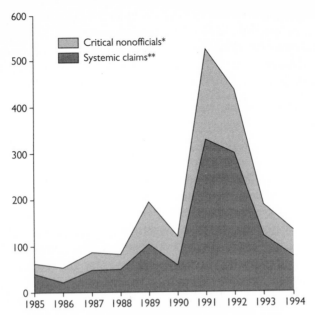

Figure 8.   Voices and Views in Coverage of Police Brutality, Selected National Print Media, 1985–94. Source: Data are compiled from the Nexis database of news and editorial items published in the *Chicago Tribune, Los Angeles Times, New York Times, Washington Post, Newsweek, U.S. News and World Report,* and *Time.*
   *Includes all items appearing in these newspapers and newsmagazines that mentioned police brutality or excessive force and also mentioned the American Civil Liberties Union (ACLU) or the National Association for the Advancement of Colored People (NAACP).
   **Includes all items appearing in these newspapers and newsmagazines that mentioned police brutality or excessive force and also contained the terms "racist," "racism," "code of silence," or "blue wall of silence."

common and widespread and caused by systemic factors such as racism or the police subculture became prominently discussed in the news.

THE STRUGGLE TO DEFINE RODNEY KING

As infused with critical claims as the news became, however, critical voices did not clearly win the struggle over meaning in the news. Ultimately, the success of black officials and critical nonofficials in designating brutality as a serious public problem was hampered by their inability to draw upon

compelling statistics. Reporters were not able to tap into officially produced data that clearly indicated widespread police abuse, because, as discussed in chapter 2, no such data exist. Thus, as the news became momentarily transfixed on defining the brutality problem by establishing its
frequency and severity, the struggle over meaning revolved around what
the Rodney King beating really represented: an isolated incident, a policing problem within Los Angeles, or a sign of wider policing problems.

In the week following the release of the LAPD patrol car transcripts,
with headlines such as "Police Brutality Triggers Many Complaints, Little
Data" and "Police Attacks: Hard Crimes to Uncover, Let Alone Stop,"
news organizations grappled with the difficulties of designating a problem whose incidence cannot be reliably quantified.[9] A *Chicago Tribune*
article, for example, began by asserting that "Police brutality, as highlighted by recent incidents in Los Angeles and New York, appears to be a
chronic problem in cities across the country, but its magnitude has yet to
be documented officially" (Campbell 1991, 16). While columnist
William Raspberry amplified Congressman Towns's claim that "A lot of
people are already coming forward to confirm what we already know:
that there is still a lot of police brutality going on" (Raspberry 1991,
A11), a *Washington Post* op-ed piece entitled "Can the Violence in L.A.
Teach Us Why Cops Lose Control?" argued that, "The Los Angeles incident is not representative of most of the metropolitan police forces
around the country. It is not necessarily even representative of Los Angeles" (DeLattre 1991, C1).

Caught on the horns of the dramatic-news-versus-no-statistics
dilemma, some news organizations struggling to define Rodney King
converged on the question, Is police brutality as bad as it *used* to be?
The *New York Times*, for example, featured the comments of Darrell
Stephens of the Police Executive Research Forum, the research arm of a
national organization of police executives. Stephens argued that the
King beating had created an impression that "most police officers are
brutal and racist, and that nothing has changed over the last 25 years."
But said Stephens, "That's clearly not the case" (Egan 1991, A1). In an
op-ed piece in *Newsday*, sociologist Jerome Skolnick wrote:

> Police brutality is like police corruption. There may be some rotten apples,
> but usually the whole barrel is rotten. Two cops can go berserk. But 20 cops
> embody a culture of policing. The written rule is clear: cops are to use no
> more force than is necessary to subdue a suspect. Where a departmental cul-
> ture condoning brutality prevails, the unwritten rule is: "Teach them a les-
> son." (Skolnick 1991, 41)

Nevertheless, Skolnick argued, "Despite current publicity given to police brutality, I believe that it has diminished in the past 50 years, even
the past 20. We need to recall how bad things used to be."

USING THE PAST TO DEFINE THE PRESENT

Thus, the struggle to define the King beating and the problem it did or
did not symbolize became in part a struggle over whether brutality was
more or less widespread than in the past. This points us toward a key dimension of how the Rodney King beating was interpreted in the news: as
a vivid reminder of America's history of racism and racial inequity. The
news portrayed the King incident not only as part of a possible contemporary pattern of police misconduct but as part of a historical pattern of
racial oppression. In a common pattern of news coverage (see Edy
1999), journalists and commentators invoked powerful collective memories to interpret the contemporary meaning of a disturbing news event.

This use of the past to define the present is evident in the references
some reporters and editorialists made to similarities between Rodney
King and Bull Connor, Selma, or other unsettling icons of the past:

> The recent Los Angeles police brutality incident, in which a group of officers
> badly beat a black man who had led them on a high-speed chase, will enter
> the annals of law enforcement as 1991's Selma, or My Lai. Like those two
> incidents, it has placed armed authority in a new, unfavorable light. (Skol-
> nick 1991, 41)

> Many people who have seen the video of the Los Angeles police beating of
> Rodney King have been reminded of the brutality inflicted on civil rights
> marchers in Selma and Birmingham, Ala. They cringe as that black man is
> mercilessly, even joyously, struck and kicked and struck again by white po-
> lice officers. (Pearson 1991, 30)

> [Gates's] intransigence sends the same signal as Bull Connor's dogs and
> hoses. (Malveaux 1991, A8)

A *Washington Post* retrospective on the major news events of 1991
observed:

> The year's most flummoxing dramas seemed . . . to be sequels—old demons
> newly packaged, Nightmare on Main Street XIII. The special effects might
> have grown more exotic, the means of destruction new, but surely these
> were still the same old ghouls that had stalked us in earlier installments. [For
> example,] the Los Angeles Police Department casually beat a black man to
> the brink of death. The only new part was that an onlooker caught Rodney
> King's attackers on video. (Williams 1991, W7)

Claims about current trends of police misconduct proved daunting to the mainstream media, for the statistical evidence needed to support such claims was sketchy and subject to interpretation, while various police and political officials, even as they condemned the King beating, were denying that it represented a current pattern of police violence. But the suggestion of a historical frame of reference resonated across the mainstream media. The result was that brutality was linked more decisively with problems of the past while the contemporary reality remained murky, the object of unresolved struggle.

HIGHLIGHTING A LATENT FRAME

The linking of Rodney King with the past was significant, for it highlighted an alternative framework for thinking about the issue of police brutality. Many incidents of police use of force do not become major news events because the claims and narratives that officials provide to reporters effectively contain the way those events are defined in the news. Official claims and narratives can succeed not only because reporters are granted privileged access to the news but because officials' claims resonate with a larger discourse of crime control. In a cultural milieu in which crime is believed to be a rampant problem of bad individuals with whom it is necessary to "get tough," police using physical force to control suspected criminals is not often seen as problematic.

But George Holliday's video provided another frame of resonance, reminding viewers of disturbing past events such as the civil rights struggles of the 1960s. The video evoked images of civil rights marchers beaten with batons, blasted with fire hoses and attacked by snarling dogs—images of Southern police protecting racial apartheid by force. Indeed, one scholar's observation about the images from Birmingham and Selma could apply equally well to how many people reacted to images from the King video: "Horrified readers could stare endlessly at police tactics so barbaric that most people assumed they could not occur in America" (Goldberg 1991, 204). This linkage of Rodney King with the past was bolstered by the communications strategies of the activists, community leaders, and black officials who claimed not only that the beating was an indicator of current trends in law enforcement but that it reflected a historical pattern of police brutality toward minorities. Representative Conyers, for example, reminded reporters that "One of the staple features of the black experience in America has been police abuse" (Campbell 1991, 16).

Thus, the video tapped into a latent civil rights discourse steeped in the bloody struggles for racial equality that have marked American history. In the Rodney King video, the cultural discourse of crime control met its match in a countertheme of due process and civil rights. As Gamson (1992b) has observed, every dominant cultural theme has its countertheme, which it can never fully erase from public discourse. The theme of technological progress butts up against fears of technology gone mad; beliefs in popular democracy compete with a recognition of the role of interest-group power in American politics. Similarly, the cultural discourse of crime control occasionally runs up against deep American distrust of the power of the state and support for due-process protections, values steeped in powerful imagery from the struggles of women and minorities for equal justice before the law. (Indeed, this conflict in our cultural values contributes greatly to the ambivalence with which Americans sometimes view police, as discussed in chapter 2.) This civil rights "master frame," as Snow and Benford (1992) label it, remains a potentially powerful frame for interpreting police use of force.

When viewed through a civil rights frame, police use of force may be seen less as a legitimate response to public disorder than as an instrument of oppression wielded by unaccountable police, sometimes for explicitly political purposes. Indeed, the national collective memory is haunted by graphic images from the American south, from the 1968 Democratic convention in Chicago, and from other events that have displayed police use of force as raw political power. On a more mundane level, the civil rights frame reflects Americans' enduring cultural ambivalence toward the coercive power of the state. The civil rights frame thus cuts against cultural preoccupations with crime control that emphasize law and order, cracking down, getting tough.

Once again, it is important to recognize that this more critical framing of the King incident was as much the product of social construction as objective fact. The connection between the events of the 1960s and the beating of Rodney King is not necessarily clear or automatic, except for the similarity of the visual images rendered by both. King was not the same kind of victim as the political protesters attacked by police in Birmingham or Selma—people who were consciously engaged in a political struggle. At the same time, the civil rights protests were often purposefully planned in hopes of creating precisely the kinds of images that filled television screens and newspapers to bolster public support for the civil rights movement (Garrow 1978). That Rodney King's altercation with the LAPD was captured on film at all was entirely accidental. Images from the King beating were easily linked to images from the civil rights movement, however, precisely because they both revealed police behavior that was shocking and outrageous to most audiences, behavior that was only rendered believable because it was captured on film. And in a way that would perhaps not have been true had King been Asian or Hispanic, the video resonated powerfully with a particularly American understanding of racism. As one set of authors has commented, the King beating "exemplified an old-style model of racial domination that, today, virtually the entire American culture opposes. The videotape reverberated with the skeletons of American apartheid" (Crenshaw and Peller 1993, 62).

Tapping into the past, therefore, opened news coverage to marginalized discourse about policing and perhaps primed the public to view police use of force from the perspective of the civil rights frame rather than in terms of crime control. This is not to argue that no other interpretations of the King beating were available in the media; indeed, some voices in the news continued to insist that King had been beaten not because he was black or because the LAPD was out of control but because he had threatened police. What is significant is the degree to which an alternative framework for understanding that event was developed in the news—a framework in which King was emblematic of a pattern of police brutality that had not disappeared since the days of Jim Crow.

This interpretation of the King beating provided a crucial nexus between problem definition and problem solution. For viewing Daryl Gates's LAPD as a contemporary manifestation of a historical pattern of racially motivated police abuse invited a particular solution: that those police be brought into the putatively more progressive present. For the advocates of this problem definition, a concept of police reform known as "community policing" had, fortuitously, already gained growing media attention prior to the King incident and provided an apparently ready-made solution. To fully understand how the King beating and the problem of brutality was defined in the news, therefore, we must look at the popularization of community policing.[10] Growing media attention to community policing in the late 1980s had defined community policing as a progressive wave of the future; what was added in 1991 was the depiction of the aggressive policing style of the LAPD as a remnant of the past.

POPULARIZING COMMUNITY POLICING

Community policing is not a new concept. In the aftermath of the wide-spread urban unrest of the 1960s—itself often triggered by incidents of alleged police brutality—community policing became a buzzword of police reform. But as budgets declined and the inner-city problems of crime and drugs worsened in the 1970s, community policing fell out of fashion. The concept was given a facelift in the early 1980s through the work of criminologists George Kelling and James Q. Wilson. In an influential piece published in the *Atlantic* in 1982, Kelling and Wilson first presented to the general public their "broken windows" theory: the notion that policing could be more effective by focusing on the problems underlying the decay of public order in troubled communities rather than by focusing exclusively on responding to individual crimes.[11]

As early as 1985, community policing was being referred to in newspapers and news magazines as "what the future holds for law enforcement in this country" (Yardley 1985, C2), but it received minimal media attention between 1985 and 1989, the year when Wilson and Kelling reprised their argument in a lengthy essay in the *Atlantic*. Yet attention to the concept spiked dramatically in 1990, the year prior to the King beating, and increased again in 1991 and 1992. Figure 9 illustrates these trends.[12]

The spike in media attention to community policing in 1990 was due most notably to the appointment of Lee P. Brown as police commissioner of the New York Police Department. Brown, a committed advocate of community policing, was a former chief of the Houston Police Department, where he had won kudos for his reforms. Shortly after beginning his tenure at the NYPD he became president of the International Association of Chiefs of Police. Brown's ascension to the NYPD and his forceful advocacy as head of the IACP helped to put community policing on the national media agenda and to cast it in a highly favorable light.

This boost in media attention to community policing in 1990 set the stage for the struggle to define the Rodney King beating the following year. In return, that event helped to stimulate further media interest in community policing in 1991 and 1992, as the data in figure 9 suggest. But the King beating did not popularize the notion of community policing only in ways that can be measured quantitatively. It not only helped to boost media attention to community policing but played an impor-

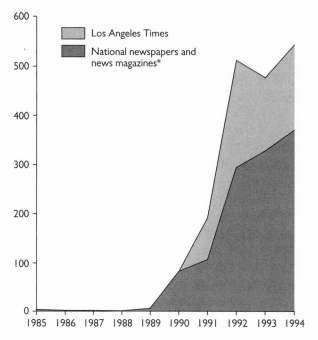

Figure 9. News Coverage of Community Policing, Selected National Print Media, 1985–94. Source: Data are
compiled from a search of the Nexis database for the
terms "community policing," "community-oriented policing," or "community-based policing" in the *Chicago Tribune, Los Angeles Times, New York Times, Washington
Post, Newsweek, U.S. News and World Report,* and *Time.*
  *Since the Rodney King beating engendered a great deal of
news coverage in Los Angeles of the community-policing reforms
set in motion there, data are shown both including and excluding
the *Los Angeles Times.* Thus, the darker area of the figure may
offer a better sense of the real magnitude of media coverage
across the country.

tant role in the evolution of popular understandings of community
policing.

COMMUNITY POLICING AS A SOLUTION FOR BRUTALITY

We can gain a sense of this interaction between the King incident and
media portrayals of community policing by looking first at the way the
media defined community policing and the shifting problems for which
it was offered as a solution. In 1990, when media attention to the concept first increased dramatically, community policing was portrayed

primarily as a better way to control crime; but in the aftermath of the King beating and of the subsequent riots in 1992, it was portrayed as a way to improve police-community relations and to improve police accountability as much as a method of crime control.

This shift is suggested by the following findings: In 1990, of the 176 news articles and editorials mentioning community policing that appeared in the eleven newspapers examined here, only 16 items also mentioned police abuse, brutality, excessive force, or misconduct; in 1991, out of 447 items mentioning community policing, 107 also mentioned police abuse, brutality, excessive force, or misconduct. The proportion of items mentioning community policing in connection with police brutality thus rose from 9 percent in 1990 to 24 percent in 1991.[13]

As these figures suggest, brutality was added to the list of problems that community policing could address. Indeed, 54 percent of these items explicitly presented community policing as a solution or antidote to police brutality.[14] These numbers are significant not only in themselves but in the fact that, as the data above indicate, the linkage of community policing with police misconduct was not common prior to the King beating. Moreover, 61 percent of references to community policing in 1991 presented it exclusively in a favorable light by mentioning its purported benefits or citing sources who favored it, while only 2 percent of items presented community policing exclusively in an unfavorable light by mentioning purported costs or problems arising from those reforms or citing sources who opposed it; 19 percent of items contained both favorable and unfavorable information.

Thus, in 1991 it became common to hear community policing described as "the real crux of change" that would address brutality problems in the LAPD and other police departments (Kelling 1991, B7). The media did not independently arrive at the notion of community policing as an antidote to brutality. Rather, that notion was endorsed by many official sources and actively promoted by certain high-profile police chiefs and police organizations that were attempting to turn negative publicity over the King beating into an impetus for nationwide police reforms. For example, on April 16, roughly five weeks after the King video first hit the airwaves, Commissioner Brown organized a "summit" of police chiefs in New York City to address the perceived crumbling of public support for police. The chiefs attending the summit issued a news release in which they defined police brutality as a problem of increasing societal violence and urban decay that put extreme pressures on police officers. The chiefs offered their own systemic framing of police misconduct, arguing that "The police are continually being left to deal with the aftermath of years of urban neglect, of the rampant drug culture, of increasing criminal victimization, and of a lost generation wandering the streets without employment or hope of a better future" (Treadwell 1991, B1). They urged the federal government to respond by, among other things, creating a center that would train local police forces in community-policing strategies. Other police sources contributed as well. Washington, D.C., police chief Isaac Fulwood Jr. contrasted the community-policing approach with the LAPD's crime-attack style by telling reporters that "the label 'war on drugs' has defined the crisis in such military terms . . . that police officers are faced with an enemy that must be defeated by 'any means possible,' contributing to the use of excessive force" (Jennings and Lester 1991, B1). Thus, the systemic framing of police misconduct emerging in the news provided an opportunity for advocates of community policing to present a systemic solution.

The notion of community policing as a solution for brutality was also powerfully endorsed when, in July 1991, the Christopher Commission, appointed by Mayor Tom Bradley to investigate the LAPD, issued a report in which it recommended a number of structural changes in the department, including the implementation of community-policing reforms. According to the *Los Angeles Times*, the Christopher Commission argued that community policing "would reduce tension between residents and police by eliminating the perception within the Police Department of 'the community as enemy' " (Murphy 1991, B3). Congress further endorsed the connection with an Omnibus Crime Control Act (which eventually died under President Bush's veto threat), which sought to fund "Cop On the Beat" grants to develop "innovative neighborhood-oriented policing programs" (U.S. Congress, House, 1991).

Then, in 1992, as Los Angeles erupted in flames after the officers charged with abusing King were acquitted, politicians scrambled to respond to that symbol of the demise of urban America while not alienating a suburban constituency increasingly obsessed with crime. Media attention to community policing spiked again as politicians, particularly the two main presidential candidates, picked up the community-policing banner. But as the Clinton team in particular adopted community policing as a prime campaign theme, the connection between those reforms and police misconduct began to fade. Community policing became increasingly conflated with the idea of putting "more cops on the beat," which continued to be a theme in the Clinton administration. By 1992 the percentage of newspaper items mentioning both community policing and police mis-conduct fell to 14 percent, down from 24 percent the year before.

The story of how the solution of community policing eventually shifted away from the problem of police brutality will have to be told elsewhere; for now, the important story to tell is how the two tem-porarily were linked in 1991. For not only was community policing of-fered as a solution for police misconduct in the wake of Rodney King, but the style of policing epitomized by the LAPD was suddenly repre-sented as an outdated remnant of the past.

LAPD-STYLE POLICING AS A THING OF THE PAST

Just as the King beating shaped prevailing representations of commu-nity policing, the rise of community policing shaped the problems that were constructed around the King beating. A predominant problem definition constructed around the King incident was that American policing, particularly at the LAPD, had not progressed out of the past. The "crime attack" model of policing exemplified by the LAPD, with its emphasis on squad car patrols, cool professionalism, and innovative high-tech tactics such as SWAT teams, was generally portrayed posi-tively in the news prior to 1991, even as the very different style of "community" policing was being popularized. After the King incident, the LAPD was portrayed as a repository of the worst in past policing practices, the exemplar of what was wrong with police departments that had not yet caught the wave of the future.

We can catch a glimpse of this transformation in newspaper and magazine articles about community policing appearing before and after the King beating. Prior to March 1991, the LAPD was invariably por-trayed positively and was even offered as an example of a department that was embracing community-policing ideas. Indeed, Wilson and Kelling's second *Atlantic* article (1989) encouragingly portrayed the LAPD as one police department successfully implementing community policing. One *Newsweek* article in 1990 even portrayed the LAPD's Operation Cul-de-Sac, in which high-crime neighborhoods were liter-ally walled off with concrete barricades, as an example of community policing. "While few municipalities have gone as far as Los Angeles," *Newsweek* reported, "Operation Cul-de-Sac is a variation on the com-munity policing efforts now underway in other blighted inner cities" (Salholz 1990, 24).

After the King beating, however, the LAPD was represented as anachronistic, exemplifying all that needed to change in American policing. For example, a *Chicago Tribune* piece on Milwaukee's transition to community policing noted that, "Like other police departments in the nation, Milwaukee's is in slow and balky transition from the 1950s model of purely incident-driven law enforcement. It is one that stresses professionalism, reactive response and a distant, 'just the facts ma'am' approach to police work" (Worthington 1991, 29). This reference to the LAPD style immortalized in the television show *Dragnet* was repeated in other news stories. A *New York Times* piece examining the Kansas City Police Department's efforts to root out abusive officers noted that many of them "wear mirrored sunglasses and other trappings of authority. Out on the street, they are humorless and approach the increasingly complex job like 1950's cardboard television characters: just the facts ma'am and no backtalk" (Terry 1991, A1). Echoing this theme yet again, a November *Washington Post* piece began with this observation about a police officer in a Brooklyn precinct that was adopting community-policing tactics: "Sgt. Andrew McGoey has seen the future of police work, and it does not look like what was pictured in the old television dramas" (Goodstein 1991, A1).

Just as prominent police sources were instrumental in linking the solution of community policing to the problem of brutality, they were also the main propagators of images of LAPD-style policing as outmoded. For example, the president of the Police Executive Research Forum told *USA Today* that while the LAPD enjoyed a good reputation for law enforcement, it practiced outdated "militaristic" methods. "It makes more sense and it's more effective for police to be partners with the community," he argued (Gerald Williams, quoted in Stewart and El Nasser 1991, A1). And Joseph McNamara, former San Jose police chief and a strong advocate of progressive police reforms, wrote an op-ed piece that appeared in both the *Los Angeles Times* and the *St. Petersburg Times* in which he argued:

> Over the last two decades, the nation's big-city police departments wrestled with reforms and gradually embraced concepts of affirmative action and community policing. But the Los Angeles Police Department and its chiefs were permitted if not encouraged to march to a different drum. (McNamara 1991, M1)

The time had come, McNamara argued, for the LAPD to abandon its outmoded crime-attack style.

Thus, the King beating coincided chronologically with a quickly proliferating media discourse about community policing, and this coincidence shaped how both police brutality and community policing were presented in the news. Even as Daryl Gates was proving unable to control the news about the King beating and the voices of police critics were being amplified in the news, other sources such as the International Association of Chiefs of Police, the Police Executive Research Forum, and individual chiefs and former chiefs such as Brown and McNamara were inviting journalists to focus on an appealing-sounding set of reforms called community policing.

Why did community policing become the solution for the brutality problem being constructed in the media around Rodney King? It was not the only proposed solution, after all. Many police critics advocated the establishment of civilian review to make police more accountable to their communities, for example. Several reasons are suggested by the case study presented above. First, community policing was favored by many high-profile police officials who had already established a media platform for their views and by prominent politicians who took up the community-policing banner. Long before Rodney King encountered the LAPD in 1991, police sources such as Lee Brown and experts such as Wilson and Kelling had been spreading their philosophy of reform through the mass media. These same sources were then able to define the Rodney King beating as an indicator of the necessity of community-policing reforms. The Christopher Commission report and the Clinton campaign added further stamps of legitimacy to the concept. Civilian review, in contrast, was not supported by police or most other officials.[15]

Equally important was the way community policing fit with the emerging problem definition surrounding the King beating. It was a short step from the media's interpretation that police brutality was an ugly vestige of American racism and a symptom of police hostility toward the communities they are supposed to serve to the media depiction of the LAPD's crime-attack style of policing as outmoded and community policing as its polar opposite. These linkages between past and present were undoubtedly strengthened by the unrest in 1992, which so clearly echoed the Watts riots and other urban rebellions of decades earlier—unrest that had spurred the first experiments in community policing. Community policing thus made even more sense as the riots created a public sense of déjà vu about police-community relations.

Finally, community policing fit especially well with the most simplistic problem definition that emerged around the King beating: Daryl Gates. Many activists, community leaders, and politicians in Los Ange-

les and beyond focused on Gates's leadership of the LAPD as the proxi-
mate cause of Los Angeles's policing problem, a perception aided by
Gates's sometimes abrasive personality and history of inflammatory
public statements. This focus on Gates allowed a systemic problem definition of police mismanagement and insulation from political control
to be understood in highly personalized terms. Thus, an intuitively appealing solution was to force Gates out of power and to replace the ves-
tiges of his leadership style with another model of policing altogether.
Community policing reforms symbolized sweeping away Gates's aggressive "crime-attack" policing along with the memories of Rodney King.

NEWS ICONS AND THE POLITICS OF
PROBLEM DEFINITION

The argument presented here has been that the beating of Rodney King
became the centerpiece of a mass-mediated struggle to define a brutality
problem and appropriate solutions for it. The widely disseminated
video of officers raining blows on King boosted the issue of brutality on
the media agenda, while news organizations defined and contextualized
the event by amplifying critical societal voices who sought to define police brutality as a widespread public problem. Because the incident was
widely perceived as a police attack on King, and because the videotaped
images evoked other filmed images from past struggles over civil rights,
the incident was interpreted as signifying a problem of police aggression that extended beyond that one event, even beyond Los Angeles.
Moreover, the King beating acted as a kind of focusing event (Kingdon
1995) that joined a program of reforms already growing in popularity
among police departments and the media with an expanded set of problems: police misconduct and poor police-community relations.

A remaining question is how the King incident can inform us about
the dynamics of event-driven problem definition in other news contexts. Several observations made here can contribute to a theory of how
news icons shape and are shaped by the politics of problem definition in
the news. In general, the event-driven problem definition surrounding
the Rodney King beating unfolded in ways similar to that of the infamous garbage barge *Mobro* (Bennett and Lawrence 1995). Both the
King beating and the garbage barge were treated as symbols of brewing
public problems, encouraged journalists to invite critical societal voices
into the mainstream, and facilitated the linkage of newly perceived
problems with "new" solutions.

Antibrutality activists and black officials, empowered with the symbolic weaponry of the King video, were able momentarily to assume center stage and become primary definers of the problem constructed around Rodney King. Yet the access they gained to the news did not guarantee them an ability to control the problem definition that emerged in the news. Whereas the *Mobro* became a vehicle for environmentalists to lead the charge toward recycling, a bandwagon that officials later jumped on, the King beating provided an opportunity not only for police critics to dramatize their concerns about patterns of brutality but for certain police sources to gain support for their preferred programs of reform. Police chiefs and former chiefs such as Brown, Fulwood, and McNamara and police organizations such as the Police Executive Research Forum were ready to capitalize on the King beating, and community policing thus won a favorable hearing in the news. This suggests that while news icons create opportunities for nonofficials and other critical societal voices to contribute to problem definition in the news, they do not erase the basic logic of news construction: the most powerful and best-organized voices gain the greatest access, and those who can lay the groundwork for their preferred problem definitions are advantaged over those who have not.

Second, the way the King video evoked symbolic associations with the past played a significant role in the problem definition that arose. The King beating resurrected a problem thought by much of white America to be a thing of the past. This suggests that an important component of event-driven problem definition is the particular historical and cultural themes that news icons evoke. Indeed, the "politics of memory" can intersect with the politics of problem definition, as the "mobilization of memory" serves as "a vital political resource" for groups competing to define the present (Schudson 1989, 112).

In the struggle to define the King beating, many questions were raised that have not been addressed here, and that event lingers uncomfortably in the public consciousness. Media scholar John Fiske (1994, xxi) has argued that "An event becomes a media event not at the whim of the media alone but also to the extent that it gives presence to abstract cultural currents that long precede it and will long outlast it." Some news icons, like the beating of Rodney King, erupt in the midst of complex streams of history and culture. The struggles such events set off are deep, long lasting, and difficult to resolve.

EIGHT

Accidents Will Happen

The News and Event-Driven
Problem Definition

Questions about the prevalence and causes of police brutality have not been dormant since the beating of Rodney King but have continued to spark controversy both in New York and Los Angeles. In the mid-1990s the NYPD adopted the trappings of the crime-attack style once championed by Daryl Gates's LAPD and has trumpeted its positive effects in impressive statistical drops in crime rates. The NYPD's beefed-up forces have also cracked down on "quality of life" offenses such as panhandling, public drunkenness, and public urination and have adopted sophisticated methods for targeting geographic areas with high concentrations of crime—crackdowns that remind some observers of the LAPD drug sweeps of the 1980s. The NYPD has even donned new uniforms patterned on the LAPD's traditional dark blue, militaristic style (Newton 1995).

The LAPD has moved in the opposite direction. In June 1992, Los Angeles voters ratified Charter Amendment F, which revamped the city's system for selecting and overseeing chiefs of police, thereby establishing the basis for greater civilian control of the department. More recently, the LAPD has embraced the now-familiar trappings of community policing, getting cops out of their cars and onto the sidewalks and encouraging them "to emphasize community contacts over arrests" (Newton 1995, A1). The more aggressive style the LAPD was once known for has not disappeared, however, and some communities have continued to complain of brutal policing tactics. In December 1995, the

NAACP held hearings in Los Angeles that yielded vociferous complaints of police harassment and brutality. The criminal trial of O. J. Simpson that year produced more images of brutal Los Angeles police, as the public heard tape recordings of LAPD detective Mark Fuhrman describing beating "niggers" and Latinos "to mush." Though Fuhrman's exploits had allegedly taken place many years before,[1] his vivid descriptions of brutality brought the issue once again to national media attention, leading the Justice Department to consider conducting an investigation of systematic brutality within the LAPD (Olivo 1995).

Continuing complaints led the Los Angeles Police Commission in May 1996 to finally enact one component of the Christopher Commission's suggested reforms by appointing an inspector general to investigate citizen allegations of police misconduct. Other reforms lagged, however, as documented in the so-called Bobb Commission report of 1996, which scrutinized the LAPD's response to the Christopher Commission's recommendations. The Bobb Commission found that the LAPD still lacked a system for tracking and analyzing the use of force by its officers, and, though complaints were down, it found that punishments for excessive force were still lenient and costs of brutality lawsuits still high (Newton 1996).[2] Long-time LAPD observer Joe Domanick observed that "The Mark Fuhrmans are a dying breed. But they are a slowly dying breed. The LAPD is a rusted vessel that's going to take a generation to turn around" (quoted in Reibstein 1995, 24). In 1999, the U.S. Commission on Civil Rights announced its recommendation, after a study that had begun in 1993, that Los Angeles appoint a special prosecutor to handle excessive-force cases, citing the poor record of the county prosecutor's office in prosecuting officers accused of brutality. The commission also recommended a federal probe of allegations of continuing brutality by the Los Angeles County Sheriff's Department. Law enforcement officials charged that the report was inaccurate and outdated (Daunt and Lait 1999). Simultaneously, a major scandal unfolded in the city's Rampart Division in which officers were found to have framed, beaten, and, in at least one case, shot drug suspects (Lait and Glover 1999).

Meanwhile, critical scrutiny of the NYPD has increased. The Mollen Commission report, issued in 1994, revealed the exploits of corrupt and brutal officers in some of New York's most troubled neighborhoods. The report asserted that "Over the years, the Department has . . . made little effort to address the full scope of the problem of brutality and its tolerance" by officers and their supervisors (Mollen 1994, 44). The New York Civilian Complaint Review Board also released a report in 1994 showing a 46 percent increase in police-brutality complaints (including 220 beatings, pistol-whippings, and other alleged incidents) in the first six months of 1994 compared with the same period the previous year. The increase in complaints was said to reflect "a renewed aggressiveness on the part of the Police Department under Mayor Rudolph W. Giuliani," including his crackdown on quality-of-life offenses (Krauss 1994a). The Giuliani administration and the NYPD countered that the increase in complaints represented the inevitable cost of cleaning up the streets and implied that many of the complaints were illegitimate. The New York Civil Liberties Union attributed the increase in complaints to the fact that the civilian review board had recently been made more independent of the police department, encouraging a greater number of legitimate complaints to be lodged. Subsequently, in 1996, Amnesty International completed a review of allegations of excessive force against the NYPD and concluded that the number of claims of police misconduct against the city increased from 977 in 1987 to more than 2,000 in 1994 (Krauss 1996b).

The issue of brutality gained sharper focus in 1997. In the early morning hours of August 9, Abner Louima, a 30-year-old Haitian immigrant, was taken into police custody after a scuffle outside a Brooklyn nightclub. By the time he left the 70th precinct station house three hours later, Louima was suffering from severe internal injuries inflicted by NYPD officer Justin Volpe, who sodomized Louima with the broken wooden handle of a broomstick.[3] The lurid details of Louima's brutalization, the racial overtones of the attack, Mayor Giuliani's hurried transfer of the 70th precinct's chief, and the angry demonstrations of thousands of New Yorkers kept the Louima case in the news for some time.

Tensions aroused by the Louima case boiled over after the shooting of Amadou Diallo in 1999. On an early February night, four officers of the highly touted Bronx Street Crimes Unit fired 41 shots at Diallo, a 22-year-old West African immigrant who worked as a street peddler, as he stood in the vestibule of his Bronx apartment building. Diallo had no criminal record and was unarmed; 19 of the bullets hit him. The shooting immediately provided journalists with an abundance of story cues that quickly drove the story to the top of local and national headlines, opening perhaps the most vigorous mass-mediated debate over policing to occur in many years.

The immediate critical reaction to the Diallo shooting was in large part driven by the apparent egregiousness of such overwhelming force used against an unarmed man. Further darkening the picture was the lack of credible evidence that Diallo had threatened the officers. The officers claimed they had believed Diallo might have been a rapist they were looking for, and police officials speculated that perhaps the officers had thought Diallo had a gun. The lawyer for the officers involved in the shooting tried to provide a narrative that would show the incident was justified, claiming that Diallo had exhibited "aggressive behavior," which the lawyer declined to describe. While the number of bullets fired at Diallo "may seem to a layman to be excessive," the lawyer argued, "it was the number required before this man stopped" (Cooper 1999, A1), and he wondered aloud "how anyone on the outside can know that this was an unjustifiable shooting. . . . Both the Police Commissioner and the Mayor recognized that the mere number of shots alone does not make this a crime on the part of the police officers" (Flynn 1999, B5). But the thoughts of one resident of the Soundview neighborhood where Diallo lived seemed to echo a wider public perception: "Forty-one shots—forty-one shots. . . . Even if he was a criminal, that's crazy" (Waldman 1999, B6). Even Mayor Giuliani, in an unusual rhetorical move, cast doubt on the police version of events by telling reporters, "We are very concerned obviously about the number of shots" (Herszenhorn 1999, B6). Four officers were subsequently indicted on charges of second-degree murder.

Local and national reaction to the case was intense. The Reverend Al Sharpton, a well-known presence in brutality allegations in New York, was joined by the president of the NAACP, Kweisi Mfume, in decrying the shooting, while Amnesty International USA charged in a press release that the slaying "raises deeply troubling questions about the use of excessive force and police brutality" (McFadden and Roane 1999, A1) and called for an independent commission to investigate. Within days, demonstrations against the shooting were drawing up to 1,000 participants in New York, and the protests continued well into the following month, when former mayor David Dinkins was arrested, along with U.S. Representative Charles Rangel, for acts of civil disobedience at NYPD headquarters. The protests moved beyond New York in April 1999, as relatives of victims of police brutality from across the country led more than 1,000 protestors in a march in front of the Justice Department in Washington, D.C. One week later, 19 police chiefs and community leaders from across the country convened in Washington to discuss how police departments might win back public confidence.

Crucial to the way the Diallo shooting was defined were the efforts of an organization called 100 Blacks in Law Enforcement Who Care. Spokesmen for this organization, which may have enjoyed greater credibility than comparable citizens' groups because its members were themselves police officers, sponsored a news conference with antibrutality groups the day the shooting was first reported. The group charged that Diallo's death demonstrated that the NYPD's Street Crimes Unit was itself the problem, since it had "been given carte blanche to do as it will to the people of the City of New York, especially the African-American community," and had "taken a more aggressive stance under [the Giuliani] administration" (McFadden and Roane 1999, A1). In response, the *New York Times* published a critical exploration headlined "Elite Force Quells Crime, But at a Cost, Critics Say." The lead paragraphs of the story explained that "the unit has become a hallmark of the aggressive policing championed by the Giuliani administration. . . . But its tactics have also been criticized by community leaders and other police officers who say the department should rein in the unit's members, who like to say they 'own the night' " (Roane 1999, B6). The problem definition widened when a coalition of politicians, labor leaders, and business executives publicly called for broader reforms of the NYPD's hiring practices, its reporting on the use of force, and its processes of civilian review, and for the creation of a special prosecutor to handle excessive-force cases. Coalition members argued that although the individual officers involved in the Diallo shooting had been indicted, "they considered it more important to pursue long-term solutions to what they described as systemic tension between police officers and black and Hispanic New Yorkers" (Hicks 1999, 41). Meanwhile, the Justice Department's Civil Rights Division widened its investigation of the NYPD, focusing on whether persistent complaints of excessive force there were the product of "systemic deficiencies in police operations" (Weiser 1999, 46).

The Diallo case thus touched off an intensive struggle to define a policing problem in New York. The *Times* observed that "Mr. Diallo's death has [drawn] national attention to what critics contend is the dark side of Mr. Giuliani's achievements in bringing down crime—the sense that aggressive police enforcement has created a climate that can breed brutality" (Bumiller and Thompson 1999, A1). Within a week, the *Times* editorial page featured an op-ed piece by civil rights lawyer Joel Berger, who argued that misconduct accusations of all kinds against police "have risen sharply in New York in the past four years, much more

so than other claims against the city" (Berger 1999, A23). Mayor Giuliani countered by charging that critics' attacks on him and the NYPD
were partisan and unfair. He blamed a "media frenzy" for poll results
showing that more than three-fourths of all New Yorkers doubted that
blacks and whites are treated equally by police and that one-third of
black New Yorkers said they had at some time felt endangered by a police officer (Barry 1999).

As this poll suggests, the problem constructed around the Diallo
shooting also hinged on claims about institutionalized forms of racism.
The debate resurrected a problem definition that had haunted the
NYPD since the shooting of Jose Garcia: the racial disparity between
the NYPD and the population of the city (Wilgoren 1999b; Wilgoren
and Cooper 1999). Beyond New York, a debate ensued about nationwide patterns of racially motivated police abuse. In a commentary on
National Public Radio, for example, Joe Davidson of the Center for
Crime, Communities, and Culture argued that "A major reason this
country can't get race relations right is a law-enforcement process that
displays such bias that many in the black community believe the
criminal-justice system is designed for 'just us' " (Davidson 1999). Police brutality, he claimed, "occurs all too frequently around the country
for black people to consider [Diallo's] death an isolated incident."
Rather, the Diallo shooting was "symbolic of a culture that places little
value on black life." This problem definition was ratified by at least one
police official. Philadelphia Police Commissioner John F. Timoney, a
participant in the Washington meeting of police chiefs, observed during
the meeting: "Frankly, there is a problem with race in policing. To solve
it, we have to deal openly with it" (Janofsky 1999, 12).

The Diallo case even made its way into the presidential campaign.
Democratic candidate Bill Bradley invoked the shooting as evidence of
continuing racial strife in America, describing it as "an extreme example
of the targeting that most African-Americans have experienced with the
police at some time in their lives." Indeed, Bradley asked, "Is a Diallo-like
incident a potential catalyst, not just toward police reform but toward
deeper understanding?" Even more unusual for a presidential candidate,
Bradley asked his audience, "Why doesn't some public official ask our
schoolchildren to observe the tragedy with a moment of silence in memory of another life lost to senseless violence?" (Nagourney 1999, A20).[4]

As the Diallo case makes clear, the dynamics that drove the Rodney
King story were not unique to that incident, and police brutality will
continue to surface in the news as long as dramatic incidents offer com-

pelling news material to journalists—and as long as concerns about police brutality continue to fester in urban and minority communities. The meaning of these future news events will be constructed out of the complex interplay of communication strategies and story cues as police, elected officials, experts, activists, and grassroots communities vie to push the story in different directions. Nor are these dynamics unique to news coverage of policing. A wide variety of "accidental events" fill the news pages from day to day and raise a wide variety of public issues. While some pass quickly out of the news, some become pivotal news events around which struggles over meaning and political battles for power are waged and, occasionally, public policy is made.

EVENT-DRIVEN VERSUS INSTITUTIONALLY DRIVEN PROBLEM CONSTRUCTION

The research and theoretical framework presented here can more closely join studies of the social construction of the news with studies of the construction of public problems. Official dominance of the public definitions of policy issues, what I call "institutionally driven" problem definition, anchors one end of a continuum of news dynamics. Anchoring the other end is what I have called "event-driven" problem definition.

The basic features of these two modes of problem definition are illustrated in table 4. Institutionally driven problem definition is pegged to the daily activities, conflicts, and debates happening on institutional news beats such as the White House or city hall. Event-driven problem construction is cued by the appearance of dramatic news events erupting within or outside these news beats and the story possibilities that those events present to journalists. The predominant frames in institutionally driven news are defined by institutional elites, and the range of official debate roughly defines the range of debate in the news. Event-driven problem definition arises sporadically, and news constructed around accidental events often draws upon a wider variety of voices and perspectives, ranging beyond the spectrum defined by official debate (though still often coming up against structural and cultural limitations on the news). In event-driven contexts, news organizations can set the official agenda rather than the usual pattern of the officially driven news agenda, and singular events can become emblematic of larger public problems. In event-driven dynamics, the problems that are designated and the ways they are defined derive as much from unfolding story developments as from the efforts of officials to frame the news.

TABLE 4. CHARACTERISTICS OF
INSTITUTIONALLY DRIVEN AND EVENT-DRIVEN
PROBLEM DEFINITIONS IN THE NEWS

Institutionally driven problem definition	Event-driven problem definition
News focuses on "routine" events: presidential speeches, congressional committees, campaign strategies, crime fighting, etc.	News focuses on unusual, unexpected, unplanned events: terrorist attacks, ship groundings, airplane crashes, police violence, etc.
Officials are key providers of news narratives and frames.	Story cues flow from characteristics and developments of events; non-officials may be key providers of news narratives and frames; news frames may also be influenced by characteristics of events themselves.
Narrative structure of news defined by key decision points within institutional processes.	Narrative structure of news defined by story "developments" that are less tightly pegged to institutional processes.
Range of official debate roughly defines range of debate in the news.	Perspectives presented in the news may range wider than present official debate.
Political institutions set the news agenda. Key "problems" in the news are those officials wish to "own" (or those they must own).	News organizations may set the institutional agenda. Key "problems" in the news are those news organizations find most newsworthy and "interesting."
Dominant problem definitions serve official interests in agenda setting, reelection, party building, mobilizing key constituencies, etc.	Problem definitions variable and volatile, depending on story; problem definitions may tend to favor advocates of "reform."

Event-driven news thus often provides a window of opportunity for advocates of social and political change. Event-driven policy debates challenge would-be reformers, community activists, and savvy politicians alike to influence public perceptions about the need for new policy solutions or political reforms. The Rodney King beating, for example, eventually brought an end to LAPD Chief Daryl Gates's policing career while it put police departments around the country on the defensive. But it also created opportunities: for Los Angeles mayor Tom Bradley to move against Gates, his long-time political enemy; for civil rights activists to put police misconduct on the public agenda and to define it as a systemic, nationwide problem; and for reformers within the policing establishment to promote the concept of community policing.

Institutionally driven problem definition stems from the officially dominated, "routine" news that has been studied and theorized extensively. Event-driven problem definition, in contrast, has not been systematically studied. And in between the institutionally driven and event-driven poles lies a fairly wide middle ground of mass-mediated discourse that is negotiated daily on contentious issues such as abortion, taxes, and the impeachment of President Clinton. This is news that is still primarily driven by the agendas and activities of officials but keyed as well to the activities of well-established interest groups and the occasionally newsworthy activities of grassroots groups. Developing a model of event-driven problem definition highlights the now-missing pole that places both official dominance of the news and this middle ground into context. Illuminating the event-driven pole, in other words, sheds light on the whole continuum of news dynamics.

Event-driven and institutionally driven dynamics are obviously ideal types: heuristic devices that help us to understand real-world phenomena. The boundaries of each type are in reality permeable. Dramatic news events can prompt policymakers to put issues on institutional agendas, which in turn triggers institutionally driven discussion of policy issues in the news. A good example of the permeability of these boundaries is found in the "drug war" of the 1980s. The appearance of crack cocaine, and in particular the highly publicized drug-related deaths of two celebrity athletes in the spring of 1986, set off a wave of media attention to this newest drug threat. Politicians climbed quickly on board, and the House of Representatives churned out a $2 billion Drug Free America Act just in time for the mid-term elections. News organizations, whose reporting on the crack menace had initially spurred officials to action, subsequently followed the decline (in 1987) and rise again (in 1988) of official attention to crack (Reinarman and Levine 1988).

Clear distinctions can sometimes be difficult to draw, therefore, between "routine" news events and institutionally driven problem definition, on the one hand, and accidental events and event-driven problem definition, on the other. News coverage of accidental events can become routinized as institutions respond; accidental events, on the other hand, can upset carefully managed institutional news. The diplomatic crisis over chemical and biological weapons inspections in Iraq in early 1998 seems a good example of how the two processes can become intertwined. The Clinton administration designated the stand-off between United Nations weapons inspectors and Iraqi officials as a serious foreign-policy problem and attempted to define it as a problem of Iraqi intransigence. Yet what started out as an accidental news event, at least from the U.S. perspective, soon became routinized, institutionally driven news. Nearly every day between late 1997 and early 1998, news organizations dutifully reported the latest developments from Iraq—what weapons sites inspectors had been granted or denied access to, what charges and countercharges had been thrown back and forth among officials in the U.S., the U.N., and Iraq.

Then, as the United States prepared to mount a military campaign to force compliance with the inspection regime, the Clinton administration took its case to the American public in a series of public forums with Secretary of State Madeleine Albright and Secretary of Defense William Cohen. One carefully staged routine news event at Ohio State University became an accidental event of sorts when members of the audience grilled the officials with highly critical questions about U.S. intentions and chanted antiwar slogans so loudly that they drowned out Albright's presentation. Meanwhile, another accidental event—the revelations of a sexual affair between the president and White House intern Monica Lewinsky—threw the administration on the defensive. That event seriously undermined the administration's ability to dictate the news narrative regarding Iraq, for the planned military mission now looked to some like an attempt to draw attention away from the Lewinsky scandal. This news context reflected a complex interplay between institutionally driven problem definitions and the sudden appearance of unpredictable and dramatic events.

The Lewinsky scandal itself repeated this pattern, for it is difficult to categorize that long-running story of presidential scandal as purely event-driven news. Clearly, much of the impetus for the Lewinsky story was provided by officials in the Office of the Independent Counsel and other institutional news beats.[5] But the story set in motion a media feeding frenzy that spun out of the control of any single institution and raised a host of questions in the news about everything from presidential character to the state of feminism in the 1990s to the meaning of "sexual harassment" and "moral leadership." Like some of the events analyzed in this study, "Monica Lewinsky" became a hotly contested political symbol whose significance was defined in widely divergent ways.

THE SOCIAL CONSTRUCTION OF ACCIDENTAL EVENTS

Even though the distinction between institutionally driven and event-driven problem definition is not always as clear in reality as it is presented in this typology, event-driven news remains a useful concept, not least because it signals a unique institutional role for the media. When events arise beyond or spill outside of institutional bounds, the news becomes an informal screening process for problems entering the formal policy process in formal institutional arenas. News events become key determinants of serious policy discussions in the mass media, for problem construction in the policy process is often set in motion by dramatic and unpredictable news events that cry out to be explained, defined, and normalized. When officials are unable to control the news concerning a dramatic unexpected event, policymaking initiatives become likely. More subtly, the way events are discussed in the news often shapes the way that public policy issues are defined within policymaking institutions. Events matter not only because they often catalyze policy debates but because those events and the problems they represent must be defined.

This dynamic has been recognized but not fully theorized in various studies by political communication and public-policy scholars. From the political communication side, studies have shown how dramatic news events, such as the deaths of Ryan White and Rock Hudson from AIDS, shape the public agenda by embodying pressing public issues (Dearing and Rogers 1996). Dramatic news events can also shape the framing of policy debates in the news. Gamson and Modigliani (1989), for example, have shown how the accident at Three Mile Island shifted the dominant frames in public discourse about nuclear power. Similarly, from the public-policy side, following on Cobb and Elder's (1983) notion of "triggering events," Kingdon (1995) has argued that "focusing events" can be crucial in pushing issues onto or further up the policy agenda. Drawing upon Kingdon, Birkland (1997) develops a model of how certain kinds of focusing events—natural disasters, oil spills, and nuclear power plant accidents—mobilize competing groups and shape public policymaking.[6]

Most of these studies have simply treated certain events as "natural" catalysts and then traced their impact on policymaking and public discourse, and they have usually treated public problems as preexisting conditions that simply surface or become submerged on the policymaking agenda. The crucial processes by which events and problems themselves are defined by policymakers, journalists, and the public have remained undertheorized. Yet to serve as catalysts, events must come to be understood as indicators of public problems—or, to use Best's (1988) term, events must be perceived as "typifications" of larger issues.

A notable exception is found in the work of Deborah Stone (1989), who develops a typology of the "causal stories" that different actors apply to policy problems, stories that shift responsibility for problems to different parties. As Stone recognizes, political actors struggling to define political issues strategically portray events in ways that lend themselves to a favored problem definition. Following Stone's approach, this study has focused on the question of how some events are socially constructed either as random and discrete occurrences or as indicators of brewing public problems that need to be addressed. Many people agree, for example, that the Rodney King incident was a disturbing event and that the police handled the altercation poorly, to say the least. But what is crucial to understand is how so many people came to see the King incident as symbolic of deeper and more pervasive problems in the American criminal-justice system.

The social construction of events is thus a crucial step in struggles to define and designate public problems. Yet the socially constructed nature of these events can be difficult to recognize. For example, in his very useful study of news coverage of political conflict in the Middle East, Wolfsfeld (1997) recognizes the important role played by news events in shaping news frames. He observes that "certain events give advantages to certain frames" because "some frames make more sense than others" for covering particular events (45). But he suggests that the objective facts of events determine what news frames become prevalent in news coverage of subjects such as police brutality, military atrocities, and human-rights violations. "When victims have been found and especially when they can be filmed [and] . . . if it is the authorities who are found at the other end of the stick, then it is they, rather than the challengers, who find themselves in an uphill battle for legitimacy" (54).

Indeed, an important theme of this study has been the opportunity that events can create for critical understandings of public issues to arise in the news. Yet it is important to remember that there is often an interpretive gap between the objective facts of an event and the significance it acquires in the news. Indeed, what frame "makes sense" is not necessarily a question that can be objectively answered, especially regarding events as ambiguous and potentially controversial as use-of-force incidents. Indeed, much of the story told in this study centers on the difficulty that critical nonofficials have in promoting a systemic frame for the issue of police brutality, even when it might seem to "make sense." For though it may be authorities who are at the other end of the stick, what they are doing with the stick will always be the key question. Police brutality is rarely self-evident and is almost never talked about in the news without the participation of police, who almost invariably claim that the "victim" is a victim of nothing other than his or her own aggression, deviance, or poor judgment. The ability of this kind of claim to win the struggle to define news events is central to the construction—or warding off—of policing problems.

Event-driven problem construction does not matter only in an agenda-setting sense, therefore. Events matter not only because they get people talking about public problems but in how they get them talking.

TOWARD A THEORY OF EVENT-DRIVEN PROBLEMS

Recognizing the inherently contested and constructed nature of many accidental events, we can begin building a theory of event-driven problem definition with a few simple propositions. The first proposition is that journalists become key mediators of problem definitions when accidental events become big news. Journalists' decisions about whose voices to include in the news are driven by journalistic values and norms. One aim of this study has been to suggest that these norms are not unidimensional. Journalists do not always try to sensationalize or suppress accidental events. The amount and type of coverage an event receives depends upon journalists' assessments of its newsworthiness, as well as on journalistic judgments about what an event "really" means. The concept of "story cues" is useful in helping us to see what journalists see when assessing an event's newsworthiness.

A second proposition, therefore, is that particular news events provide journalists with particular story cues that push emerging problem definitions in particular directions. These sometimes idiosyncratic event characteristics or story developments become the building blocks of new or redefined public problems, often independent of clear statistical evidence or agreement among the experts. The way that event-driven problems are defined in the news depends to a considerable degree on the unique mix of symbolism, context, and compelling imagery surrounding and arising out of accidental events.

Story cues also arise from the competing claims and reactions of various groups. Journalists continue to take cues from officials when writing about dramatic accidental events. But as this study has shown, they also look elsewhere for evidence and claims that help to make sense of those events, and they take cues from the reactions of communities and grassroots organizations most affected by events. Thus, while minority activists, for example, may rarely be able to independently set the agenda of institutionally driven news about policing, they can be invited in to define alleged-brutality incidents that arouse strong reaction in their communities. A third proposition, therefore, is that the problem definitions that arise from dramatic news events depend in part upon the strategies used by both official and nonofficial groups to provide journalists with definitive frames for accidental events. And a fourth proposition follows from the first three: The problem definitions that arise in the media arena are variable and contingent.

The best example from within this study of these propositions is of course the Rodney King beating. News organizations across the country presented the incident as a clear and unambiguous case of brutality—a presentation quite unlike that given to any other use-of-force incident examined in this study. The seeming unambiguousness of the video encouraged reporters to immediately turn to activists and black officials to define the event. The King beating thus engendered the first nationwide public conversation about policing, race, and justice to occur in many years. Yet had King been white, or had the beating not been videotaped and played on television, or had the videotape captured a different segment of the incident, the story line and hence the problem definition that emerged in the news would certainly have been qualitatively different. Similarly, had grassroots groups in Los Angeles not reacted strongly to the incident, or had civil rights organizations such as the ACLU not been poised to struggle over its meaning, the public definition of the event and its implications for public policy might well have been different.

These propositions are applicable to news domains beyond policing and crime, as well. One example is found in the grounding of the *Exxon Valdez* in March 1989, which became a key turning point in a long-term policy struggle over federal oil policies and in the larger struggle of environmentalists to shape public attitudes toward the environment. It was not merely the fact of the event but the way its meaning was struggled over that shaped the policy environment. As it happened, the most newsworthy characteristics of the story conferred symbolic advantages on environmentalists. Environmental groups used the media imagery of oiled sea otters, dead birds, and workers cleaning oiled rocks with towels to illustrate their argument that the spill was an act of needless and possibly irreversible human destruction of the environment. These images trumped the symbol-poor arguments of the oil industry that the spill was not serious and should not be seen as an indicator of any need for stricter regulation of the oil industry. As images of oil-soaked otters flooded television screens (and adorned the advertisements and mass-mailings of environmental groups), the issues of oil-spill policy, oil extraction, and oil consumption gained more prominent places on media and governmental agendas, and environmentalists won a seat at the policymaking table that had previously been denied them. In this event-driven context, the seeds of the 1990 Oil Pollution Act were sown in Congressional committees (Birkland 1997; Lawrence and Birkland 1999). The *Exxon Valdez*, meanwhile, became a lasting symbol of environmental degradation that shaped the context of future environmental debates.

Similarly, the crash of ValuJet Flight 592 in May 1996 culminated in a redefined public problem of aviation safety. The public definition of the crash was not contained by official claims that simple oxygen generators mistakenly loaded in the cargo hold were the extent of the problem. Rather, the story of ValuJet was not brought to a close until the FAA had all but admitted that its oversight of this and other cut-rate airlines had been lax. More interesting, perhaps, is how the crash stimulated a prolonged and wide-ranging struggle over problems and solutions. Transportation Secretary Federico Peña responded to the crash by defining structural underpinnings of the problem: the conflict of interest inherent in the FAA's dual role as both regulator and promoter of air travel. Members of the House of Representatives met that broadened problem definition with an even broader solution: the removal of the FAA from the Department of Transportation altogether. Though such restructuring never took place, that it was discussed at all illustrates the power of accidental events to invite the redefinition of policy issues. As one *New York Times* story reported, "Like few accidents before it, the ValuJet crash has become a kind of Rorschach test, affording the opportunity for many people involved in aviation safety to see something in the accident and its aftermath that reflected long-standing concerns" (Bryant 1996, A8).

The dynamics of event-driven problem construction are not limited to major accidents. Sometimes, even the smallest of accidental events can become major news icons. Such was the case of Stella Liebeck, who is probably best remembered as "the McDonald's coffee lady." Ms. Liebeck suffered third-degree burns when she spilled a cup of coffee she had just purchased at a drive-through window. What made Ms. Liebeck's case a national news story was a jury's decision to award her $160,000 in compensatory damages and $2,700,000 in punitive damages. Though the trial judge subsequently reduced the punitive damages to $480,000, far fewer news organizations reported this stage of the story. Instead, "the news media reported the damages as if Ms. Liebeck had just won the litigational lottery," transforming the highly unusual award into a symbol of litigation run wild. "Proponents of tort-reform . . . appropriated the coffee verdict to support their claims" about "a tort-system out of control" (Aks, Haltom, and McCann 1997, 5–7). The McDonald's coffee lady thus became a vivid typification—a symbol that aided proponents of "tort reform" seeking to curtail personal damage claims against corporations.

One final example again illustrates that even minor events can take on major importance and spur problem construction in the media and reminds us that accidental events can arise even on routine news beats. That is the infamous state dinner held in Tokyo in 1992 as part of George Bush's highly publicized trade mission to Japan. What became newsworthy was not the dinner but the moment when President Bush vomited in the lap of Prime Minister Kiichi Miyazawa. The event, captured on film, was mentioned in numerous news stories that year—not a surprising fact, given that it was highly unusual and, at least initially, raised concerns about the President's health. What is fascinating, however, is the way the event was used by journalists to tell stories about the decline of American global economic superiority. Bush's illness became a metaphor for the country's failing vigor and for his own questionable success at improving the foreign balance of trade. The Japan trip, which quickly became dubbed "Bush's ill-fated mission" or the "messy summit," thus came to represent the putatively awkward and vulnerable position of the United States in the post-cold war era. As business reporters were simultaneously revealing in the financial pages of major newspapers, it was perhaps Japan that was more economically ill. Yet the accidental event at the state dinner was apparently too irresistible a metaphor for political reporters to resist (Dahl and Bennett 1996).

As some of these examples suggest, dramatic news events can contribute not only to the construction of public problems but to the rise of new policy "solutions" to newly defined (or redefined) public problems, as when community policing was presented as a solution to the brutality problem constructed around the King beating. This is where the study of how news events are defined meets more traditional studies of policymaking: depending on how they are defined, accidental events can act as "focusing events"—windows through which problems and solutions are joined (Kingdon 1995). By stimulating public angst and anger, accidental events invite officials to normalize troubling situations by announcing reforms. Event-driven debates can invite fresh thinking about solutions to public problems or allow solutions that have been languishing in the wings to take center stage.

The political impact of event-driven policy debates both within and outside of the media arena is uneven and often short-lived, however, for several reasons. Beyond the constraints identified here such as privileged official access to the news and the norm of media professionalism, event-driven problem construction is also constrained by the limited carrying capacity of the media arena (Hilgartner and Bosk 1988), which creates intense competition among issues and events for limited media attention. High-profile accidental events may kick off a struggle in the media arena among competing event and problem definitions that may never be fully resolved before the media turn their attention to other news stories. As Anthony Downs recognized long ago, as the media spotlight swings from one dramatic news event to the next, the public's attention may be drawn away from one event-driven policy debate to another (Downs 1972). Meanwhile, power relations may not shift as easily in policymaking arenas as they can in the media arena. While marginalized groups and perspectives may win a greater hearing by journalists, that may not translate into a greater presence in policymaking institutions. And as noted above, dramatic news events may stimulate largely superficial or symbolic responses in policymaking arenas. Indeed, for all its considerable impact on the news, the Rodney King affair did not engender a concrete, federal-level policy response to the newly recognized problem of police brutality. Congress did eventually pass legislation increasing the federal government's power to investigate and seek injunctions against police departments in which there is a "pattern and practice" of brutality—but only after another extraordinarily dramatic event, the Los Angeles riots, reiterated the messages of the King beating over a year later. Thus, event-driven policy debate in the news is not necessarily a prelude to real changes in public policy.

Moreover, even though event-driven debates can illuminate overlooked dimensions of societal conditions and may even create consensus in the media around particular problem definitions, any new consensus produced through event-driven news may be tenuous and the
new problem definitions flawed or incomplete. Even the prolonged and
relatively intensive examination of policing that followed the Rodney
King beating did not produce a complete picture of policing problems.
Activists and other police critics did bring to the news a perspective on
policing that is often confined to troubled inner-city communities and
the minority press. The new problem definitions that emerged rested on
a better sense of some of the systemic roots of brutality. Yet it is open to
question how well the King beating served as a thinking tool for understanding the problem of police brutality.[7] Claims about racist brutality
made for compelling news scripts because of the racial identity of King
and the officers, and because the videotaped images reminded journalists and their audiences of iconic moments from American history.
Claims about racism also caught on because they offered a familiar
script involving easily recognized characters: old-fashioned racist cops
and their hapless black victims.

But racism is not the only cause or necessarily the deepest or most
pervasive cause of police brutality. Police officers who are themselves
members of minority groups can and do treat minority citizens in ways
those citizens perceive as brutal. In fact, two well-publicized cases of alleged brutality to surface after the Rodney King beating involved videotaped altercations in which African American officers were filmed repeatedly striking minority suspects.[8] Other systemic factors that are not
as easily scripted in the news contribute to police brutality, such as the
unwillingness of many police chiefs to seriously limit the discretion of
rank-and-file officers to use force, the unwillingness of many prosecutors to bring excessive-force charges against police except in the most
clear-cut or egregious cases, and the expressive rather than instrumental
nature of some police violence. While these factors may be connected to
institutionalized racism, racism alone is an incomplete basis for understanding the phenomenon of police brutality.

In fact, images from George Holliday's video seem to have generated
only a shallow consensus around policing reform. The widely televised
incident shifted attention toward one dimension of police use of force—
racially motivated abuse—and away from the dimension more commonly talked about in the news—the fight against crime. The video
may have united most of the public momentarily in agreement that the

force used against King was illegitimate and that it pointed to a problem—police racism—that needed correcting. But the largely negative public and media reaction to the Rodney King beating did not supplant the widely shared discourse of crime control. While demands for police reforms may have increased as the graphic imagery filled television screens across the country, a large portion of the public remained willing to give police considerable discretion to use force. The new consensus also did not include many in the law-enforcement community itself.[9] Thus, the long-term effects of the King beating on general public support for improved police accountability aren't clear. It may be that, as one Los Angeles-based writer observed, "In theory, they think the King beating was wrong. In practice, they're willing to accept it as collateral damage in the war on crime" (Curran 1991, M1). Incomplete and impermanent consensus around event-driven problem definitions is probably quite common, especially given that event-driven news can be, like the cases analyzed in chapter 6, highly mutable.

Nevertheless, even if it does not lead to real policy changes, event-driven problem definition can have an important impact on public discourse and politics. Event-driven news can alter the political contexts in which policy is made. Even if officials are able to regain control of a police-brutality story, as officials in New York City were able to do after the deaths of Federico Pereira and Jose Garcia, event-driven news still constrains officials' options and makes at least tentative moves toward policy change more likely. Of course, officials may merely mouth soothing platitudes or engage in purely symbolic gestures, as Edelman would likely predict (see Edelman 1977; 1988). But even "symbolic" official responses can have real-world effects by validating the criticisms that made them necessary. While officials may respond superficially to an accidental event, that they respond at all can sustain rather than silence their critics. And though subsequent reforms instituted in departments around the country may not have rooted out police brutality, George Holliday's video nonetheless altered the political and symbolic terrain in which police operate. Among other things, it increased the newsworthiness of police-brutality stories and may have increased the supply of brutality stories to the media.[10] As one *Los Angeles Times* reporter told me, people alleging police brutality became more willing after the Rodney King incident to contact reporters with their stories (Newton 1997).[11]

Moreover, event-driven debates can leave a legacy of symbolic landmarks that exert a lasting influence on subsequent policy debates.

Once new territory has been staked out or old terrain altered by high-profile news events, politicians, journalists, and publics can incorporate those landmarks into their thinking about policy issues. The Rodney King beating made many minority communities' fear of the police more salient and credible to white, middle-class audiences. Once reporters and the public became accustomed to treating the King video as shorthand for the problem of racist police brutality, it became easier to take for granted certain critical perspectives on policing. Thus, over time, defining events can add up to changes in public consciousness; from small rivulets can flow a sizable stream of collective "common sense" about what public problems we face, who they happen to, and why.

THE PROMISE AND PITFALLS OF EVENT-DRIVEN NEWS

As the discussion above suggests, the difference between event-driven and institutionally driven problem construction does not necessarily lie in the quality or accuracy of the problem definitions produced by each. Event-driven problem definitions are not necessarily "better" than those produced by institutionally driven news. Both institutionally driven and event-driven news can, at least in theory, approximate normative ideals of public discourse in a democratic society. Institutionally driven news is pegged to legislative deliberation, general elections, and other institutional processes in which politicians grapple, however imperfectly, with public-policy issues. As the framers of our Constitution hoped, public officials often have superior knowledge of the issues and certainly have ample opportunities to test their ideas against the arguments of other politicians, affected groups, and the general public. Thus, the news can allow officials to lead the public in needed directions; taking its cues from official debate, institutionally driven news can present competing perspectives on public problems and help the public to deliberate about policy alternatives being considered by government officials.

Event-driven news also has democratic promise. Accidental events are dramatic because they disturb our complacency, suggesting unresolved conflicts in our politics and our political values. With the help of journalists looking for good stories and story angles, voices and perspectives that politicians may be disinclined to represent can gain a hearing in the news, producing a more vigorous and well-rounded debate. So, while institutionally driven discourse can invite the public to debate issues making their way along institutional avenues, event-driven discourse can raise attention to issues that may otherwise be overlooked by politicians and the constituencies they court. Event-driven news, in other words, can help us to examine problems that our formal political institutions alone may not. Moreover, event-driven news is often the mechanism—however imperfect and messy—by which officials are subjected to public scrutiny and their accountability to the public enforced.

But both types of discourse have their less attractive possibilities as well. Institutionally driven news can simply reproduce the narrow concerns and political machinations of politicians. Unless cued by serious official debate, institutionally driven problem construction will not necessarily be well rounded or include competing perspectives on public issues. Indeed, as the official-dominance model of the news maintains, news that is too closely indexed to the topics and perspectives that officials are willing to address is news that falls short of its democratic promise (Bennett 1990). At the same time, as Patterson (1994), Fallows (1997), and Cappella and Jamieson (1997) have shown, mainstream national news has become increasingly oriented toward the "game" of official politics. Institutionally driven news can, therefore, be shallow, cynical, and lacking in substance.

Event-driven news, on the other hand, is often sensationalized, hyperbolic, and overheated; at the least, it may be based on erroneous first impressions and irresistible but misleading metaphors. In the rush to "get the story" and to hold audience attention, events can take on greater significance than they may deserve and be defined in inaccurate ways. And in an effort to squeeze as much market value as possible from dramatic news events, news organizations can construct problems that are less the result of real analysis than of breathless instant commentary (observations that should hardly strike any reader as harsh in the post-Lewinsky era).

The key distinction between institutionally driven and event-driven policy news, therefore, is not necessarily the quality of problem definitions they produce. The distinction is useful, rather, because each type of discourse has its particular dynamics and implications for public problem construction and signals a different institutional role for the media in democratic politics. Recognizing event-driven problem definition as a unique and important political phenomenon is also important because it shows signs of increasing as the commercial pressures on mainstream news organizations intensify and the relative strength of competing norms within mainstream journalism shift. Officially staged routine events may be less dominant in the news today than when Molotch and Lester (1974) first identified them as the touchstone of daily news. As new media have exploded and tabloid media increasingly influence the content of the mainstream media, officials have lost some of the control over the news that they used to enjoy. Presidents, congressmen, mayors, and police chiefs are no longer quite as privileged in "asserting the importance and factual status of 'their' occurrences" (ibid., 108). As the battle among the media for market share of a steadily declining audience becomes more heated, the incentives increase for saturation coverage of dramatic news events, in the process sometimes creating full-blown public problems out of ambiguous or even trivial events.

Patterson's (1994) analysis of two decades of political news, for example, found the number of "urgent" stories increasing—stories billed by news organizations as crises of one sort or another. Likewise, Fallows (1997) cites an "endless stream" of artificially intensified "emergencies" in news coverage of the White House; indeed, he counted 30 such emergencies during the first two months of the Clinton presidency alone. As the media have become more inclined to designate situations as crises, they have become more adept at exploiting the news value of unexpected, nonroutine events—from Clinton's runway haircut to his Oval Office sexual exploits.

At the same time, there is growing evidence that the media have become more inclined to treat news events as jumping-off points for thematic exploration of social issues. One recent study of news spanning 100 years discovered that the focus of the daily news has shifted from covering the who, what, when, and where of discrete events to covering the issues underlying breaking news events. The authors conclude that "The basic recipe for news—the report of events new to the hearer— has acquired a third ingredient: For a story to qualify as news, journalists now supply a context of social problems, interpretation, and themes" (Barnhurst and Mutz 1997, 27). Indeed, they argue, "many things that happen to people, although novel, must now get ignored unless reporters can link them to something bigger" (51). Therefore, dramatic news events may increasingly be serving as invitations for the news media to grapple, however gracefully or clumsily, with political and social issues. Media scholars have often bemoaned the event-focused orientation of most news. As Patterson (1994, 180) observes, "By tradition, the news is found in particular events rather than the underlying forces in society that create them." But the dynamics of event-driven news explored here reveal that events can be the starting point—sometimes the only starting point—for news coverage of those underlying forces.

Therefore, it appears that the mass media today are more inclined to make considerable meaning out of "accidental" news events. These events—dramatized, serialized, and thematized by the media—can come to represent significant "problems" in the news and in the public mind, sometimes, though not necessarily, creating better understandings of those problems and what can be done to address them.

This trend toward event-driven problem definition should not be exaggerated. Institutionally driven problem construction remains a predominant mode of policymaking and public discourse. Officials are the primary definers of many public problems—from drug abuse to terrorism to communism, from health-care costs to welfare queens to balancing the budget. But accidental events happen, and they produce news dynamics less firmly pegged to official sources, news that allows journalists thematic license, news that offers opportunities to reshape the public definitions of problems we face as a society.

Research Strategy

The first phase of the research reported here aimed at generating a comprehensive overview of coverage of the issue of police use of force in both the *New York Times* (*NYT*) and the *Los Angeles Times* (*LAT*) across the period of 1985–94. Thus, the first round of data was gathered from both newspapers' indexes, which provide brief summaries of all news and editorial items appearing in the paper each year, organized by subject matter. All index entries pertaining to any aspect of police use of force—everything from brief mentions of use-of-force incidents to legislative debates about police weaponry—appearing under the heading "Police" in the *NYT* index and either "Police" or "Police Brutality" in the *LAT* index were coded (the *Los Angeles Times* index uses the heading "Police Brutality" to categorize some stories, but the *New York Times* index does not). Based on this method, 1,195 *NYT* index entries and 1,433 *LAT* index entries were compiled, out of approximately 3,900 total entries regarding U.S. police in the *New York Times* index, and approximately 4,100 total entries regarding U.S. police in the *Los Angeles Times* index. Each of these entries was coded according to the protocol exhibited in figure A.1 below.

These index entries were then used to construct a database of the 198 use-of-force incidents reported in the *NYT* and the 354 use-of-force incidents reported in the *LAT*. A profile of the coverage of each of these incidents was obtained by coding the information available in index items mentioning each incident. The protocol for this stage of coding is displayed in figure A.2 below. Much of the data displayed in tables and figures throughout the book are derived from this database. These data represent the universe of coverage of use-of-force incidents during this time period: inferential statistics are included in the text and figures from time to time for the reader's interest.

The third phase of the content analysis involved coding the full text of all news and editorial coverage of a sample of 114 use-of-force incidents (UFIs), 56 that were reported in the *NYT* and 58 that were reported in the *LAT*. These incidents received varying amounts of news coverage, totaling 423 news and editorial items, which were read and coded in their entirety. Text was downloaded from the Lexis-Nexis database.

A few considerations entered into the construction of this sample of incidents. Because a primary method of analysis in this study is to analyze differences in news coverage across subgroups of UFIs, based on the amount of news coverage they received, it was important to construct a sample that would neither over- nor under-sample from any one group. Therefore, I sought to construct a random sample of each subgroup rather than a random sample of the overall population of incidents. I also sought to construct samples of subgroups that would not equal more than 50 percent of the UFIs in that group and that would be roughly equal in terms of the proportion of cases sampled from each group and each newspaper. Therefore, roughly one-fourth of cases from each subgroup was selected at random.

The coding of full text items and of index entries was subjected to tests of intercoder reliability by having two different graduate student coders, neither of whom was familiar with the hypotheses of the research, code a sample of index entries and of full text items. Specific reliability scores for various coding tasks are reported in each chapter.

Finally, to supplement the content analysis, twelve lengthy, open-ended telephone interviews were conducted with crime reporters at the *New York Times* and the *Los Angeles Times*, as well as with other sources that could provide some insight on the police-reporter relationship (e.g., policing experts, police-media liaison officers, and police media consultants).

FIGURE A.I CODING PROTOCOL FOR *NEW YORK TIMES* AND *LOS ANGELES TIMES* INDEX ENTRIES

All *New York Times* and *Los Angeles Times* index entries pertaining to police use of force were coded according to the following protocol:

Variable name	Value
storynum	assign number to entry
date1	day/month
date2	month/year
placesec	1 = section I or A 0 = other
placepg	1 = page 1 0 = other
newsed	1 = news 0 = editorials, letters, columns
epthem*	1 = episodic 0 = mixed −1 = thematic
locnat	1 = local story 0 = other
off	1 = official mentioned 0 = no official mentioned
nonoff	1 = nonofficial mentioned (other than victims/suspects in use of force incidents) 0 = no nonofficial mentioned
noncrit	1 = activists, community leaders, community residents, academic experts mentioned 0 = no such sources mentioned
indvw	1 = individualizing claim mentioned 0 = no individualizing claim mentioned
sysvw	1 = systemic claim mentioned 0 = no systemic claim mentioned
casement	1 = particular UFI mentioned 0 = no particular UFI mentioned
case	suspect/victim name (string variable)
polact	1 = mention of policy action in a political institution or by institutional actors, or by candidates for political office 0 = no mention of such action
citizact	1 = mention of citizen political action (not including activities associated with filing complaints/charges) 0 = no mention of citizen political action

*The distinction between "episodic" and "thematic" news items is borrowed from Iyengar (1991) and modified somewhat for this analysis. The following index entries provide examples of each type of story focus:

Episodic: "Two Buena Park police officers shot and killed a man who led them on a short chase on July 3, 1994, and threatened employees at the Buena Park Mall with a handgun, authorities said." (*Los Angeles Times*, July 4, 1994)

Mixed: "Questions of double jeopardy are raised in second Rodney King trial; criminal justice system itself is seen on trial in Los Angeles, with one side arguing that Fed Govt must try to heal wounds left by Simi Valley acquittals and others maintaining that officers are caught in political witch hunt." (*New York Times*, February 19, 1993)

Thematic: "Clifton section of Staten Island, where Ernest Sayon died resisting arrest, is enclave of blacks and Hispanics whose trouble with economic hardship and crime seem to have followed them across Narrows to suburban-like borough; residents of Park Hill Apartments, which has reputation for drugs and prostitution, say they feel alienated from police and white community." (*New York Times*, May 1, 1994)

FIGURE A.2 PROTOCOL FOR COMPILING DATABASE OF USE-OF-FORCE INCIDENTS

A database of all UFIs reported in the *New York Times* and *Los Angeles Times* was constructed using the following protocol:

Variable name	Value
casename	string variable
locnat	1 = local case 0 = other
numstory	number of Index entries mentioning the case
frontpg	1 = any front-page coverage 0 = no front-page coverage
frontsec	1 = any I or A section coverage 0 = no I or A section coverage
thematic	1 = any thematic coverage (including mixed) 0 = no thematic coverage
vicrace	1 = victim/suspect described as minority (full text Nexis search to verify) 0 = victim/suspect not described as minority
vicgend	1 = victim/suspect described as female or female gender otherwise indicated 0 = victim/suspect described as male or male gender otherwise indicated
vicage	1 = victim/suspect described as under the age of 16, as an adolescent, as over the age of 60, or as a senior citizen 0 = victim/suspect not described as under the age of 16, as an adolescent, as over the age of 60, or as a senior citizen
viccrim	1 = victim/suspect described as having criminal record or engaged in criminal act 0 = victim/suspect not described as having criminal record or engaged in criminal act
typforce	1 = force other than beating or shooting described, or more than three officers participating 0 = no force other than beating or shooting described, and no more than three officers participating
vicdead	1 = victim/suspect described as dead 0 = victim/suspect not described as dead
video	1 = event reportedly videotaped 0 = event not reportedly videotaped
leglproc	1 = DA investigation, grand jury, criminal trial, or civil suit reported 0 = no DA investigation, grand jury, criminal trial, or civil suit reported
polact	1 = at least one item mentioning this UFI coded "1" on "polact" in first round of coding 0 = no stories coded "1" on "polact" in first round of coding
citizact	1 = at least one story mentioning this UFI coded "1" on "citizact" in first round of coding 0 = no stories coded "1" on "citizact" in first round of coding

FIGURE A.3 PROTOCOL FOR CODING FULL TEXT

News and editorial items covering a sample of UFIs (423 items total) were each coded according to the following protocol:

Variable name	Value
storynum	assign number to story
date	day/month/year
placesec	1 = section I or A 0 = other
placepg	1 = page 1 0 = other
jrnlist	reporter's name (news only) (string variable)
stolngth	length of story, by number of words
newsed	1 = news 0 = editorials, letters, columns
regnews	1 = home edition, not news brief (including editorials) 0 = nonhome edition story or news brief
epthem	1 = episodic 0 = mixed −1 = thematic
locnat	1 = local story 0 = nonlocal story
case	victim/suspect name (string variable)
caselink	0 = no other UFI mentioned 1 = other UFI mentioned
nonoff	1 = nonofficial source mentioned 0 = no nonofficial source mentioned
noncrit	1 = activists, community leaders, community residents, academic experts mentioned 0 = no such sources mentioned
nonhead	1 = mention of nonofficials in headline 0 = no mention of nonofficials in headline
nonlead	1 = mention of nonofficials in lead 0 = no mention of nonofficials in lead
typattr	type of attribution of nonofficial sources 1 = citizen as subject of action; no paraphrase or quote 2 = nonofficial paraphrased 3 = nonofficial directly quoted
sysvw	1 = systemic claim reported 0 = no systemic claim reported
syshd	1 = mention of systemic claim in headline 0 = no mention of systemic claim in headline
sysld	1 = mention of systemic claim in lead paragraphs 0 = no mention of systemic claim in lead paragraphs

FIGURE A.3 *(continued)*

Variable name	Value
polact	1 = mention of response by a political institution, officials, or candidates for political office 0 = no mention of such action
citizact	1 = mention of citizen political action (not including activities associated with filing complaints/charges) 0 = no mention of citizen political action

Notes

1. MEDIATING REALITIES

1. I adopt the "contextual" rather than the "strict" constructionist perspective on social problems in general and police brutality in particular. Contextual constructionism, as defined by Best (1993), utilizes social-construction theory as a means to better understand phenomena in the empirical world—that is, the success of some claims and the failure of others—without going so far as dismissing the facticity of all claims or refusing to make one's own claims about reality. However, I attempt in this study to remain agnostic regarding the "truth" of various claims about the prevalence of police brutality. The point of this study is not primarily to establish whether there are or have been brutality problems in particular locales at particular times but rather to understand when brutality is presented in the news as a possible problem and why.

2. This definition of a "public problem" follows that offered by Kingdon (1995, 90–115). Problems have been defined similarly by other scholars as "situations that are experienced by people as painful [which] become matters for public activity and targets for public action" (Gusfield 1981, 3), or simply as "troubling conditions that persist" and that are not "accepted as inevitable or unproblematic" (Edelman 1988, 12).

3. I use the term "journalists" broadly here to designate all those involved in the production of news, including not only reporters but their editors; though I often employ the term for the sake of simplicity, I always intend that "journalists" be understood as members of news organizations more than as individual actors. It is the collective behavior of journalists in constructing the news and the collective behavior of news organizations in the political arena, more than the behavior of individual reporters and editors, that is of interest here.

4. Variations on this more dynamic and less officially dominated view of the

news have been suggested by scholars such as Patterson (1994), Schlesinger (1990), and Wolfsfeld (1997).

5. For the sake of simplicity, under the term "accidental event" I include several kinds of events that Molotch and Lester (1974) distinguish from "accidents." "Scandals," in their formulation, are public events arising out of activities purposely undertaken but not intended for public consumption (such as the official who sexually harasses a co-worker and then is found out by the media); terrorist attacks are a type of event they label as a "disruptive routine event"— a characterization that begins to cloud the distinctions among these categories. In my formulation, the term "accidental" stands for any unexpected news event that is not the "purposive accomplishment of elites." "Accidental" may thus refer to an event's status as a public event (an event that is either not intended to occur or not intended for public consumption) or to the channels through which an event arises (off the beaten path of standard news gathering).

6. See the appendix for further details about methodology.

7. That newspaper coverage can be systematically analyzed more easily than television coverage offers a further advantage. The content of all newspapers analyzed here is catalogued in the Lexis-Nexis database, making data retrieval and analysis for a long historical time period more feasible than for a comparable analysis of television news.

8. Police departments generally retain tight control of such records for a variety of reasons, including legal restrictions arising from police-union contracts, ongoing litigation against the department, or both. Consequently, researchers are generally not allowed full access to such records. Indeed, in his recent book on police abuse, Chevigny (1995) was unable to obtain most of his data directly from the NYPD or the LAPD but instead relied upon information available from independent monitoring agencies, from attorneys seeking to prosecute police, and from the media (Chevigny 1996). Moreover, in the view of William Geller, an experienced researcher with the Police Executive Research Forum and co-author of a major study on police use of deadly force, obtaining systematic police records for an adequate sample of police use-of-force incidents would simply be "unprecedented" (Geller 1997). I contacted both the NYPD and the LAPD, inquiring about the public availability of records regarding police use of force, and was told that I could submit written requests for information pertaining to individual cases. The number of cases analyzed in this study (over 550) obviously precludes pursuing this line of inquiry for the full sample of cases analyzed here. Moreover, even if they release pertinent records, the departments retain control over what kinds of information these records include. For reasons discussed further in chapter 2, therefore, police records are not necessarily an objective or reliable starting place for analyzing police use of force.

2. MAKING A PROBLEM OF BRUTALITY

1. Distinguishing between "police use of force" and "police brutality" is both extremely important and quite difficult; see the discussion below for the definitions that will be employed here.

2. One indication of this ambiguity is that police generally fear the "second-guessing" that almost inevitably accompanies any use of significant or deadly force that is made public. One San Antonio police officer who shot a man in 1982, for example, said that his first reaction after firing the fatal shot was fear of how his superiors would interpret his use of force, especially as his assailant was found to have been carrying only a can of spray paint and a sharpened stick. He also recalled with some bitterness the local newspaper's headline the following day: "Officer Slays Man Holding Stick" (Mangum 1995).

3. Former LAPD Chief Daryl Gates expressed this view perhaps more openly than most when he defended giving his officers latitude in the use of force: "If I think they were doing their very best to deal with a tough situation, and they used some force, and perhaps they got the last whack in . . . , [it can be] tough to distinguish whether the last whack was necessary. I give them the benefit of the doubt. I think they deserve it" (quoted in Shah 1991, 60).

Since Gates gained an ugly reputation for condoning brutality, using his words here may seem to unfairly tar all police officials with Gates's brush. While attitudes about the use of force undoubtedly vary across departments and police chiefs, most police most of the time do tend to believe that the use of force is essential to the job of policing and that the general public cannot accurately evaluate its appropriate use. In fact, the Mollen Commission found in many New York City precincts that police—from street cop to brass—generally tolerated what others would label police brutality. "Unlike serious corruption, which most cops outwardly tolerate but inwardly deplore and resent," the commission reported, "officers seem fairly tolerant—both outwardly and inwardly—of occasional police brutality. While most officers are genuinely sickened by . . . extreme brutality . . . , many do not seem to believe that anything is really wrong with a few blows and bruises now and then" (Mollen 1994, 49).

4. In general, the public often does give police the benefit of the doubt. Survey data indicate that the public is highly supportive, at least in the abstract, of police officers' discretion concerning the use of force. The General Social Survey has asked people since the 1970s whether "there are any situations in which you would approve of a policeman striking an adult male citizen." On average, 72 percent of respondents have answered "yes," with very little fluctuation across time (*General Social Survey Cumulative Codebook* [National Opinion Research Center, University of Chicago, 1994]). The single significant fluctuation appears to have been a temporary decline after the Rodney King incident in 1991. The percentage agreeing that there are situations in which they would approve of police striking an adult declined from 77 percent to 67 percent of white respondents, and from 48 percent to 36 percent of black respondents (Sigelman et al. 1997). The percentages have since returned to roughly their pre-1991 level.

As these data suggest, the benefit of the doubt extended to police is not unlimited. In a recent Gallup poll, 80 percent of respondents disagreed with the statement that "It is wrong to second-guess [police] by prosecuting or punishing them for wrongdoing which occurs in the course of their job performance" (Gillespie 1999). Other research has indicated that blacks are less likely than whites to support police discretion to use deadly force (Cullen et al. 1996); the same Gallup poll found that 21 percent of nonwhites, versus 5 percent of whites, believe that police officers in their community use their guns too frequently.

5. Of course, these attitudes may have been based as much on personal experiences or experiences of friends, family, and associates as on the King video. While irrefutable statistical evidence about the frequency of brutality in minority communities is not often available (as discussed below), evidence does indicate that minorities are more likely to be subjected to police use of force, particularly deadly force. Indeed, "virtually all of the studies that have examined the race of civilian victims of shootings by the police have shown that blacks are shot in numbers significantly disproportionate to their proportion of the local population" (Geller and Scott 1992, 147).

6. Indeed, because the filing of incidence reports is the job of individual officers making arrests, any information police departments may have on the frequency of physical altercations not involving deadly force or the discharge of firearms is often entirely dependent upon the information provided by police officers themselves. See Geller and Scott (1992), chapter 2, for a thorough review of the limitations of available data on police use of deadly force.

7. The Justice Department pledged, in the aftermath of the Rodney King beating, that it would begin to compile such a database. It did complete, in 1991, a review of 15,000 complaints of police misconduct received by its Civil Rights Division over the previous six years. The study, which was not made public until the civil unrest in Los Angeles in 1992 again brought the issue of brutality to the fore, concluded that no "statistically significant patterns of police misconduct" were discernible across the agencies examined (U.S. Congress, House, 1992, 101). It is worth noting that, as Skolnick and Fyfe (1993, 212–13) observe, the study ignored a simple conclusion suggested by the data: "a pattern in which some cities accounted for an inordinate number of complaints," suggesting that some police departments are more brutal than others. The 1994 Omnibus Crime Bill included a provision mandating that the Justice Department begin compiling a database on excessive force; in response, the Bureau of the Census has begun including questions about police-citizen contacts in its annual victimization survey. The results of the latest Police-Public Contact Survey were reported in November 1997. This survey of 6,000 randomly sampled Americans found that less than 1 percent (fourteen) of the respondents claimed to have been subjected to police use of force, with a majority of those agreeing with the survey question that "some of their own actions, such as threatening the police or resisting being handcuffed, may have provoked police" (Greenfeld, Langan, and Smith 1997, v). Due to the random nature of the sample and the minimal data collected, however, little in this survey sheds light on patterns of police use of force in different geographic areas or against different types of people (ibid.). Even this limited effort to collect national data on excessive force may not continue, as the bureau reported that no funds had been appropriated or sought for the subsequent fiscal year.

8. However, the number of persons filing untrue complaints may well be offset by the number of people who lack the resources or temerity to file a complaint. Police brutality expert Jerome Skolnick has argued that,

Just as rape is underreported, so is police brutality—and for similar reasons. Excessive-force victims may fear retaliation by their police assailant and his or her fellow officers. And as in rape cases, it is the brutality victim's word against the perpetrator's. Like the sexually active rape victim, the brutality victim who is an ex-con . . . often assumes that he will lose in a swearing contest against a cop—and he is usually right. (Skolnick 1991, 41)

9. For instance, the San Francisco Police Department registered more citizen complaints in 1990 than did the Los Angeles Police Department, though San Francisco had 2,000 officers and the LAPD 8,000. However, San Francisco also had a more independent civilian review process than Los Angeles, and this may have encouraged more complaints—or discouraged fewer—than the system in Los Angeles (ACLU 1992).

10. Journalists with the *Washington Post* discovered these data limitations when they attempted to assess whether the rate of police shootings in their city was higher than that of other cities. It took four reporters assisted by two researchers eight months to piece together enough data to draw defensible conclusions; "as the project progressed," one reports, "we decided against relying on the FBI's justifiable homicide records to calculate police killings, both those in D.C. and those we compared with the District." Instead, the *Post* combined FBI data with U.S. Census data, data provided by the National Institute for Computer-Assisted Reporting, and data from its own survey of police departments (Craven 1999).

11. As former Minneapolis police chief Anthony Bouza has said, when a police chief is called "at 3:30 in the morning and told, 'Chief, one of our cops has just shot a kid,' the chief's first questions are: 'What color is the cop? What color is the kid?' " If the answers are white, and black, respectively, Bouza said, "He gets dressed" (quoted in Geller and Scott 1992, 1).

12. The shooting of Jose Garcia is discussed further in chapter 6.

13. Chermak (1994), for example, finds that in news coverage provided by six newspapers and three television stations across the country, approximately 11 percent of all news items were about crime, making crime the fourth largest category of news, behind sports, business, and general interest stories. When sports and business were excluded, crime comprised 16 percent of all remaining news items. The newspapers contained an average of nine crime stories per day, and the television stations produced an average of four per day. Chermak also finds that police performance was evaluated in less than 4 percent of crime stories (115).

14. My use of the term "use-of-force incident" serves the purpose of describing coercive police actions without evaluating the motives of the officers involved or the appropriateness of their actions. The term "use of force" allows me to discuss news representations of these activities without passing judgment on whether police actions in any particular incident were necessary, proper, or motivated by good faith or bad. The use-of-force incident involving motorist Rodney King, which will be mentioned often in this study, is referred to here as both an "incident" and by its more familiar label: "the Rodney King beating." Regarding the persons subjected to police use of force, when I do not use that awkward and lengthy phrase, I alternate between the terms "suspect" and "al-

leged victim." This is to acknowledge that the persons subjected to police use of force are often involved in criminal or threatening activities but not always (for example, people may be "roughed up" by police simply for verbally challenging officers' authority or insisting that police adhere to legal procedures for conducting arrests and searches). Alternating these terms also serves to acknowledge that some of these people see themselves—or are seen by others—as victims of illegitimate police behavior. The reader should also note that the use-of-force incidents analyzed here overwhelmingly involved police using force against civilians; a handful of the cases involved police beating or shooting other police officers, either accidentally (so-called friendly fire situations) or purposefully (as when undercover officers were not recognized as police officers).

15. These figures reflect police shootings that were reported in each newspaper's index; see discussion of methodology in the appendix.

16. There are several likely reasons that most use-of-force incidents never become news. Most basic is the fact that reporters simply never learn about most of them, and an unknown number of incidents they do learn of probably do not fit journalistic notions of newsworthiness or do not offer the kinds of "story cues" described in chapter 5. This screening process by which some potential news events become nonevents is, unfortunately, difficult to study, especially given that police records of individual use-of-force incidents are not made available to the public, as discussed above.

3. NORMALIZING COERCION

1. Readers familiar with the work of Deborah Stone (1989) will recognize similarities between her theory of "causal stories" and the system I construct here for categorizing discourse about police use of force. While I owe a clear intellectual debt to Stone's thinking, her typology of causal stories does not work particularly well for analyzing discourse about police use of force because the primary rhetorical struggle over use-of-force incidents fundamentally involves questions of whether police have acted *appropriately*. Thus, the main axes of debate are not whether the cause of an incident was "accidental" or "inadvertent," for example, but rather if an *intentional* incident was precipitated by a suspect or by police. In those few cases where police are defined as the precipitators of violence (rather than as merely reacting to the violence or defiance of a suspect), the debate then focuses on what causes police to use excessive force.

Readers familiar with the work of Herbert Packer will recognize a similarity between what I call "individualized" versus "systemic" views of police use of force, and Packer's "two models of the criminal justice system." Packer contrasts a pyramidal view of criminal justice, in which police discretion at the street level is crucial to accomplishing legitimate crime-control objectives (a model which underpins the "individualizing" claims about police use of force generally offered by officials), with an inverted-pyramid view in which police discretion must be constrained in order to protect due process rights (a model which sometimes underpins the "systemic" claims of police critics and antibrutality activists). See Packer (1968).

2. The woman, a black transient, was shot 18 times.

3. The death of the 19-year-old college student, by compression of the neck during restraint, was ruled a homicide by the Los Angeles County coroner.

4. The officer quoted here was discharged after he allegedly kicked a drunken man in the groin, struck him in the ribs with his baton, and sprayed mace in his face. The officers on the scene asserted that the man's wife was inciting others present to shoot them.

5. Washington, D.C., police Sgt. Chris Archer (1996) has argued that officers are undertrained in many U.S. police departments. Therefore, although they are taught to escalate their level of coercion only as far along the "continuum of force" as necessary to control a suspect's resistance, they lack adequate training in *how* to do so. Consequently, according to Archer, many police-citizen encounters escalate needlessly into violence.

6. The same point is made by a former LAPD detective quoted in Skolnick and Fyfe (1993, 8), who claims that many arrest records are enhanced with invented or deleted facts in order to construct the preferred version of events.

7. The phenomenon of the cover charge has been noted by a variety of observers. The Mollen Commission, which investigated the New York City Police Department in 1994, reported that "When cops come to the stationhouse with a visibly beaten suspect, supervisors, we were repeatedly told, often do not question the story they hear [from the arresting officers]. And the story, or 'cover' as some put it, is fairly standard: resisting arrest" (Mollen 1994, 49). An Orange County assistant district attorney told a reporter in 1991 that "We'll see them with black eyes and bruises and then look at the police report, where it says 'necessary force was used and the person had to be taken to the hospital.' That's code for: 'We beat 'em up' " (Lichtblau and Johnson 1991). And an attorney who represents brutality victims for the New York Civil Liberties Union told another reporter that "The cops call it sending them down The ROAD: Resisting arrest, Obstruction of justice, Assault and Disorderly conduct": the four crimes with which brutality victims are most often charged (Kocieniewski and Levitt 1991). Of course, police officers are well aware that their narratives will generally hold sway with their bosses, the courts, and the media. As one officer allegedly told a Los Angeles family during a raid on their home, according to court records, "I could blow your (obscenity) head off right here and nobody can prove you did not try to do something" (Weinstein 1991).

8. Similarly, a commission charged with investigating police use of force in New York in the mid-1980s found "much evidence of low-level abuse," including the use of racial epithets. But the commission maintained that the use of deadly force was not a systemic problem, reporting that New York state law-enforcement officers generally showed restraint in their use of deadly force and that race was not a significant factor in police shootings (Barron 1987).

9. According to the same news article, "El Cajon police initially said Geiger was shot when he refused to surrender, but on Wednesday they revised their version of the incident, saying he was shot accidentally while resisting arrest."

10. Daniels was shot by police officers a month after the 1992 Los Angeles riots. The shooting touched off an angry impromptu demonstration; the officer stood trial for murder in 1993, the first such trial in Los Angeles County in over

a decade. The prosecution argued that Daniels was shot for no reason other than that he "affronted" the officer.

11. The kinds of claims made by victims of alleged brutality are constrained by legal norms, for only some kinds of claims are recognized by courts as valid and by lawyers as strategically viable. For example, the argument that local political officials are responsible for a problem of brutality is legally valid only if proof can be provided that a department's official policy encouraged or tolerated unconstitutional actions by officers. Aside from this specialized claim, which can be difficult to sustain, federal law permits the filing of civil suits only against individual officers, not against the departments or governments they work for (see U.S. Congress, House, 1992, testimony of Jon O. Nelson).

12. The commission contended that "The LAPD has a number of tools . . . to promote and enforce its policy that only reasonable and necessary force be used by officers. . . . The commission believes that the department has not made sufficient efforts to use these tools effectively to address the significant number of officers who appear to be using force excessively and improperly."

13. To obtain a broad picture of the prominence of different kinds of voices and views in the news, I analyzed the index entries for ten years' worth of *New York Times (NYT)* and *Los Angeles Times (LAT)* coverage. Index entries are brief summaries of all news and editorial items published by a newspaper, compiled monthly. Index entries reflect the central action of each news item and identify the key actors in the story; in general, they mirror the lead paragraphs of news items and convey the main argument of editorials, op-ed pieces, and letters to the editor. Index entries provide a good source of data regarding the prominence of various sources in the news and can be used by researchers to "reproduce the broad contours of policy debate" (Althaus et al. 1998). Therefore, I will refer to claims appearing in the index entries as "prominent" claims. Of course, "prominence" should be understood in relative terms, since index entries are only story summaries and cannot reflect all the sources that may be mentioned in the full text of a news story.

Each *NYT* and *LAT* index entry regarding police use of force was coded as to whether it mentioned official sources, nonofficial sources, individualizing claims, or systemic claims. All coding reported here was done by the author; samples of coded items were submitted to two graduate student coders to test inter-coder reliability; inter-coder agreement of 90 percent was established. One-sample t-tests show the difference in both newspapers between the proportion of items mentioning official sources and the proportion mentioning critical nonofficial sources to be statistically significant (p < .01); the same is true of differences in the proportions mentioning individualizing and systemic claims.

14. Since index entries are only summaries of news items, they do not always indicate the full range of sources and views that may appear in the news. Therefore, these data about claims found in the news are based on analysis of the full text of all news and editorial items about a randomly-selected sample of use-of-force incidents. Coverage of 56 incidents in the *NYT* and 58 in the *LAT*—a total of 423 news and editorial items—was coded, using the same coding scheme used to code the index entries. Agreement among coders was 92 percent on full text items.

15. The distinction between "episodic" and "thematic" news items is borrowed from Iyengar (1991) and modified somewhat for this analysis. Thematic reporting links events, examines broader social phenomena, and more explicitly seeks to explain or contextualize events. The typical episodic news item is event-bound, examining only one event and/or its immediate impact on other events, persons, or institutions. The typical thematic story, in contrast, moves beyond specific events to discuss issues in more abstract or conceptual terms and is less time-bound than episodic stories, which tend to focus on "what happened today." Items coded "episodic" in this study included reports of use-of-force incidents, reports about developments in their aftermath (e.g., the filing of charges; the beginning of a trial), as well as reports of other discrete events having to do with police use of force (e.g., legislative hearings on police policies; court rulings regarding police policies). Items that looked at police use of force or police brutality in the broader terms described here were coded "thematic."

16. The data in figure 1 are based upon the coding of index entries described above. Index entries are not perfect measures of the exact number of times any one incident is mentioned in each newspaper, because events are sometimes mentioned in passing in the full text of news stories in ways that are not picked up in the index. Index entries do provide, however, a relatively accurate assessment of the *comparative* newsworthiness of various news events.

17. As reported above, critical nonofficials were prominent in only 19 percent of *NYT* and 17 percent of *LAT* index entries. They appeared in a larger percentage of stories when read in full—43 percent of *NYT* and 25 percent of *LAT* stories mentioned these kinds of sources. But in only 29 percent of the full-text *NYT* articles analyzed here and 21 percent of *LAT* articles were critical nonofficial sources actually quoted in their own words, as opposed to being either simply mentioned or paraphrased.

18. These figures are derived from the full text data. The figures are similar for the *Los Angeles Times*: While 19 percent of items citing no critical nonofficials mentioned systemic claims, 29 percent of items citing critical nonofficials also mentioned systemic claims. The differences regarding critical nonofficials are statistically significant for both newspapers (p < .01).

19. The Mollen Commission which investigated the NYPD in 1994 found that brutality

> occurred . . . to show power, out of fear and hostility towards a person or the community that person represents, to vent frustrations and anger, or in a misplaced attempt to compel respect in the community. Officers also told us that it was not uncommon to see unnecessary force used to administer an officer's own brand of street justice: a nightstick in the ribs, a fist to the head, to demonstrate who was in charge of the crime-ridden streets they patrolled and to impose sanctions on those who 'deserved it' as officers, not juries, determined. As was true of other forms of wrongdoing, some cops believe they are doing what is morally correct—though 'technically unlawful'—when they beat someone who they believe is guilty and who they believe the criminal justice system will never punish. (Mollen 1994, 47)

20. One exception to this general rule is that of former NYPD officer and current sociologist James Fyfe, who has authored numerous works on policing

and police violence. Fyfe seems to have gained a place on the "golden rolodex" of newspaper reporters, appearing in many of the news items analyzed in this study which did include a critical academic view.

21. Ericson and his co-authors found several motivations for this new openness on the part of Canadian police: changes in management philosophy; a sense of public responsibility; a perceived need to "sell" the police department to maintain fiscal resources; a perceived need to avoid the image of having something to hide; and a belief that building cooperative relationships with journalists would lead to favors, such as voluntary self-censorship, in the future (Ericson, Baranek, and Chan 1989, 96). It appears that American police departments have become more "media savvy" for many of the same reasons. In departments embracing a "community policing" approach, for example, the perceived need to create a more "open" image for the department can lead to efforts to improve media relations.

22. As the chief of one sheriff's association said in a letter to former Judiciary Committee Chairman senator Joseph Biden, such groups "incite the community" against the police (Weinstein and Hall 1994), endangering police officers and making policing that much more difficult. As one police officer told a *Los Angeles Times* reporter in the aftermath of the Rodney King beating, "You ought to go out into the street and talk to some of the coppers out there. . . . Because I get the impression that some officers are really feeling a tremendous amount of stress and pressure with every contact they make with the public" (Serrano 1991a).

23. In one notable exception, one *Los Angeles Times* reporter told me that his stories about police use-of-force incidents almost never come from his contacts within the LAPD. Rather, he said, people who claim to have been victimized by police, or lawyers working for alleged victims, are his primary sources for such stories (Newton 1997). In part, this difference appears to stem from his position as a well-placed and well-respected reporter who has won from his editors considerable autonomy to pursue stories of interest to him; and in part it stems from the fact that he assumed that position in the aftermath of the Rodney King beating. As a result, he told me, people seem more willing to contact reporters with allegations of police abuse. Notably, however, this reporter also said he would "always" talk to police sources before writing a story about a use-of-force incident.

24. The political power of police and their unions is further illustrated by the passage in 1994 of a bill for which the NYPD union, the Patrolmen's Benevolent Association, was the sole lobbying group. The bill removed from the police commissioner powers to discipline officers involved in misconduct; tellingly, the bill passed the state legislature in the *aftermath* of a major corruption scandal that rocked the NYPD and filled headlines for months (Sexton 1994).

25. In choosing the phrase "media professionalism," I do not mean to imply that norms associated with commercialism or reformism, explored in later chapters, are somehow "unprofessional." Nor do I mean to ignore the fact that journalistic professionalism, as understood by journalists, includes many dimensions, like the careful documenting of information; it even includes, according to common usage in the profession, exactly the opposite of what I am

contending, for journalists often critique other journalists for a lack of professionalism when they fail to exhibit independence from powerful sources. Conscientious reporters generally consider it unprofessional to jump on any bandwagon, or slavishly to adopt the perspective of any particular societal group in their reporting. In practice, however, that type of professionalism is more carefully adhered to with regard to certain kinds of news sources and certain kinds of topics than others. Put simply, mainstream journalists more readily label as "unprofessional" news stories that uncritically convey the complaints of alleged brutality victims or antibrutality activists than news stories that uncritically convey the narratives and claims of police spokesmen. I wish to highlight the fact that journalistic understandings of professionalism hinge particularly on the "responsible" exercise of power.

26. Survey researchers have traced a steady decline in Americans' faith in the objectivity of the news media. A Pew Center poll conducted in 1999 found that the percentage of respondents agreeing that the media are "politically biased" increased from 45 to 56 percent since 1985, while the percentage believing the media are "careful not to be biased" decreased from 36 to 31 percent (Pew Center 1999). A 1994 cross-national poll found, paradoxically, that while nearly 70 percent of Americans found newspapers "believable" and even higher proportions said that of television, the primary criticism most Americans lodged against the news media was its "lack of objectivity" (Meisler 1994).

27. While Ochs's statement, made in 1931, might seem too dated to provide insight into contemporary journalistic norms, the *Columbia Journalism Review* featured it in a 1996 publisher's note. The *Review* introduced Ochs's words by observing that, "The ethos of journalism. . . . informs the work of all journalists who would call themselves professionals, and it is the commitment that inspires this magazine."

28. Another anecdote suggests that this way of thinking about sources' legitimacy extends beyond reporters at the *Times*. Antibrutality activist Don Jackson has related the story of being on the scene of the Dalton Avenue drug sweep in South Central Los Angeles in 1988, a high-profile case in which Los Angeles police engaged in extensive vandalism, and, according to a suit brought by residents, brutality. According to Jackson, a television reporter on the scene exclaimed, "But look at these people—they're all drug-heads." Though one rifle, 18.6 grams of rock cocaine and five ounces of marijuana were seized in the raid, and thirty-three people were arrested, the only narcotics possession charges brought were against two teen-agers who did not live in the apartments raided (Jackson 1997; Sahagun 1991).

29. Data are compiled from the *General Social Survey Cumulative Codebook* (National Opinion Research Center, University of Chicago, 1994).

4. SETTING THE AGENDA

1. What any of these institutions may have been able to do about Gates's policing policies is unclear, because all lacked the authority, under the city charter, to discipline or fire him—a fact that became a major element in the problem-definition process following the Rodney King beating.

2. Mayor Bradley moved only rarely and tentatively against Gates prior to the King beating. In June 1990, Bradley ordered the Police Commission to investigate police actions in subduing a janitors' strike at Century City, during which about two dozen people were injured. In September 1990, Gates testified to the Senate Judiciary Committee that casual drug users "should be taken out and shot." The comment received considerable local and national news coverage, and Bradley responded by appointing two political allies to the Police Commission. This action was also prodded, observers believe, by evidence that the LAPD had devoted considerable man-hours to gathering evidence for the defense of officers accused of vandalism in a drug raid on an apartment building at 39th and Dalton Avenue and by evidence that some members of the Police Commission had willfully looked the other way on the Dalton case (Domanick 1994, 357–58).

3. The jury in the civil trial awarded the Larez family $260,000, including $90,000 in punitive damages, which they ordered Gates to pay out of his own pocket. The city council voted to pay the damages out of city funds, but a federal appellate court later threw out the punitive damages altogether.

4. These figures are based on coding of *Los Angeles Times Index* entries. See chapter 3, note 13.

5. The story reported that because of increased political pressure and improved training, police killings of African Americans had dropped by 50 percent since the 1970s.

6. The suit named as defendants not only the 80-odd officers who carried out the raid but their supervisors, Chief Daryl Gates, Mayor Tom Bradley, and other local officials. It alleged that the damage done "was the result of the policy of gang sweeps, which has been implemented by the city of Los Angeles, by Mayor Bradley, by Chief of Police Daryl Gates" (Freed 1989, sec. 2, p. 1).

7. That reporters from the *Times* could have accessed the residents' allegations much sooner is evidenced by coverage in the *Los Angeles Sentinel*, a local black-owned newspaper. In contrast to the *Times'* coverage, the *Sentinel* immediately reported in great detail residents' claims that they had been beaten, left handcuffed for hours, and made to whistle the tune from Andy Griffith—all details that eventually came out in the *Times* (Lawrence 1996b). Moreover, one witness to the scene, local activist Don Jackson, told me that at least one television reporter was on the scene when the Dalton story broke (Jackson 1997), indicating that mainstream reporters had access to the residents' views.

8. For example, an op-ed by freelance journalist Joe Domanick cited the Dalton Avenue raid as an example of a police department unconstrained by accountability to the public:

> The reluctance of the mayor, City Council and Los Angeles County Board of Supervisors to speak up on these matters is, to be sure, rooted in the special autonomy enjoyed by both the police chief and the sheriff, and in the historically conservative political nature of Southern California. . . . It has also to do with the benign neglect of a mayor, City Council and Board of Supervisors who watched South Central and other areas fester and erupt in terrible gang violence, then told the cops to get in there and do something about it. Police accountability—always on shaky ground here—has once again gotten lost in the shuffle. (Domanick 1990, B5)

9. The data reported in figure 3 are based on the coding of *Los Angeles Times Index* entries. The coding scheme used here was the same as that reported in chapter 3; see the appendix for details. It bears repeating here that index entries are imperfect indicators of the exact number of nonofficial voices and systemic claims appearing in the news. Therefore, the data in figure 3 are best viewed as comparative data on the relative prominence of such voices and claims over time.

10. For example, in 1988 San Bernardino sheriffs' deputies were videotaped striking and kicking five Mexican citizens at a party. The video, shot by a neighbor and made public by Latino activists, led to a criminal suit in which a jury awarded the men $1 million (the award subsequently was reduced by a judge). The arrest of Kevin Dunbar, a white homeless man, was videotaped and released to news stations in 1990. The tape appeared to show a Laguna Beach police officer kicking Dunbar in the face, though the view was obscured by a police car. Dunbar sued the department and the city for $10 million; in the largest settlement in Orange County history to that date, the city subsequently offered Dunbar $100,000. Neither of these cases became very big news at the *Los Angeles Times*: the "Victorville 5" case was mentioned in six stories over two years; Dunbar's case was mentioned in only two stories in 1990, the year it occurred, and in 32 stories in 1991, though all but one of these were in the Orange County rather than the Home edition of the paper. One southern California videotaped case that became a major news event, the case of Don Jackson, is discussed below; the impact of videotaping on both *Los Angeles Times* and *New York Times* coverage in general is discussed further in chapter 5.

11. At the criminal trial, the defense claimed that most of Rodney King's head and facial injuries occurred from his initial fall to the pavement; where this first blow actually hit King remains disputed. The expert in police use of force who testified on behalf of the prosecution asserted that this first blow was in self-defense and fully justifiable (Parloff 1992, 78).

12. California Highway Patrol officer Melanie Singer testified that some of these blows hit King in the face, which would have violated LAPD policy. According to Parloff (1992, 79), this testimony is inconsistent with other testimony, with the medical evidence, and with what is discernible in the videotape. In any case, as Parloff points out, the bulk of King's injuries were sustained during this initial portion of the beating, the portion that was hardest for the jury in the criminal trial to second-guess.

13. The in-focus portion of the video shows Powell hitting King 27 times and Wind delivering 15 baton blows along with five kicks to King's upper body. Parloff (1992) essentially agrees with one juror who had commented to reporters after the criminal trial in 1992 that King had been in full control of the situation. "King could have avoided or stopped the beating by assuming a prone position.... Every time King assumed that position, the beating stopped" (Parloff 1992, 80). Responding to Sergeant Stacy Koon's comment to a reporter that during the altercation King kept rising off the ground like "a Bobo doll," journalist Joe Domanick observed, "Of course, Rodney King *was* popping up and down like a Bobo doll. What could Koon or anyone else ex-

pect? People are tied down when they're whipped. That's the way the human body reacts when it's hit" (Domanick 1994, 374).

14. The defense in the criminal trial countered the apparently clear narrative offered by the video by "deconstructing" it frame by frame, allowing them to make the official story—that King was responsible for his own beating—more compelling. The defense asserted that Officers Powell and Wind regularly stopped hitting King in order to evaluate his response, and that every time King further resisted arrest, the blows resumed.

15. In fact, a total of 27 police officers were on the scene, 23 from the LAPD and four from the California Highway Patrol.

16. Moreover, the police narrative clashed with the accounts of civilian witnesses on the scene who told reporters that King had not resisted arrest. As one initial *Los Angeles Times* story put it, "Witnesses said King was already lying on the ground when a police officer shot him with a stun gun, delivering an electrical shock of 50,000 volts. Officers then clubbed him wildly. There was a brief lull and King lay silent until one officer stomped on his head" (Wood and Fiore 1991, A1).

17. One message recorded in the transcripts described the scene of a domestic dispute involving African Americans to which officers had responded that evening as being "right out of 'Gorillas in the Mist.' " The squad car that received the message responded: "HaHaHaHa. Let me guess who be the parties." The transcripts also suggested that the violence visited on Rodney King was not quite an aberration, as in this exchange between Sergeant Stacy Koon and a watch commander:

> *Koon:* You just had a big time use of force . . . tased and beat the suspect of CHP pursuit, big time.
> *Officer at desk:* Oh well . . . I'm sure the lizard didn't deserve it . . . HAHA I'll let them know, O.K.

In addition, one message recorded from the patrol car of Laurence Powell and Timothy Wind, two of the four officers that eventually stood trial for the beating, said, "I haven't beaten anyone this bad in a long time" (Wood and Stohlberg, 1991, A1).

18. That Bradley waited a full month before publicly calling for Gates to resign reflects both his own characteristically cautious style and the fact that he lacked the power to actually remove Gates from office. Thus, Bradley had to wait for public pressure to peak before essentially asking Gates to leave office. Indeed, roughly two weeks earlier, Bradley had told reporters that the only way for the LAPD and the city to resolve the crisis generated by the King beating would be for Gates to "remove himself" from office, but he had cast his remark as a suggestion, not an official pronouncement. Bradley's action on April 1 was followed by more serious political conflict when, three days later, the Police Commission announced it was placing Gates on temporary leave. Two days later, the City Council voted to reinstate Gates, setting off a court battle over the city's proper chain of command.

19. Later *Los Angeles Times* polling more closely indexed the public voice to official action but also contributed to the expansion of official conflict. On

March 20, the day after the release of the police radio transcripts was reported, the *Los Angeles Times* conducted another poll. It found that a third of Angelenos now thought Gates should resign immediately, and a majority believed that Gates was substantially responsible for the beating. The paper also asked again if racist feelings were common among police officers; this time, two-thirds of respondents said they were. Thus on March 22, one day before the first nonminority elected officials (three California Congressmen, including Henry Waxman) would directly call for Gates's resignation, prompting Bradley's open call one week later, the *Los Angeles Times* reported that this option would have considerable public support.

20. For example, Ryan's (1991, 224) model of potential "upward spirals" in media coverage of activists' concerns does not include a potentially crucial variable—the spontaneous appearance of dramatic news events that resonate with claims activists are trying to raise. The model places full responsibility for making an issue "hot" on activists increasing their level of activities. Certainly well-organized and committed activism is a crucial variable in the construction of many public problems in the news, especially those that officials wish to ward off. But, arguably, journalists' assessments of the newsworthiness of activists' claims are driven as much or more by the context provided by current events dominating the news pages as by activists' own efforts.

21. Activist groups became primary definers of the King beating, but they were not exclusive definers. The *Los Angeles Times* (particularly on its editorial pages) provided a forum not only for the LAPD's critics but for its supporters. One letter to the editor, offering a starkly individualized understanding of police use of force in general and the King beating in particular, provides a glimpse of the range of the debate:

> Thank you . . . for Patrick Buchanan's remarks reminding us that all this outbreak of histrionics over the apprehension of a law breaker is just that—hand-wringing by the brothers of the criminal, prospecting by the Police Misconduct Lawyers Referral Service, publicity seeking by the American Civil Liberties Union.
> . . . Please tell the urban warrior that it is very easy to avoid unpleasant encounters with the police. Just don't break the law! (Graham 1991, B6)

The struggle to define the Rodney King incident is analyzed further in chapter 7.

22. Since the incident described here, Jackson has changed his name to Diop Kamau.

23. Jackson's sting was met with a fairly low-key and unified official response in Long Beach. Some local city council members responded to Jackson's video by supporting the establishment of a civilian review board to oversee the police department, an initiative the department had resisted in the past. Rather than fight, however, the department immediately got on board, supporting the creation of the board and providing a blueprint for its structure. The initiative passed the council in 1989 and was put before the city in a general election the following year. Meanwhile, the case triggered little if any official response outside of Long Beach.

24. Molotch and Lester's (1974) typology of news events would probably categorize the Jackson video as a "routine disruptive event." I have chosen to

characterize it as an "accidental" event for reasons explained in chapter 1, note 5.

5. MAKING BIG NEWS

1. While the existence of journalistic norms cannot really be "proven," their existence can be strongly suggested by empirically demonstrated patterns of representation in the news. All other things being equal, patterns in the way journalists represent political issues and events stem from the routines that shape their daily work and the normative orders that underlie it. Like Wolfsfeld (1997) observes of his own arguments about media behavior, even when we cannot know if journalists consciously perceive particular norms, we can demonstrate that news organizations behave *as though* they are performing these roles. The importance of journalistic norms to the construction of the news has been suggested by a variety of scholars, including Tuchman (1978), Gans (1979), and Bennett (1990; 1996). For a contemporary debate on the nature and content of journalistic norms, see *Political Communication* 13 (1996).

2. The three competing normative orders identified here draw from and differ from those identified by Weaver and Wilhoit (1992) in their surveys of journalists. What I define as the "professionalism" norm fits well with what they identify as the "disseminator" role in that both emphasize neutrally transmitting information; my formulation also captures journalists' concern with exercising power responsibly. Similarly, what they define as the "adversarial" role is somewhat narrower than what I point to with the "reformism" label. For Weaver and Wilhoit, adversarialism is confined to those journalists who identify "being an adversary" of government or business as an important role; in my formulation, reformism includes a broader tendency of journalists to recognize problems, especially problems caused by official hypocrisy or malfeasance or the failure of democratic political processes, as good stories. Finally, what they identify as the "interpretive" role is in some ways roughly analogous to what I label "commercialism." With the concept of media commercialism, I focus on a powerful storytelling role that journalists are sometimes reluctant to identify with openly, perhaps because it is to some degree at odds with the expectations of the neutral disseminator role. Indeed, Weaver and Wilhoit's surveys suggest that journalists publicly embrace the commercial, storytelling norm less often than either the professional "disseminator" or the reformist "adversarial" roles. Thus, Weaver and Wilhoit's surveys suggest but do not necessarily confirm the norms identified here, at least in part because survey research is necessarily limited by what journalists are conscious of and will openly say about their profession (by the same token, my own formulation is subject to the criticism that it may be difficult to confirm with survey research).

3. The ideal of journalistic adversarialism has been critiqued from two perspectives. Critical media scholars of the "official dominance" school see a news media that too readily identifies with elites and the status quo to be very adversarial. These critics argue that media adversarialism, to the degree that it exists, is timid and trivialized. Only when official consensus has broken down, ac-

cording to this argument, will mainstream news organizations challenge official claims or actively set the agenda (Bennett 1990; Gitlin 1980; Hallin 1986). Other critics, in contrast, focus on the contemporary media's apparent eagerness to attack public officials. They criticize in particular media "feeding frenzies" (Sabato 1991), in which evidence or even rumor of official scandal often leaves official careers ruined, public policies in tatters, and public trust in government severely strained. One particularly powerful critique argues that the contemporary mainstream media have become so thoroughly cynical that they treat politics as a game and official actions and rhetoric primarily as ploys to be exposed (Fallows 1997; Patterson 1994). Thus, media adversarialism has been criticized both for being too weak and for being too strong. Indeed, according to the second critique, media adversarialism has mutated and now crowds out the steady, neutral professionalism of an earlier era. Viewed from either perspective, the "watchdog" ideal may be largely a popular myth.

4. High-profile use-of-force incidents win not only more news stories but longer ones, according to data obtained from the full text of coverage of a sample of cases. The average length of news items about low-profile cases in the *New York Times*, for example, was 370 words, compared with 644 words for mid-profile and 884 words for high-profile cases. Higher-profile cases also appear more often on the front page or in the front section of the newspaper.

5. The findings reported in figure 5 are based on coding of each newspaper's index. Findings based on coding of the full text of news stories about a random sample of incidents display similar patterns. Systemic claims about police brutality, for example, appeared in coverage of only 13 percent of low-profile cases reported in the *New York Times*, in contrast with 78 percent of mid-profile and 100 percent of high-profile cases. In the *Los Angeles Times*, 12 percent of low-profile cases were the subject of at least one systemic claim, compared with 50 percent of mid-profile and 100 percent of high-profile cases. In contrast, individualizing claims casting the use of force as an appropriate response to violent or threatening behavior appeared in the lead paragraphs of 30 percent of low-profile stories but in only 7 percent of high-profile stories in the *New York Times*. Similarly, 43 percent of *Los Angeles Times* items about low-profile cases contained these claims in their lead paragraphs, compared with 19 percent of items about mid-profile and 11 percent about high-profile cases (p < .05).

6. Items coded as "editorials" include masthead editorials, op-ed pieces, and letters to the editor; all were clearly identified as editorial-page items in their respective index entries. The distinction between "episodic" and "thematic" news items is borrowed from Iyengar (1991) and modified somewhat for this analysis. As Iyengar (1991, 14) recognizes, some news items display both kinds of focus; these items were coded as "mixed" but were counted as thematic items in the data displayed here. It is important to point out that the content of thematic news items and editorials may not necessarily be unremittingly critical of police. Indeed, as chapter 6 will illustrate, some editorials in particular attempt to normalize controversial situations. The appearance of thematic news nevertheless represents critical moments in the news—moments when the use of force is not being easily normalized.

7. Differences in coverage across these groups are statistically significant (p < .001 for the *New York Times* and p < .01 for the *Los Angeles Times*). Events are not always linked independently by journalists. In some cases, linkages are suggested to journalists by their sources. In the *New York Times*, for example, 15 percent of linkages between events were attributed by a reporter to an outside source, while 39 percent of linkages were made by sources and elaborated on by journalists. But in 45 percent of cases, the linkages were introduced by reporters without being attributed to any outside source. These commonly took the form of brief paragraphs that contextualized current events by reference to past events, such as a reporter's observation regarding one high-profile New York City case in 1991 that the incident "follows a national uproar over the beating of a California motorist, Rodney G. King, by a group of Los Angeles policemen" (Blumenthal 1991b, 21).

8. This argument contradicts Skolnick and Fyfe's (1993, 42) assertion that "most of the brutality cases that have drawn wide public attention and have led to expensive litigation have been characterized by truly outrageous police conduct rather than by borderline misbehavior."

9. According to Los Angeles prosecutors, for example, "unless an officer's use of force is blatantly excessive and confirmed by credible, independent witnesses, it is virtually impossible to establish what is unreasonable" in terms of the use of force. And "more often than not . . . the officer's accuser has been taken into custody on criminal charges and may have a prior arrest record, both of which can be used in court to impugn his integrity." Finally, "unless a person can prove that he received demonstrable and lasting injury at the hands of the police, the chances of winning an assault case against an officer are slim" (Freed 1991, A1).

10. One might assume that those use-of-force incidents that are filmed are the most newsworthy. The reporters I interviewed often mentioned the presence of video as an element of newsworthiness, and videotaping has certainly made big news out of some incidents. But most of the high-profile cases analyzed in this study were not videotaped. And, contrary to what the Rodney King case might lead us to expect, the relationship between videotaping and the amount of newspaper coverage a case receives is not strong. In the *New York Times*, 5 percent of all reported use-of-force incidents between 1985 and 1994 were reportedly videotaped; 3 percent of the low-profile incidents were videotaped, compared to 11 percent of both the mid- and high-profile incidents. In the *Los Angeles Times*, 3 percent of all incidents covered were reportedly videotaped; 2 percent of the low-profile and 6 percent of the mid-profile incidents were videotaped, compared to a third of the high-profile incidents (two out of six). Thus, some relationship between videotaping and newsworthiness is indicated in the *Los Angeles Times*, but very little is indicated in the *New York Times*. Regression analysis reveals no statistically significant relationship between incidents that were reportedly videotaped and the number of stories they received in the *New York Times*, excluding the Rodney King case (B = .725, p = .64), but some relationship in the *Los Angeles Times* (B = 2.43, p = .001).

11. One example is found in the arrest of Kevin Dunbar, a white homeless man, which was videotaped and released to news stations in 1990. The tape ap-

peared to show a Laguna Beach police officer kicking Dunbar as he lay on the ground but did not show clearly whether Dunbar was actually kicked, because he was lying behind a police car and was surrounded by a group of officers. The tape then showed Dunbar being lifted to his feet, with blood underneath his right eye. Did the video show a case of excessive force? A grand jury refused to file charges against the officer; in August 1991, the city agreed to settle with Dunbar for $100,000 if he would drop his federal lawsuit. But neither the department nor the officer admitted to any wrongdoing, claiming that the officer kicked Dunbar in the arm after Dunbar resisted arrest.

12. Gamson and Modigliani (1989) provide an example of mainstream journalists' reluctance to independently designate public problems in their account of a partial meltdown at the Enrico Fermi nuclear reactor outside of Detroit in 1966. Despite its seriousness (the plant was shut down manually after the automatic operating system failed, followed by a six-month period in which officials tried to figure out ways to remove the damaged fuel rods from the plant), the accident was barely reported, registering its first mention in the *New York Times*, where it was described as a "mishap," five weeks after it occurred. Gamson and Modigliani contend that no oppositional spokespersons were available to journalists that would enable them to construct the story as anything other than a mishap.

13. It is worth noting that story cues are not always as distinct in reality as they appear in the typology presented below. The purpose of constructing this typology of cues is not to exhaustively list and firmly categorize them but rather to point to underlying norms structuring news representations and to suggest ways in which those norms are engaged by unfolding real-world events.

14. Occasionally, stories do appear in the news about legal proceedings against police in cases that have not received much previous attention. Generally, however, such news items are "fillers": stories filed by reporters on the courtroom beat that editors deem just interesting enough to fill a few column inches of the news hole and that primarily serve organizational needs to fill space in the newspaper (see Chermak 1994).

15. Other scholars have also studied the tendency of journalists to construct "waves" around key news events (see Wolfsfeld 1998; Kepplinger and Habermeier 1995).

16. Further evidence of this reportorial dynamic is found in Skolnick and Fyfe's (1993, 14–15) account of a press conference held by Daryl Gates immediately after the Rodney King beating. Reporters at the press conference peppered the chief with questions about a variety of other use-of-force incidents, from the shooting of Eulia Love in 1979 to the more recent arrests of sports stars Jamaal Wilkes and Joe Morgan. Clearly, at that early juncture, reporters were already linking the King event with other incidents.

17. Remarkably similar dynamics are evident in a series of police shootings in the Los Angeles area in 1991, on the heels of the Rodney King beating. The deaths of Arturo Jimenez, David Angel Ortiz, Keith Hamilton, and Steve Clemons, all shot by Los Angeles county sheriff's deputies in the space of one month, were decisively linked in the pages of the *Los Angeles Times* and led to demands for reform of the LASD along lines that had been applied to the LAPD.

18. See chapter 4.

19. ANOVA is chosen as the method of statistical analysis here for ease of visual presentation. The relationships suggested in figure 6 hold up under more rigorous causal analysis, however. Bivariate regression, conducted with an index of critical story cues as the independent variable and an index of critical coverage as the dependent variable, shows a statistically significant relationship between the story cues illustrated in figure 6 and the amount of critical coverage each use-of-force incident received (the dependent variable being an index of critical news characteristics present in coverage of each case): For the *New York Times*, B = .558 (p < .000); for the *Los Angeles Times*, B = .331 (p < .000).

The limitations of the sources of these data, however, should be borne in mind. The presence or absence of various story cues is measured here simply by information available in each newspaper. No external source of information has been consulted, because no external sources exist that could provide reliable information about all the incidents examined here (as discussed in chapter 1, police records of these incidents are not publicly available, nor would they necessarily provide full and reliable information on the variables of concern). This raises obvious difficulties with making statements about the relationship between cues and coverage. For example, the presence or absence of witnesses and others willing to provide competing accounts cannot be unproblematically inferred from news coverage. For journalists may be unaware of or choose not to publicize the accounts of some victims or witnesses of police use of force. The same problem applies to the citizen-action cue: the data are based on reported citizen action, while it is possible that some citizen activism goes unreported. Similarly, the data reported in figure 6 do not address the possibility that some minority suspects were simply not identified as such by the police or by reporters; therefore, the point of the data in figure 6 is not that only 30 percent of *New York Times* incidents, for example, involved ethnic minorities but that in only 30 percent of cases was the race of the subject made known to the public. Nevertheless, the patterns are striking and do suggest that incidents involving racial or ethnic minorities, and incidents met with competing accounts, legal proceedings, citizen action, and official responses, gain greater and more critical news coverage.

20. Indeed, the proportional differences in reported competing accounts and legal proceedings across groups of incidents are not statistically significant for the *New York Times*, precisely because of the high baseline.

21. The importance of official action as a cue to critical news coverage is illustrated by the following: 20 percent of use-of-force incidents reported in the *New York Times* that were reportedly met with citizen action but no official concessionary response became the subject of thematic news stories and editorials—key indicators of critical news. Yet every incident but one that was met both with citizen action and with an official response gained that kind of news coverage. In the *Los Angeles Times*, these patterns were similar but less dramatic: 72 percent of incidents to which both citizens and officials responded became the subject of thematic news and editorials, compared with 52 percent of incidents to which only citizens responded.

The importance of official responses is also suggested by regression analysis, which reveals that official responses are the single most powerful predictor of the amount of coverage an incident receives (though not of the type of coverage it receives). In a multiple-regression model with story cues as independent variables and the number of stories garnered by various incidents as the dependent variable, only the official response variable proved statistically significant (for the *New York Times*, B = 6.83, p < .05; for the *Los Angeles Times*, B = 5.622, p < .000).

6. STRUGGLING FOR DEFINITION

1. The "stun gun cases" of 1985, which are analyzed briefly in chapter 5, collectively garnered more news coverage in the *Times* than any use-of-force incidents other than the Rodney King beating. The three cases analyzed here, however, were the individual use-of-force incidents occurring in New York to gain the greatest amount of coverage from 1985 to 1994. Occurring in relatively quick succession, they allow for a natural experiment of sorts in event-driven problem definition.

2. The Mollen Commission report stated that "Until now there has always been a distinction drawn between corruption and brutality. . . . [But] that distinction has in some cases blurred. The corruption we found sometimes involved abuse of authority and unnecessary force, and the violence we found sometimes occurred to facilitate thefts of drugs and money" (Mollen 1994, 45). Indeed, the commission argued, brutality "strengthens aspects of police culture and loyalty that foster and conceal corruption," serving as a rite of passage or initiation into corruption (7).

3. The reader may notice that there is no direct insight included here from the reporters who wrote the stories analyzed. This is because, in some cases, the relevant journalists no longer work for the *Times* and could not be tracked down; in other cases, the reporters I interviewed told me they did not remember the specific stories I tried to ask them about. For example, the reporter who produced many of the stories on the Pereira case claimed to have no recollection of the case at all, even when I provided him with specific details. This happened regularly with regard to the stories that got only minor attention at the *Times*, but it is surprising that it happened with regard to some major stories as well. A few reporters did shed some light on the specifics of these stories, but nothing that suggested conclusions other than those drawn here.

4. The *Times* published only one news item on Pereira's death in the one-month period after he died and before the Rodney King beating became national news and the NYPD announced its new investigation.

5. One witness's lawyer countered with accusations that the police had tried to coerce his client into supporting the official account of Pereira's death.

6. I could find no indication in the pages of the *Times* whether the promised investigation of the Queens precinct ever took place, or whether the special nonlethal-force units were ever created.

7. Of course, this editorial reflects an acceptance of the King video as defin-

itive proof of excessive force—long before the Simi Valley jury's decision would forever place the King video itself in question.

8. In a later thematic story appearing after the officer charged in Pereira's death was acquitted, the *Times* again quoted Dr. Davis, who said that when expert witnesses offer conflicting medical testimony, judges and juries turn their attention to the rest of the evidence in the case (Fried 1992b, 18).

9. Indeed, the Washington Heights disturbances were described as a "surprise" (Dao 1992b, A1) and a "splash of ice-cold water" (Gonzalez 1992, B2) to a city that thought it had been spared the violent racial unrest that had rocked other cities in the wake of the Rodney King trial.

10. The *Times* did not initially report Garcia's prior criminal record—one arrest for selling a small "personal use" packet of cocaine—for several days. A Dinkins administration official later claimed he had made Garcia's drug record public just two days after Garcia's death, but for some reason this information did not appear in any stories about the Garcia case until three days later.

11. This is the one instance in which a reporter I interviewed shed significant light on how a brutality story was covered. According to Krauss (1996b), one reason the Sayon story may have acted as a vehicle for critical community voices is that the *Times* sent a black reporter into Clifton to gather the typical "reaction" quotes. Community residents in the heavily black areas of Clifton, he surmised, may have been more willing to speak candidly with a black reporter.

12. It is interesting to note that how the *Times* presented this resident's claim seems to subvert its meaning. The resident appears to be saying that the police are there to make sure the residents (most of whom in this case were black) don't "spill over." The reporter amends this notion by substituting "the ills."

13. At least two observers have suggested that the *Times* consistently "plays ball" with the NYPD and refuses to publicly make problems for the NYPD (Chevigny 1996) and that, during the early 1990s, the *Times* Metro Bureau, which covers the NYPD, was the paper's "weakest" bureau (Kocieniewski 1997). These critiques suggest that the *New York Times'* relationship with the NYPD is more cooperative (some might say co-opted) than the norm. By the same token, one *New York Times* reporter I talked with voiced the opinion that the *Los Angeles Times'* relatively aggressive coverage of the political turmoil engendered by the King beating simply evidenced that it was "out to get Daryl Gates" (Krauss 1996b).

But it would be easy to spuriously attribute critical *Los Angeles Times* coverage of the Rodney King incident to that paper's willingness to "get Gates" when what mainly drove its coverage was the strong narrative power of the video and the political dynamics it set in motion. In fact, there are reasons to doubt the view that the *Los Angeles Times* has been significantly more critical of the LAPD than the *New York Times* has been of the NYPD, at least before the King incident. As evidence presented in chapter 4 indicated, coverage of police misconduct was quite muffled in the years prior to 1991, indicating that the *Los Angeles Times* was hardly willing to "get Gates" before the King beating occurred. Indeed, David Shaw, the *Times'* own media critic, wrote a series of pieces in 1991 outlining how the *Times* had missed or ignored a simmering brutality problem until the King beating became a major news event (see Shaw 1992).

7. INTERPRETING RODNEY KING

1. The analysis presented here is based upon the author's coding of selected national newspapers and newsmagazines, which were accessed via the Nexis database. To construct an efficient yet representative search, I chose to analyze those publications that have been included in the Nexis database over a sufficient period of time to make comparisons of coverage before and after the King beating possible. A variety of analyses of these publications' content was conducted; see footnotes throughout for details. In most cases, the quantitative analyses presented here are based on the entire universe of coverage in these media; accordingly, inferential statistics are included only as appropriate or for the reader's interest.

2. Data in figure 7 reflect all news articles that mentioned the phrases "police brutality" or "excessive force" three times or more. The figure includes only media included in the Nexis database for the entire time period of 1985–94: the *Chicago Tribune, Los Angeles Times, New York Times, Washington Post, Newsweek, U.S. News and World Report,* and *Time.* Items pertaining to foreign locales, such as South Africa, were omitted.

3. These figures were derived by coding a sample of references to the King beating in all 11 newspapers examined here; a random sample of 124 out of 395 total items were coded. All items were also submitted to a second coder; intercoder agreement was 89 percent.

4. As Parloff (1992) argues, it was not at all clear to the officers on the scene that King was indeed unarmed. Los Angeles Police Department policy required officers to subdue suspects before searching them, and the preferred method of subduing suspects was to require them to "prone out." Therefore, the officers claimed that they were simply trying to subdue King in the usual manner before searching him. As Parloff also notes, however, the officers could have chosen sooner to forgo forcing King to prone out and simply swarm on him, as they eventually did. Nevertheless, the Simi Valley jury saw King's resistance as inviting the level of force officers used against him.

5. Similarly, a *New York Times* editorial comparing a local case of alleged excessive force (the death of Federico Pereira) to the King beating claimed that "The New York case is more serious than the police beating in Los Angeles [and] more ambiguous. *With no videotape, it remains for the court to sort out evidence on the extent of police brutality*" (Police brutality, public trust, 1991, emphasis added). Even the venerable *Times,* it appears, viewed the videotape as unambiguous evidence of police misconduct and did not feel it necessary to await an official investigation.

6. President Bush was more equivocal: though he condemned the officers' behavior, he was more circumspect about what the incident represented. Bush told reporters in mid-March that "It was sickening to see the beating that was rendered, and there's no way in my view to explain that away. It was outrageous" (Rosenthal 1991, A16).

7. Between March 5 and March 18, 1991, the national news media analyzed here collectively published 11 news stories mentioning Rodney King that were longer than 1,000 words in length and only one story that focused the-

matically on the issue of police brutality. After the transcripts were released, between March 19 and March 31, these media published 24 lengthy stories mentioning King and nine thematic explorations of police brutality.

8. The data in figure 8 are based on relatively simple indicators. The phrases "racist or racism" and "code of silence" or "blue wall of silence" were searched for in conjunction with the terms "police brutality" or "excessive force." This search reveals the prevalence of ideas about the connection between racism or the police subculture and police brutality. Similarly, the names of the two most prominent nationwide civil rights groups concerned with police brutality—the ACLU and the NAACP—were searched for in conjunction with the phrases "police brutality" or "excessive force." Since many more antibrutality groups exist around the country, and since many systemic claims could be made about brutality that would not be found with these search terms, the data in figure 8 are best viewed as a measure of the relative prevalence of such voices and views across time. Since the content of some of the newspapers examined in this study is not available via the Nexis database prior to 1990, figure 8 includes only those that are included in Nexis for the entire time period of 1985–94. Items pertaining to foreign locales, such as South Africa, were omitted.

9. These in-depth examinations of brutality could have appeared during the previous week, when the Justice Department announced it would review federal brutality complaints—seemingly providing a legitimate cue for stories about possible patterns of brutality across the country. But instead, they appeared after the LAPD transcripts were released, suggesting again that the release of the transcripts was the most important story cue for the national news media. One explanation for this finding is that it took time to prepare such reporting. But an equally plausible explanation is that, even as the Justice Department agreed to conduct a probe, it was cautioning that such a study would take time and that patterns of police misconduct would be hard to detect. The transcripts, in contrast, strongly suggested a pattern of racist brutality among Los Angeles police, providing easily comprehensible problem definitions and, more important, highly dramatic news material.

10. The philosophy associated with community policing is also referred to as "community-based," "community-oriented," or "problem-oriented" policing. For simplicity's sake, I use the term "community policing" to stand in for all of these various labels.

11. Kelling and Wilson's article both reflected and reinforced the growing popularity of community policing in academic and policing circles, a popularity that has persisted despite (or perhaps because of) its considerable ambiguity. As one recent study observes, "Perhaps the most unavoidable conclusion one can draw from a study of community policing is that it means different things to different people" (Lyons 1995, 38). But most commentators agree that the fundamental principles of the community-policing philosophy include shifting the focus of policing from crime response or crime attack to community problem solving, moving police officers out of patrol cars and into established beats with more face-to-face contact with the community, and establishing better relationships between police and communities to facilitate both crime control and problem solving (see Lyons 1999).

12. Again, since the content of some of the newspapers examined in this study is not available via the Nexis database prior to 1990, figure 9 includes only those media that are included in Nexis for the entire time period of 1985–94. Data from the full set of national media examined here (11 newspapers plus three newsmagazines) mirrors the significant increases in attention to community policing from 1990 through 1992: the number of items that mentioned community policing increased from 11 items in 1989 to 89 items in 1990 to 194 items in 1991 and 512 items in 1992.

13. These findings are based on a search of the Nexis database for the phrases "community policing" (and cognates) and "police brutality" (and cognates) in the 11 newspapers examined here.

14. These findings are based on the author's coding of the full text of all newspaper items mentioning both community policing and police brutality, excessive force, or misconduct, in 1991. Excerpts of all items ("KWIC" cites downloaded from Nexis) were submitted to a second coder; agreement between coders was 87 percent on descriptions of community policing and 88 percent on community policing as a solution for brutality.

15. Though the concepts of community policing and civilian review received a roughly equal amount of coverage in 1991, most news coverage of civilian review in the aftermath of Rodney King focused as much on its possible drawbacks as on its possible benefits. Thus, while community policing was portrayed overwhelmingly positively in the news, civilian review received much more mixed news coverage.

8. ACCIDENTS WILL HAPPEN

1. In May 1997, an LAPD investigation concluded that Fuhrman had grossly exaggerated his own and other officers' brutality. Los Angeles Police Department chief Willie Williams told reporters that "the statements Mark Fuhrman made regarding systematic misconduct are simply not true" (Purdum 1997, A22). Apparently, the investigation's conclusions rested primarily on a lack of police records of the events Fuhrman described.

2. The Bobb Commission noted that the falling number of excessive-force complaints against the LAPD must be analyzed with care, because as of 1996 the department still lacked a computerized database of use-of-force incidents and complaints of excessive force—a fact that hindered the Bobb Commission's investigation (Newton 1996). By 1999, LAPD chief Bernard Parks had toughened discipline against officers involved in misconduct, to the considerable consternation of many rank-and-file officers (Terry 1999).

3. Volpe's lawyer, Marvin Kornberg, initially suggested to reporters that Louima's injuries could have been sustained during a homosexual encounter. Volpe changed his plea to guilty during his trial and claimed that he had been enraged because he believed Louima had hit him in the earlier scuffle; testimony at trial showed that he was wrong. In December 1999, Volpe was sentenced to 30 years in prison. Another officer was convicted of helping to hold Louima down during the assault, while other officers were charged with conspiracy in trying to cover up the assault.

4. This problem definition was furthered by an apparent pattern linking at least some of the officers involved in the Diallo shooting with other violent incidents. Three of the officers had been involved in shootings in the previous two years, one of which was under review by the Brooklyn District Attorney's office at the time that Diallo was shot. Three of them had also been accused of excessive force and racial insensitivity in the past, though those charges had not been substantiated. Police Commissioner Howard Safir later announced that the Street Crimes Unit would be broken into eight smaller units, but not before a federal lawsuit filed on behalf of six black and Hispanic men sought to force the city to abolish the unit altogether, claiming that it had unconstitutionally stopped and searched thousands of New Yorkers without reasonable suspicion that they had committed crimes.

The apparent egregiousness of the force used against Diallo also led to critical discussions in the news about the semiautomatic weaponry provided to NYPD officers. This problem definition was short-lived, however, for it was immediately countered by police and elected officials and rejected by academics and law-enforcement experts. The International Association of Chiefs of Police told the *New York Times* that crime fighting had "escalated to where [criminals] carry little machine guns. You've got to be prepared to meet the threat"; Mayor Giuliani defended the use of 9-millimeter guns and praised the NYPD for "being just about the most restrained Police Department in the country" (Wilgoren 1999a, 43). "Whatever the gun is . . . the bigger problem is the quick trigger," said David Lerner, a spokesman for the Center for Constitutional Rights, while Paul Chevigny of New York University told the *Times*, "It's much more about training, accountability and protocol than it is about the weapon" (ibid.).

5. Indeed, in one sense the initial allegations themselves were not an "accidental event" at all, since they were part of the independent prosecutor's strategy for catching President Clinton in a web of his own half-truths.

6. In their exploration of long-term trends in agenda building, Baumgartner and Jones (1993) also note that dramatic events, when exploited by policymakers, can help to change the policy issues on the government agenda and the ideas that underlie established policies—though they are skeptical about the power of events alone to act as catalysts for policy change.

7. For an examination of how historical events may serve as "thinking tools," see Edy 1999.

8. In July 1991, a videotape was released to the media that showed Fort Worth police officer Edward James Parnell III striking a black suspect in his custody at least 28 times with his baton. Parnell claimed that striking the man, who had broken the window of the patrol car, was the only way to keep him from escaping, but he was dismissed from the force three months later. In the other case, Compton, California, police officer Michael Jackson was filmed striking a Latino youth by the name of Felipe Soltero in the face with his baton in August 1994. A jury found that Jackson had violated Soltero's rights but that the injuries he sustained were not serious enough to warrant compensatory damages. Media coverage of both cases, in the *New York Times* and *Los Angeles Times*, respectively, emphasized the racial angle of the cases.

9. Police across the country, particularly those who did not favor community-policing reforms, complained that the national furor set off by the King video unfairly tarnished all police with the same brush while ignoring what police often view as the real problem: an increase in criminals and deviants who are willing to violently resist arrest. A column in a 1991 issue of *The Police Chief* magazine exemplifies this perspective:

> A segment of the media, some politicians, and traditional anti-police groups and personalities are making it appear as though there is an epidemic of police misconduct that desperately cries out for controlling measures.
>
> The truth is that [police] face a dramatic increase in disrespect for the uniform and violence against police. There is a common thread running through most excessive use-of-force cases—including the Rodney King case. That common thread is the unwillingness on the part of the public to cooperate with the police, followed by active resistance. (Spector 1991, 13)

This argument foreshadowed a backlash, as police unions and their supporters looked for ways to protect officers against a perceived environment in which officers are increasingly threatened not only by violent criminals but by unfounded excessive-force allegations. Thus in 1996, Rep. Carlos Moorhead, Republican from California, introduced a bill entitled the Law Enforcement Officers Civil Liability Act, which would limit awards in civil excessive-force suits. This effort was echoed in state legislatures around the country. In New Jersey, for example, police unions helped write the Law Enforcement Officers Protection Act, which would protect officers from lawsuits arising out of altercations in which they discharged weapons or chased suspects in motor vehicles, provide for officers to be reimbursed for legal costs, and expunge records of departmental or criminal charges of excessive force in which officers were found not guilty. In California, a bill passed by the state assembly erased unproven misconduct allegations from officers' files. And in Philadelphia, the police union petitioned the state Labor Relations Board to end public access to disciplinary hearings involving officers accused of misconduct, arguing that the "humiliation" of publicity damaged officer morale (Fazlollah 1996).

10. For example, the furor over Rodney King appears to have increased the newsworthiness of a subsequent series of shootings of African American and Latino men by Los Angeles County sheriff's deputies in the summer of 1991. Activists and community leaders demanded an investigation of that department similar to the Christopher Commission's investigation of the LAPD, demands met by the formation of the Kolts Commission in 1992. The Kolts Commission found that a pattern of excessive force by sheriff's deputies had been officially sanctioned by inadequate departmental discipline. The commission recommended thorough departmental reforms.

11. At the same time, police have increasingly complained that, since the King incident, civilians have become more willing to resist arrest and then press brutality charges. After the King beating, some LAPD officers began to carry small tape recorders while on duty as protection against illegitimate complaints of excessive force, a practice that had become more widespread by 1996. Said Police Foundation president Hubert Williams, "Police see themselves under attack . . . and they see the tapes as a defense" (Shuster 1996, B1).

References

Aks, Judith, William Haltom, and Michael McCann. 1997. Symbolic Stella: On media coverage of personal injury litigation and the production of legal knowledge. *Law and Courts* (Summer): 5–7.

Althaus, Scott L., Jill A. Edy, and Patricia Phelan. 1998. Which text is best? Using newspaper indexes for political communication research. Paper presented at the annual meeting of the American Political Science Association, Boston, Mass., September 2–6.

American Civil Liberties Union (ACLU). 1992. *Fighting police abuse: A community action manual*. New York: American Civil Liberties Union.

Archer, Chris. 1996. Comments on police brutality. Morning Edition, National Public Radio, November 20.

Bagdikian, Ben H. 1992. *The media monopoly*. 4th ed. Boston: Beacon Press.

Baker, Russ W. 1994. Bratton's beat. *New York Times*, May 11, A25.

Balz, Dan. 1991. Beating by L.A. police "outrageous," Bush says. *Washington Post*, March 22, A4.

Barak, Gregg. 1994. Media, society, and criminology. In *Media, process, and the social construction of crime*, edited by Gregg Barak. New York: Garland Publishing.

Barbanel, Josh. 1990a. Stand on police killings could shape Lee Brown's future. *New York Times*, February 2, B1.

———. 1990b. Some 911 calls to be shifted so officers can get to know areas. *New York Times*, February 3, 29.

Barnhurst, Kevin G., and Diana Mutz. 1997. American journalism and the decline of event-centered reporting. *Journal of Communication* 47(4): 27–53.

Barron, James. 1987. New York study of police finds no wide misuse of deadly force. *New York Times*, May 19, A1.

Barry, Dan. 1999. Giuliani says Diallo shooting coverage skewed poll. *New York Times*, February 17, B3.

Baumgartner, Frank R., and Bryan Jones. 1993. *Agendas and instability in American politics*. Chicago: University of Chicago Press.

Bearak, Barry, and Eric Harrison. 1989. Protest seen turning into mayhem. *Los Angeles Times*, January 19, 1.

Bennet, James. 1992. A neighborhood bonded by turmoil. *New York Times*, July 7, B4.

Bennett, W. Lance. 1990. Toward a theory of press-state relations. *Journal of Communication* 40(2): 103–25.

———. 1996. *News: The politics of illusion*. 3d edition. New York: Longman.

Bennett, W. Lance, and Regina G. Lawrence. 1995. News icons and the mainstreaming of social change. *Journal of Communication* 45(3): 20–39.

Bennett, W. Lance, and Jarol Manheim. 1993. Taking the public by storm: Information, cuing, and the democratic process in the Gulf conflict. *Political Communication* 10: 331–51.

Berger, Joel. 1999. The police misconduct we never see. *New York Times*, February 9, A23.

Berger, Peter L., and Thomas Luckman. 1967. *The social construction of reality*. Garden City: Anchor Books/Doubleday & Company.

Bessent, Alvin E., and Letta Tayler. 1991. Police brutality: Is it no problem? *Newsday*, June 2, 5.

Best, Joel. 1988. *Images of issues*. New York: Aldine de Gruyter.

———. 1993. But seriously folks. In *Constructionist controversies*, edited by Gale Miller and James A. Holstein, 109–27. New York: Aldine de Gruyter.

———. 1999. *Random violence*. Berkeley: University of California Press.

Birkland, Thomas. 1997. *After disaster*. Washington, D.C.: Georgetown University Press.

Bishop, Katherine. 1991. Police attacks: Hard crimes to uncover, let alone stop. *New York Times*, March 24, section 4, page 1.

Blair, Jayson. 1999. Police official blames news coverage for murder increase. *New York Times*, October 9, 5.

Blumenthal, Ralph. 1991a. Murder case against 5 officers: Accounts clash on many points. *New York Times*, March 22, A1A.

———. 1991b. Police feel haunted by specter of brutality. *New York Times*, March 30, 21.

———. 1996. Telephone interview by the author. October 2.

Bonner, Christie-Lynne, public information officer for the Seattle Police Department. 1996. Personal interview by the author, April 23, Seattle Police Department.

Boylan, James. 1986. Declarations of independence. *Columbia Journalism Review*, November/December, 30–45.

Bradley blasts "bigotry" of police officers. 1991. *Los Angeles Times*, March 20, A12.

Bragg, Rick. 1994. Two views of police presence in Clifton. *New York Times*, May 2, B3.

Bryant, Adam. 1996. F.A.A. chief admits mistakes on ValuJet. *New York Times*, June 26, A8.

Bumiller, Elisabeth, and Ginger Thompson. 1999. Giuliani cancels political trip amid protest over shooting. *New York Times*, February 10, A1.

Bunting, Glenn F., and Andrea Ford. 1991. ACLU figure named to police board. *Los Angeles Times*, March 16, A25.

Campbell, Linda P. 1991. Police brutality triggers many complaints, little data. *Chicago Tribune*, March 24, 16.

Cappella, Joseph N., and Kathleen Hall Jamieson. 1997. *Spiral of cynicism*. New York: Oxford University Press.

Chermak, Steven. 1994. Crime in the news media: A refined understanding of how crimes become news. In *Media, process, and the social construction of crime*, edited by Gregg Barak. New York: Garland Publishing.

———. 1995. *Victims in the news*. Boulder: Westview Press.

Chevigny, Paul. 1969. *Police power*. New York: Vintage Books.

———. 1995. *Edge of the knife*. New York: The New Press.

———. 1996. Telephone interview with the author. August 28.

Chibnall, Steven. 1977. *Law-and-order news*. London: Tavistock Publications.

Christopher Commission report excerpts. 1991. *Los Angeles Times*, July 10, A12.

Civilian Complaint Review Board, New York City Police Department. 1996. Semi-Annual Status Report. New York.

Clifford, Frank, and John L. Mitchell. 1991. Incident gives city a national black eye. *Los Angeles Times*, March 7, B1.

Cobb, Roger W., and Charles D. Elder. 1983. *Participation in American politics*. 2d ed. Baltimore: Johns Hopkins University Press.

Cocaine found in dead suspect. 1987. *New York Times*. February 14, 31.

Cohen, Bernard C. 1963. *The press and foreign policy*. Princeton: Princeton University Press.

Cohen, Stanley. 1996. Crime and politics: Spot the difference. *British Journal of Criminology* 47(1): 1–21.

Cook, Timothy E. 1994. Domesticating a crisis: Washington newsbeats and network news after the Iraq invasion of Kuwait. In *Taken by storm*, edited by W. Lance Bennett and David L. Paletz. Chicago: University of Chicago Press.

———. 1996. Afterword: Political values and production values. *Political Communication* 13, 469–81.

———. 1998. *Governing with the news*. Chicago: University of Chicago Press.

Cooper, Michael. 1999. Officers in Bronx fire 41 shots, and an unarmed man is killed. *New York Times*, February 5, A1.

Cornfield, Michael B. 1992. The press and political controversy: The case for narrative analysis. *Political Communication* 9: 47–59.

Corrigan, Don. 1994. The police vs. the media. *St. Louis Journalism Review* 23(May): 17–19.

Cose, Ellis. 1997. Joe Frazier for the prosecution. In *The Darden dilemma*, edited by Ellis Cose. New York: HarperPerennial.

Craven, Jo. 1999. Questioning the cops. *Columbia Journalism Review*, March/April, 25–26.

Crenshaw, Kimberlé, and Gary Peller. 1993. Reel time, real justice. In *Reading Rodney King, reading urban uprising*, edited by Robert Gooding-Williams. London: Routledge, Inc.

Cullen, Francis T., Liqun Cao, James Frank, Robert H. Langworthy, Sandra Lee Browning, Renee Kopache, and Thomas J. Stevenson. 1996. Stop or I'll shoot: Racial differences in support for police use of deadly force. *American Behavioral Scientist* 39: 449–60.

Curran, Ron. 1991. Heavy collateral damage in war on crime? *Los Angeles Times*, April 7, M1.

Dahl, Megan, and W. Lance Bennett. 1996. Media agency and the use of icons in the agenda-setting process: News representations of George Bush's trade mission to Japan. *Press/Politics* 1(3): 41–59.

Dao, James. 1992a. Police report on slaying is challenged. *New York Times*, July 6, B1.

———. 1992b. Tension in Washington Heights: Amid Dinkins's calls for peace, protesters skirmish with police. *New York Times*, July 8, A1.

———. 1992c. Police accelerate efforts to expand their presence in Washington Heights. *New York Times*, July 12, 28.

Darnton, Robert. 1975. Writing news and telling stories. *Daedalus* 2: 175–94.

Daunt, Tina, and Matt Lait. 1999. Special prosecutor urged for police abuse. *Los Angeles Times*, May 5, A1.

Davidson, Joe. 1999. N.Y. city police. Commentary on Morning Edition, National Public Radio, March 9.

Davis, Mike. 1990. *City of quartz*. New York: Verso.

Dearing, James W., and Everett M. Rogers. 1996. *Agenda-setting*. Thousand Oaks: Sage.

Death of arrested man is linked to drug use. 1989. *New York Times*, February 9, B2.

DeLattre, Edwin J. 1991. Can the violence in L.A. teach us why cops lose control? *Washington Post*, March 24, C1.

Denton, Robert E., Jr., and Garcy C. Woodward. 1990. *Political communication in America*. 2d ed. New York: Praeger.

DeStefano, Anthony M. 1991. No. 1 in cops, not complaints. *Newsday*. April 1, 5.

Domanick, Joe. 1990. Safer streets are priceless; less painful law enforcement would be too. *Los Angeles Times*, February 6, B5.

———. 1994. *To protect and to serve*. New York: Pocket Books.

Donahue, George A., Phillip J. Tichenor, and Clarice N. Olien. 1995. A guard dog perspective on the role of media. *Journal of Communication* 45(2): 115–32.

Downs, Anthony. 1972. Up and down with ecology: The "issue attention cycle." *The Public Interest* 28 (Summer): 38–50.

Edelman, Murray. 1977. *Political language*. New York: Academic Press.

———. 1988. *Constructing the political spectacle*. Chicago: University of Chicago Press.

———. 1993. Contestable categories and public opinion. *Political Communication* 10, 231–42.

Edy, Jill A. 1997. Ashes to ashes: The Watts riots as a thinking tool. Paper presented at the annual meeting of the International Communication Association, Montreal, Quebec, May 22–26.

———. 1999. Journalistic uses of collective memory. *Journal of Communication* 49(2): 71–85.

Egan, Timothy. 1991. New faces, and new roles, for the police. *New York Times*, April 25, A1.

Entman, Robert M. 1993. Framing: Toward clarification of a fractured paradigm. *Journal of Communication* 43(4): 51–58.

Entman, Robert M., and Andrew Rojecki. 1993. Freezing out the public: Elite and media framing of the U.S. anti-nuclear movement. *Political Communication* 10: 155–73.

Ericson, Richard V., Patricia M. Baranek, and Janet B. L. Chan. 1989. *Negotiating control: A study of news sources*. Toronto: University of Toronto Press.

———. 1991. *Representing order: Crime, law, and justice in the news media.* Milton Keynes: Open University Press.

Ettema, James S., and Theodore L. Glasser. 1988. Narrative form and moral force: The realization of guilt and innocence through investigative journalism. *Journal of Communication* 38(3): 8–26.

Ettema, James S., David L. Protess, Donna R. Leff, Peter V. Miller, Jack Doppelt, and Fay Lomax Cook. 1991. Agenda-setting as politics: A case study of the press-public-policy connection. *Communication* 12, 75–98.

Fallows, James. 1997. *Breaking the news.* New York: Vintage Books.

Fazlollah, Mark. 1996. FOP asks state board to close police disciplinary hearings. *Philadelphia Inquirer*, March 15, 2.

Finder, Alan. 1992. Dinkins, amid crowd, nurtures fragile peace. *New York Times*, July 9, A1.

Fishman, Mark. 1978. Crime waves as ideology. *Social Problems* 25: 531–43.

———. 1980. *Manufacturing the news.* Austin: University of Texas Press.

Fiske, John. 1994. *Media matters.* Minneapolis: University of Minnesota Press.

Flynn, Kevin. 1999. Police killing draws national notice. *New York Times*, February 8, B5.

Ford, Andrea. 1993. Officer to stand trial in truck driver's death. *Los Angeles Times*, December 16, 1(B).

———. 1997. Telephone interview by the author. March 11.

Freed, David. 1988. Gates defends his officers' search methods in court. *Los Angeles Times*, November 30, section 2, page 3.

———. 1989. "Orgy" of police violence in drug raid is alleged. *Los Angeles Times*, March 23, section 2, page 1.

———. 1991. Police brutality claims are rarely prosecuted. *Los Angeles Times*, July 7, A1.

Fried, Joseph P. 1991a. Five officers charged with murder in slaying of a suspect in Queens. *New York Times*, March 21, A1.

———. 1991b. Defense says autopsy helps Queens police. *New York Times*, March 23, 25.

———. 1991c. Experts differ on autopsy in police murder case. *New York Times*, March 31, 23.

———. 1991d. Prosecutor presses dropping murder charges for 4 officers. *New York Times*, June 26, B4.

———. 1992a. Police officer is acquitted in the killing of a suspect. *New York Times*, March 25, B3.

———. 1992b. In deaths in custody, cocaine is the suspect. *New York Times*, March 29, section 4, page 18.

Fyfe, James. 1991. Confident in brutality. *Los Angeles Times*, March 21, B7.

Gallup Organization. 1997. Black/white relations in the U.S. http://www.gallup. org. June 12.

Gamson, William A. 1992a. The social psychology of collective action. In *Frontiers of social movement theory*, edited by Aldon D. Morris and Carol McClurg Mueller. New Haven: Yale University Press.

———. 1992b. *Talking politics*. Cambridge: Cambridge University Press.

Gamson, William A., and Andre Modigliani. 1989. Media discourse and public opinion on nuclear power: A constructionist approach. *American Journal of Sociology* 95(1): 1–37.

Gans, Herbert J. 1979. *Deciding what's news*. New York: Vintage Books.

Garcia, Kenneth J. 1989. Was roughed up by police, former Bradley aide says. *Los Angeles Times*, January 11, 3(2).

Garrow, David J. 1978. *Protest at Selma*. New Haven: Yale University Press.

Geller, William A., associate director of the Police Executive Research Forum. 1997. Telephone interview by the author. March 25.

Geller, William A., and Michael S. Scott. 1992. *Deadly force: What we know*. Washington, D.C.: Police Executive Research Forum.

Gillespie, Mark. 1999. One third of Americans believe police brutality exists in their area. The Gallup Organization, March 22, http:www.gallup.com/ poll/releases/pr990322.asp.

Gitlin, Todd. 1980. *The whole world is watching*. Berkeley: University of California Press.

Giuliani, Rudolph. 1992. Rumor and justice in Washington Heights. *New York Times*, August 7, A27.

Glasser, Theodore L., and James S. Ettema. 1989. Investigative journalism and the moral order. *Critical Studies in Mass Communication*, 6(1): 1–20.

Goldberg, Vicki. 1991. *The power of photography*. New York: Abbeville Publishing Group.

Gonzalez, David. 1991. The death of a suspect: In officers' murder case, a tangle of contradictions. *New York Times*, March 24, 1.

———. 1992. Tension in Washington Heights: Events don't surprise Dominican residents. *New York Times*, July 8, B2.

Gonzalez, David, and Jane Fritsch. 1992. Shared streets, crossed paths, and a death. *New York Times*, July 12, 1.

Goodman, Adrianne. 1991. NAACP official criticizes venue change in King case. *Los Angeles Times*, December 5, B3.

Goodstein, Laurie. 1991. New "philosophy" of policing. *Washington Post*, December 23, A1.

Graber, Doris A. 1980. *Crime news and the public*. New York: Praeger Publishers.

———. 1993. *Mass media and American politics*, 4th ed. Washington, D.C.: CQ Press.

Graham, T. Bruce. 1991. Rockwell on police beating. *Los Angeles Times,* March 21, B6.

Greenfeld, Lawrence A., Patrick A. Langan, and Steven K. Smith. 1997. *Police use of force: Collection of national data.* Washington, D.C.: Bureau of Justice Statistics.

Gurevitch, Michael, and Mark R. Levy. 1985. Preface. *Mass Communication Review Yearbook* 5, ed. Michael Gurevitch and Mark R. Levy. Beverly Hills: Sage.

Gusfield, Joseph. 1981. *The culture of public problems.* Chicago: University of Chicago Press.

Haberman, Clyde. 1996. Policing issue: Who guards the guards? *New York Times,* October 15, B1.

Hall, Stuart. 1980. Encoding/decoding. In *Culture, media, and language,* edited by the Centre for Contemporary Cultural Studies. London: Hutchinson.

Hall, Stuart, Chas Critcher, Tony Jefferson, John Clarke, and Brian Roberts. 1978. *Policing the crisis.* New York: Holmes & Meier Publishers, Inc.

Hallin, Daniel C. 1986. *The uncensored war.* Berkeley: University of California Press.

———. 1994. *We keep America on top of the world.* New York: Routledge.

Hampton, Ronald. 1996. Why do we still have police brutality? May 16, Langston Hughes Cultural Arts Center, Seattle, Washington.

Harrison, Eric. 1991. Has the videotape of the King beating exposed a dirty little secret? *Los Angeles Times,* April 4, A1.

Held to a higher degree of integrity. 1991. *Newsday,* April 10, 93.

Herbert, Bob. 1996. Grief and justice. *New York Times,* July 19, A15.

———. 1997. A brutal epidemic. *New York Times,* April 28, A5.

Herman, Edward S., and Noam Chomsky. 1988. *Manufacturing consent.* New York: Pantheon Books.

Hernandez, Raymond. 1994. S.I. man dies after injury in struggle with an officer. *New York Times,* April 30, 25.

Herszenhorn, David M. 1999. Giuliani's response shows a world of differences between two shootings. *New York Times,* September 1, B6.

Hicks, Jonathan P. 1999. Varied group lists demands for the police. *New York Times,* March 28, 41.

Hilgartner, Stephen, and Charles L. Bosk. 1988. The rise and fall of social problems: A public arenas model. *American Journal of Sociology* 1 (July): 53–78.

Holloway, Lynette. 1994. Juries back police in cases like S.I. death, experts say. *New York Times,* December 11, 54.

Holmes, Steven A. 1991. Poll finds most satisfied with police. *New York Times,* April 5, A16.

How to police the police. 1991. *New York Times,* March 30, 18.

Irwin, Lew. 1991. Cops and cameras: Why TV is slow to cover police brutality. *Columbia Journalism Review,* September/October, 15–17.

It's not the Rodney King case. 1992. *New York Times,* July 9, A21.

Iyengar, Shanto. 1991. *Is anyone responsible?* Chicago: University of Chicago Press.

Iyengar, Shanto, and Donald Kinder. 1987. *News that matters*. Chicago: University of Chicago Press.

Jackson, Don. 1989. Imaginary weapon, real corpse. *Los Angeles Times*, June 19, section 2, page 5.

———. 1997. *See* Kamau, Diop.

James, George. 1990. Thirteen-year-old boy killed by police as he chases another with gun. *New York Times*, February 3, 31.

———. 1994. Bratton faults police rules for arrests. *New York Times*, May 12, B1.

Janofsky, Michael. 1999. Police chiefs say criticism of departments is valid. *New York Times*, April 10, 12.

Jennings, Veronica T., and Avis Thomas-Lester. 1991. The difficult task of policing the police. *Washington Post*, April 28, B1.

Johnson, David. 1991. U.S. inquiry sought in police beating. *New York Times*, March 13, A22.

Kamau, Diop (formerly Don Jackson), former Long Beach police officer and antibrutality activist. 1997. Telephone interview by the author. March 27.

Kaniss, Phyllis. 1991. *Making local news*. Chicago: University of Chicago Press.

Katz, Jon. 1994. Is police brutality a myth? *New York*, July 11, 38–40.

Kelling, George. 1991. The blue-uniformed fear of "social work." *Los Angeles Times*, July 11, B7.

Kennedy, Randall. 1997. *Race, crime and the law*. New York: Pantheon Books.

Kepplinger, H. M., and J. Habermeier. 1995. The impact of key events on the presentation of reality. *European Journal of Communication* 10: 371–90.

Kingdon, John W. 1995. *Agendas, alternatives, and public policies*. 2d ed. New York: HarperCollins Publishers.

Kocieniewski, David. 1997. Telephone interview by the author. April 30.

Kocieniewski, David, and Leonard Levitt. 1991. A tracking dilemma: NYPD's way of watching cops comes under attack. *Newsday*, November 19, 6.

Konner, Joan. 1996. Without fear or favor. *Columbia Journalism Review*, July/August, 4.

Kopetman, Roxana. 1991. Charges against officers in video "sting" dismissed. *Los Angeles Times*, May 14, A1.

Krauss, Clifford. 1994a. Complaints to review unit about police increase 46%. *New York Times*, November 5, 25.

———. 1994b. Anger and relief as S.I. inquiry ends. *New York Times*, December 10, 27.

———. 1996a. Rights group finds abuse of suspects by city police. *New York Times*, June 26, B4.

———. 1996b. Telephone interview by the author. August 24.

Kurtz, Howard. 1993. *Media circus*. New York: Times Books.

L.A. police beating prompts U.S. study of brutality complaints. 1991. *Chicago Tribune*, March 15, 8.

Lacey, Marc, and Davan Maharaj. 1989. Student's death after arrest ruled homicide. *Los Angeles Times*, December 29, B3.

Laguna chief gives police integrity a lift. 1990. *Los Angeles Times*, December 30, B8.

Lait, Matt, and Scott Glover. 1999. Court orders release of man based on corruption inquiry. *Los Angeles Times,* November 18, B1.

Lawrence, Regina G. 1996a. Accidents, icons, and indexing: The dynamics of news coverage of police use of force. *Political Communication* 13: 437–54.

———. 1996b. Constructing brutality: Causal stories and problem definition in the white and black press. Paper presented at the Western Political Science Association Annual Meeting, San Francisco, Calif., March 14–16.

Lawrence, Regina G., and Thomas A. Birkland. 1999. The Exxon Valdez and event-driven policy discourse. Paper delivered at the 1999 Annual Meeting of the International Communication Association, San Francisco, Calif., May 28–31.

Lehrer, Jim. 1999. Blurring the lines hurts journalism. *Nieman Reports.* Summer, 60–61.

The lesson of Washington Heights. 1992. *New York Times,* section 4, page 20.

Levy, Clifford J. 1994. Residents of S.I. neighborhood see schism. *New York Times,* May 1, 52.

Lichtblau, Eric, and Kevin Johnson. 1991. Report is a "learning device" for O.C. officials. *Los Angeles Times,* July 10, A19.

Livingston, Steven. 1994. *The terrorism spectacle.* Boulder: Westview Press.

———. 1995. Reporting U.S. ties to Latin American paramilitary organizations: Evolving post-cold war news norms? Paper presented at the 1995 Annual Meeting of the International Communication Association, Albuquerque, N. Mex.

Looking into a police raid. 1988. *Los Angeles Times,* August 10, section 2, page 6.

Lyons, William T. 1995. *Taking community seriously: Policing reform in southeast Seattle.* Ph.D. diss., University of Washington.

———. 1999. *The politics of community policing.* Ann Arbor: University of Michigan Press.

Malveaux, Julianne. 1991. Gates must go to signal police change. *USA Today,* April 4, A8.

Mangum, Roger. 1995. Interview by Terri Gross. Fresh Air, National Public Radio, September 27.

Massaquoi, Hans J. 1991. How to stop police brutality. *Ebony,* July, 58–60.

Mastrofski, Stephen D. 1988. Community policing as reform: A cautionary tale. In *Community policing: Rhetoric or reality?* edited by Jack R. Greene and Stephen D. Mastrofski. New York: Praeger.

McChesney, Robert W. 1999. *Rich media, poor democracy.* Urbana: University of Illinois Press.

McCombs, Maxwell E., and Dennis Shaw. 1972. The agenda-setting function of the mass media. *Public Opinion Quarterly* 36: 176–87.

McDonnell, Patrick. 1989. Border agent cleared in death of Mexican boy. *Los Angeles Times,* October 17, A3.

McFadden, Robert D. 1992. Coping with race and rage in the New York Police Department. *New York Times,* September 19, 1.

McFadden, Robert D., and Kit R. Roane. 1999. U.S. examining killing of man in police volley. *New York Times,* February 6, A1.

McKinley, James C. 1990a. "Tough call" for police on when to fire. *New York Times*, February 2, B3.

———. 1990b. Brown appoints panel to review gun guidelines. *New York Times*, March 22, B3.

———. 1990c. The best time to stop a crime is before it happens. *New York Times*, August 12, section 4, page 5.

———. 1991a. Police officers cleared on their word. *New York Times*, March 21, B6.

———. 1991b. Debate on New York police board heats up while complaints fall. *New York Times*, March 27, A1.

———. 1992. Tension in Washington Heights: The suburban presence in uniform. *New York Times*, July 9, B6.

McMillan, Penelope. 1992. Effort launched to reduce costs of liability suits. *Los Angeles Times*, December 4, B1.

McNamara, Joseph D. 1991. Report just underlined the obvious. *Los Angeles Times*, July 14, M1.

McQuiston, John T. 1994a. Student dies in struggle with officer. *New York Times*, December 5, B1.

———. 1994b. No misfiring of officer's gun in death, police say. *New York Times*, December 14, B4.

Meisler, Stanley. 1994. Trust in media high, but curbs favored, poll finds. *Los Angeles Times*, March 16, A1.

Meredith, Robyn. 1996. Officers' trial in slaying stirs racial tensions. *New York Times*, October 18, A10.

Merina, Victor. 1989. Families of victims shot by police call for inquiry. *Los Angeles Times*, July 12, section 2, page 3.

Miraldi, Robert. 1990. *Muckraking and objectivity*. New York: Greenwood Press.

Mollen, Milton. 1994. See *Report of the commission to investigate allegations of police corruption and the anti-corruption procedures of the police department.*

Molotch, Harvey. 1979. Media and movements. In *The dynamics of social movements*, ed. Mayer N. Zald and John D. McCarthy, 71–93. Cambridge, Mass: Winthrop.

Molotch, Harvey, and Marilyn Lester. 1974. News as purposive behavior: On the strategic use of routine events, accidents, and scandals. *American Sociological Review* 39:101–12.

Molotch, Harvey L., David L. Protess, and Margaret T. Gordon. 1987. The media-policy connection: Ecologies of news. In *Political communication research: Approaches, studies, assessments*, edited by David L. Paletz. Norwood, N.J.: Ablex.

Morley, David. 1992. *Television audiences and cultural studies*. New York: Routledge.

Mr. Bratton's wise policing. 1994. *New York Times*, May 13, A30.

Muir, William Ker, Jr. 1977. *Police: Streetcorner politicians*. Chicago: University of Chicago Press.

Murphy, Dean. 1991. Officers cite lack of control for excessive force cases, survey finds. *Los Angeles Times*, July 20, B3.

Mydans, Seth. 1991a. Tape of beating by police revives charges of racism. *New York Times*, March 6, A18.

———. 1991b. Videotaped beating by officers puts full glare on brutality issue. *New York Times*, March 18, A1.

Nagourney, Adam. 1999. Bradley, in first of issue talks, turns to Diallo shooting and race. *New York Times*, April 21, A20.

National Association for the Advancement of Colored People (NAACP). 1995. *Beyond the Rodney King story*. Boston: Northeastern University Press.

Navarro, Mireya. 1991. Charges relieve dead man's family. *New York Times*, March 12, B6.

———. 1996. St. Petersburg mayor calls racial unrest calculated. November 15, A12.

Nelson, Jill. 1994. Blue plague. *New York Times*, May 20, A27.

Neuman, Russell, Ann Crigler, and Marion Just. 1993. *Common knowledge*. Chicago: University of Chicago Press.

Newton, Jim. 1995. The NYPD: Bigger, bolder—and better? *Los Angeles Times*, December 24, A1.

———. 1996. LAPD reforms fall far short. *Los Angeles Times*, May 31, 1(A).

———. 1997. Telephone interview by the author. March 18.

New York Civil Liberties Union (NYCLU). 1996. *A Third Anniversary Overview of the Civilian Complaint Review Board*. New York: New York Civil Liberties Union.

The numbers. 1991. *Los Angeles Times*, March 24, M4.

Olivo, Antonio. 1995. Complaints against police cited at hearing. *Los Angeles Times*, December 2, B3.

Oswald, John A. 1988a. LAPD to investigate raid damage. *Los Angeles Times*, August 5, section 2, page 1.

———. 1988b. Opinion about data on police misconduct gets mixed reactions. *Los Angeles Times*, August 18, section 2, page 1.

Packer, Herbert. 1968. *The limits of the criminal sanction*. Stanford, Calif.: Stanford University Press.

Page, Benjamin. 1996. *Who deliberates?* Chicago: University of Chicago Press.

Paletz, David L. 1999. *The media in American politics*. New York: Longman.

Paletz, David L., and Robert M. Entman. 1981. *Media power politics*. New York: Free Press.

Parloff, Roger. 1992. Maybe the jury was right. *American Lawyer*, June, 7–11.

Pasternak, Judy. 1989. Ex-officer's crusade against discrimination: 'Star' of police video seizes spotlight. *Los Angeles Times*, May 27, 1.

Patterson, Thomas. 1994. *Out of order*. New York: Vintage Books.

Pearson, Hugh. 1991. The beatings may be ending, not the pain. *Newsday*, April 14, 30.

———. 1994. Black America's silent majority. *New York Times*, May 26, A23.

Perlez, Jane, and Selwyn Raab. 1985. Rising brutality complaints raise questions about New York police. *New York Times*, May 6, A1.

Pew Research Center. 1999. Big doubts on news media's values. http://www.people-press.org/feb99rpt.htm.

Police brutality, public trust. 1991. *New York Times*, March 25, A16.

Police kill man who attempted to stab officer. 1992. *Los Angeles Times*, August 20, B8.

The police, month by month. 1985. *New York Times*, April 25, A26.

Police shoot man to death. 1994. *New York Times*, April 2, section 1, page 23.

Protess, David L., Fay Lomax Cook, Jack C. Doppelt, James S. Ettema, Margaret T. Gordon, Donna R. Leff, and Peter Miller. 1991. *The journalism of outrage*. New York: The Guilford Press.

Public Agenda. 1998. Crime: A nation divided? http://publicagenda.org/issues.

Purdum, Todd S. 1997. Los Angeles police report says Fuhrman overstated brutal exploits. *New York Times*, May 6, A22.

Rainey, James. 1989a. Officer hits the prime time with video camera. *Los Angeles Times,* January 20, 1.

———. 1989b. Secret appeals of disciplinary cases sought in Torrance. *Los Angeles Times*, March 19, section 2, page 4.

Raspberry, William. 1991. It's clear that L.A. beating was not an isolated event. *Atlanta Journal and Constitution*, March 19, A11.

Reeves, Jimmie L., and Richard Campbell. 1994. *Cracked coverage*. Durham: Duke University Press.

Reeves, Richard. 1995. The cops we deserve. *Los Angeles*, December, 40–42.

Reibstein, Larry. 1995. Up against the wall. *Newsweek*, September 4, 24–25.

Reinarman, Craig, and Harry G. Levine. 1988. The crime attack: Politics and media in America's latest drug scare. In *Images of issues*, edited by Joel Best. New York: Aldine de Gruyter.

Reiner, Robert. 1985. *The politics of the police*. New York: St. Martin's Press.

Reinhold, Robert. 1991a. Los Angeles chief assailed by mayor. *New York Times*, April 3, 17.

———. 1991b. Groping for ways to break the siege mentality of the police. *New York Times*, July 14, section 4, page 6.

Reiss, Albert J. 1971. *The police and the public*. New Haven: Yale University Press.

Report of the commission to investigate allegations of police corruption and the anti-corruption procedures of the police department. 1994. By Milton Mollen, Chairman. New York: City of New York.

Retana, James. 1991. The squeaky-clean badge that is little more than a self-serving icon. *Los Angeles Times*, October 6, M1.

Ricker, Darlene. 1991. Behind the silence. *ABA Journal*, July, 45–48.

Ridley-Thomas, Mark. 1990. No longer a sacred cow. *Los Angeles Times*, November 20, B7.

Roane, Kit R. 1999. Elite force quells crime, but at a cost, critics say. *New York Times*, February 6, B6.

Robinson, John P., and Mark R. Levy. 1996. News media use and the informed public: A 1990s update. *Journal of Communication*, 46(2): 129–35.

Rochefort, David A., and Roger W. Cobb. 1994. *The politics of problem definition*. Lawrence: University of Kansas.

Roeh, Itzhak. 1989. Journalism as storytelling, coverage as narrative. *American Behavioral Scientist* 33(2), 162–68.

Rogers, Everett M., James W. Dearing, and Soonbum Chang. 1991. AIDS in the

1980s: The agenda-setting process for a public issue. *Journalism Monographs* 126 (April).

Rohrlich, Ted. 1991. Majority says police brutality is common. *Los Angeles Times*, March 10, A1.

Rohter, Larry. 1991. Police beating unsettles world of make-believe. *New York Times*, March 26, A14.

Rosenberg, Howard. 1991. Media coverage of the King case: Guilty or innocent? *Los Angeles Times*, April 8, F1.

———. 1992. Home videotape at 11!—newsworthy or not. *Los Angeles Times*, April 3, F28.

Rosenthal, Andrew. 1991. Bush calls police beating "sickening." *New York Times*, March 22, A16.

Rosenthal, Rick, police media consultant, RAR Communications. 1997. Telephone interview by the author. April 29.

Rotella, Sebastian. 1989. D.A. clears 3 deputies in slaying of armed woman in Lancaster. *Los Angeles Times*, July 20, section 2, page 8.

Rubenstein, Jonathan. 1973. *City police*. New York: Farrar, Straus, and Giroux.

Ryan, Charlotte. 1991. *Prime time activism*. Boston: South End Press.

Sabato, Larry. 1991. *Feeding frenzy*. New York: Free Press.

Sacco, Vincent F. 1995. Media constructions of crime. *The Annals of the American Academy of Political and Social Science* 539: 141–54.

Sadd, Susan, and Randolph Grinc. 1994. Innovative neighborhood-oriented policing: An evaluation of community policing promises in eight cities. In *The challenge of community policing: Testing the promises*, edited by Dennis Rosenbaum. Thousand Oaks: Sage.

Sahagun, Louis. 1991. Vandalism trial opens for 3 LAPD officers. *Los Angeles Times*, April 2, B3.

Salholz, Eloise. 1990. The "walled cities" of L.A. *Newsweek*, May 14, 24.

Sanchez, Raymond L. 1988. Police shot him for no reason, man says. *Los Angeles Times*, January 28, 1.

Schattschneider, E. E. 1960. *The semi-sovereign people*. New York: Holt, Rinehart, and Winston.

Scheingold, Stuart. 1984. *The politics of law and order*. New York: Longman.

———. 1991. *The politics of street crime*. Philadelphia: Temple University Press.

Schlesinger, Philip. 1990. Rethinking the sociology of journalism: Source strategies and the limits of media-centrism. In *Public communication: The new imperatives*, edited by Marjorie Ferguson. London: Sage.

Schneider, Anne, and Helen Ingram. 1993. Social construction of target populations: Implications for politics and policy. *American Political Science Review* 87: 334–47.

Schudson, Michael. 1978. *Discovering the news*. New York: Basic Books.

———. 1989. The present in the past and the past in the present. *Communication* 11: 105–13.

Scott, Janny. 1991. Violence born of the group. *Los Angeles Times*, March 28, A1.

Segal, Debra. 1993. Tales from the cutting-room floor. *Harper's*, November, 50–57.

Serrano, Richard A. 1989. Ex-San Diego police officer says political pressure caused his firing. *Los Angeles Times*, May 12, section 2, page 7.

———. 1991a. Two cleared of beating charges. *Los Angeles Times*, November 15, B3.

———. 1991b. Pivotal year lies ahead in push for reform of LAPD. *Los Angeles Times*, December 31, A1.

Severely injured suspect resisted arrest, police say. 1985. *Los Angeles Times*, October 20, 34.

Sexton, Joe. 1994. Anger and grief over use of force. *New York Times*, May 10, B4.

Shah, Diane K. 1991. Playboy interview: Daryl Gates. *Playboy*, August, 55–69.

Shaw, David. 1992. Media failed to examine alleged LAPD abuses. *Los Angeles Times*, May 26, A1.

Shuster, Beth. 1996. More police tape arrests in fear of false claims. *Los Angeles Times*, June 3, B1.

Sigal, Leon V. 1973. *Reporters and officials*. Lexington, Mass.: D.C. Heath and Company.

Sigelman, Lee, Susan Welch, Timothy Bledsoe, and Michael Combs. 1997. Police brutality and public perceptions of racial discrimination: A tale of two beatings. *Political Research Quarterly* 50(4): 777–791.

Skolnick, Jerome H. 1966. *Justice without trial*. New York: Wiley.

———. 1991. A police culture of brutality is on the wane. *Newsday*, March 24, 41.

Skolnick, Jerome H., and James J. Fyfe. 1992. The dark blue code of silence. *New York Times*, May 2, I22.

———. 1993. *Above the law*. New York: Free Press.

Smith, Chris. 1996. The NYPD guru. *New York*, April 1, 28–34.

Snow, David A., and Robert D. Benford. 1992. Master frames and cycles of protest. In *Frontiers in social movement theory*, edited by Aldon D. Morris and Carol McClurg Mueller. New Haven: Yale University Press.

Spector, Elliott B. 1991. Police brutality hysteria. *The Police Chief*, October, 13.

Stewart, Sally Ann. 1991. L.A. chief calls for review from civilian panel. *USA Today*, March 28, A3.

Stewart, Sally Ann, and Haya El Nasser. 1991. L.A. police chief Daryl Gates: "I don't expect to run away." *USA Today*, July 10, A1.

Stohlberg, Sheryl. 1991a. Hundreds of protesters demand that Gates resign. *Los Angeles Times*, March 10, B1.

———. 1991b. Officers offer support for Gates amid more attacks. *Los Angeles Times*, March 14, B1.

Stone, Deborah A. 1989. Causal stories and the formation of policy agendas. *Political Science Quarterly* 104 (2): 281–300.

Sullivan, Ronald. 1992. A policeman is cleared and street violence defused. *New York Times*, September 3, section 4, page 2.

Surette, Ray. 1992. *Media, crime, and criminal justice: Images and realities*. Pacific Grove, Calif.: Brooks/Cole.

Tanay, Emanuel. 1991. We expect the police to give out punishment. *New York Times*, March 22, A32.

Terry, Don. 1991. Kansas City police go after own "bad boys." *New York Times*, September 10, A1.

———. 1999. Unyielding chief for the Los Angeles police. *Los Angeles Times*, January 17, 14.

Thomas, Pierre. 1995. Bias and the badge. *Washington Post National Weekly Edition*, December 18, 6.

Tobar, Hector. 1991. Training: A casualty on street. *Los Angeles Times*, March 18, A1.

Tobar, Hector, and Leslie Berger. 1991. Tape of LA police beating suspect stirs furor. *Los Angeles Times*, March 6, A1.

Tobar, Hector, and Michael Connelly. 1990. Robber a victim, wife says. *Los Angeles Times*, February 19, B1.

Tough cops, not brutal cops. 1994. *New York Times*, May 5, A26.

Treadwell, David. 1991. Police chiefs seek U.S. panel on crime. *Los Angeles Times*, April 17, B1.

Tuchman, Gaye. 1978. *Making news*. New York: Free Press.

Turow, Joseph. 1985. Cultural argumentation through the mass media. *Communication* 8: 139–64.

Underwood, Doug. 1993. *When MBAs rule the newsroom*. New York: Columbia University Press.

U.S. Congress. House. 1991. *Omnibus Crime Control Act of 1991*. 102d Cong., 1st sess., H.R. 3371.

U.S. Congress. House. Committee on the Judiciary. Subcommittee on Civil and Constitutional Rights. 1992. *Federal Response to Police Misconduct*. 102d Cong, 2d sess.

Waldman, Amy. 1999. In a quest for peace and opportunity, West Africans find anger. *New York Times*, February 6, B6.

Watson, Carol A. 1991. Complaints meet a wall of silence. *Los Angeles Times*, March 10, M5.

Weaver, David H., and G. Cleveland Wilhoit. 1992. *The American journalist in the 1990s*. Mahwah, N.J.: L. Erlbaum.

Weinstein, Henry. 1991. Punitive award against Gates is overturned. *Los Angeles Times*, September 28, B1.

Weinstein, Henry, and Carla Hall. 1994. L.A. brutality case lawyer's road to judgeship blocked. *Los Angeles Times*, December 17, A1.

Weiser, Benjamin. 1999. Federal authorities grow more aggressive in examining police nationwide. *New York Times*, March 28, 46.

Whitely, Peyton, reporter for the *Seattle Times*. 1996. Telephone interview by author, February 16.

Wilgoren, Jodi. 1999a. Fatal police barrage renews debate over safety of semiautomatics. *New York Times*, February 7, 43.

———. 1999b. After Diallo shooting, new focus on hiring city residents for police. *New York Times*, February 28, 25.

Wilgoren, Jodi, and Michael Cooper. 1999. Police trailing other cities in diversity. *New York Times*, March 8, B1.

Williams, Marjorie. 1991. Divided we stand. *The Washington Post*. December 29, W7.

Wilson, James Q., and George L. Kelling. 1989. Making neighborhoods safe. *The Atlantic*, February, 46.

Wilson, Kinsey. 1991. Video cameras bring power to the people. *Newsday*, April 2, 49.

A wise promise from Lee Brown. 1990. *New York Times*, February 7, A24.

Wolff, Craig. 1992. Feeling betrayed, police grow wary. *New York Times*, July 8, B2.

———. 1994a. Bratton says drug sweeps are to continue on S.I. *New York Times*, May 2, B3.

———. 1994b. Mayor vows investigation of incident. *New York Times*, 3 May 3, B1.

Wolfsfeld, Gadi. 1997. *Media and political conflict: News from the Middle East*. Cambridge: Cambridge University Press.

———. 1998. Political waves and democratic discourse: Terrorism waves during the Oslo peace process. Paper presented at the annual meeting of the American Political Science Association, Boston, Mass., September 2–6.

Wood, Tracy, and Faye Fiore. 1991. Beating victim says he obeyed police. *Los Angeles Times*, March 7, A1.

Wood, Tracy, and Sheryl Stohlberg. 1991. Patrol car log in beating released. *Los Angeles Times*, March 19, A1.

Woodyard, Chris. 1989. Citizen review of police urged after taped "sting." January 17, *Los Angeles Times*, section 2, page 1.

Worsnop, Richard L. 1991. Police brutality. *CQ Researcher*, September 6, 635–39.

Worthington, Rogers. 1991. Milwaukee police chief under fire. *Chicago Tribune*, September 26, 29.

Yardley, Jonathan. 1985. The thoughtful police. *The Washington Post*, February 27, C2.

Zaller, John, and Dennis Chiu. 1996. Government's little helper: U.S. press coverage of foreign policy crises, 1945–1991. *Political Communication* 13: 385–405.

Zimring, Franklin E., and Gordon Hawkins. 1992. *The search for rational drug control*. Cambridge: Cambridge University Press.

Index

academic experts: on civilian review in New York, 116; as critical nonofficials, 47–48, 132; frequency of journalists' use of, 97, 205–6n20; scholars on social construction of public problems, 3, 5, 177; on semiautomatic weaponry for crime fighting, 222n4

accidental events, 14–15, 69, 186–87, 198n5, 222nn5,6; anomalous, 103–5, 108; commercial and reformist journalism with, 92, 103, 104, 107; creation of, 82–84; critical story cues, 86–111; event-driven problem definition by, 9, 63, 64, 77–82, 111, 134–36, 143–44, 165–89; marginalized groups' views exposed by, 6, 7–8, 63–64, 79–85, 92–93, 140, 157, 174–75, 183; to news icons, 8, 140–43; patterned, 103–5, 108, 154–55, 157; social construction of, 177–79. See also contained meaning of news events, official; King, Rodney (beating)

"accurate" representation, 12

ACLU (American Civil Liberties Union), 22, 77–78, 81 fig, 180, 220n8

activists: accidental news events' exposing views of, 6, 79–85, 93, 174–75; antibrutality, 80–84, 81 fig, 92–93, 116, 151; "antipolice," 51; beat reporters wary of, 55; after King beating, 77–82, 107, 150, 155, 174–75, 180, 211n21; marginalized claims of, 6, 49, 84, 107; as primary definers, 16,

77–79, 86, 93, 123, 127–30, 166, 180, 211n21; Ryan's "upward spirals" model and, 211n20. See also citizen action; civil rights; community leaders; critical nonofficials

adversarialism, journalistic (reformist norm), 87–88, 90–93, 103, 106, 107, 108, 212–13nn2,3

African Americans, 67, 82–84, 171, 184; as critical officials after King beating, 75, 150–53, 155, 180; LAPD brutality toward, 65, 67, 77, 167–68, 210n17; in police, 13, 171, 184; police killings dropped since 1970s, 208n5; polled on King beating, 72; polled on L. A. brutality, 144; polled on NYPD brutality, 172; polled on police discretion to use deadly force, 199–200n4; racism in use-of-force incidents toward, 21–24, 42, 72–73, 77, 98, 150, 154–57, 172, 184–85, 210n17; systemic claims, 42, 150–51, 155, 168; Ward as first black NYPD commissioner, 13. See also King, Rodney (beating)

agenda setting, by media, 9–10, 53–54, 62–85, 158, 174–75, 177–79

Albright, Madeleine, 176

Alexander, Fritz, 121

Amnesty International, 169, 170

Anderson, Edward, 22

anomalous news events, 103–5, 108

"antipolice" label, 51, 134

Archer, Chris, 203n5

Atlanta Journal and Constitution, 141

Text: 10/13 Sabon
Display: Sabon
Composition: Binghamton Valley Composition
Printing and binding: Maple-Vail Book Manufacturing Group